W9-ADD-975

MILTON
AND THE DEATH
OF MAN

MILTON AND THE DEATH OF MAN

Humanism on Trial
in *Paradise Lost*

Harold Skulsky

DELAWARE

Newark: University of Delaware Press
London: Associated University Presses

Associated University Presses
440 Forsgate Drive
Cranbury, NJ 08512

Associated University Presses
16 Barter Street
London WC1A 2AH, England

Associated University Presses
P.O. Box 338, Port Credit
Mississauga, Ontario
Canada L5G 4L8

The paper used in this publication meets the requirements of the American National Standard for Permanence of Paper for Printed Library Materials Z39.48-1984.

Library of Congress Cataloging-in-Publication Data

Skulsky, Harold.
    Milton and the death of man : humanism on trial in Paradise lost / Harold Skulsky.
      p. cm.
    Includes bibliographical references (p.) and index.
    ISBN 0-87413-719-5 (alk. paper)
    1. Milton, John, 1608–1674. Paradise lost.   2. Christian poetry, English—History and criticism.   3. Epic poetry, English—History and criticism.
4. Milton, John, 1608–1674—Religion.   5. Free will and determinism in literature.   6. Man (Theology) in literature.   7. Humanism in literature.
8. God in literature.   I. Title.
PR3562.S56   2000
821'.4—dc21   99-051869

Contents

Introduction

By "humanism" In what follows, I will mean the belief that persons, unlike many other kinds of object, cannot go unmentioned (or dispensed with by paraphrase) in an adequate description of what there is; that persons are elementary parts of reality. If you are a person, at least these three things are true of you:

1. The things you do and suffer are facts about the whole you, not facts about your parts. In particular, the following is false: that deeds and sufferings rightly ascribed to you are "really" (that is, literally) interactions among the things you're made of; that they are yours only figuratively.[1]
2. Among the irreducible facts about the whole you, in addition to your deeds and sufferings, are your duties, rights, and deserts.
3. There are things you do—the things worth praising or blaming, rewarding or punishing—that nothing and nobody *made* you do; in the usual jargon, you do them of your own "free will."

Naturally, nearly all the terms in these propositions are in urgent need of clarification—not least the notion of the "whole you." I will tie up these loose ends in chapter 2. For my present purposes—a sketch of what this book is about—approximation does no harm. I will be arguing that *Paradise Lost* is among the central literary documents of a crucial moment in European thought: the early stages of the decline and fall of humanism.

Intellectual history, as I aim to practise it, is an interpretative discipline that fuses literary criticism and philosophical analysis. It adds to the synoptic ambitions of Lovejoy or Cassirer or Kristeller or Berlin a respect for the power of a body of belief to ensnare the believer in the trammels of its logic, and above all a wary respect for the logic. The focus here is not so much on the genealogy of a writer's ideas as on his struggle with the fear he shares with earlier

7

members of the running symposium of his intellectual tradition—
the fear that those ideas will turn out to be as contradictory or vacuous as they are impossible to get on without. In this focus on the
fine texture of argument, my models are those recent working philosophers (like Anthony Kenny, Gilbert Ryle, and Bernard Wil-
liams) who have brought analytical precision as well as critical tact
and historical scholarship to the task of sending a bright light into
the dark corners of older thought. I hope that my readers will join
me in the work, and the exhilaration, of analyzing the interplay of
ideas and inferences that lets the story told in *PL* serve the teller as
a kind of proof.

Intellectual history, as I aim to practise it, also respects the power
of expressive and persuasive strategies, of figurative language and
complex acts of speech, to shape or warp the logic of ideas. So I
also hope to engage my readers in the work of analyzing the rhetoric of *PL*.

My recent predecessors in this line of Miltonic questioning include notable works by Fallon and Marjara.[2] Since I count the doc-
trinal and Biblical background as part of my purview, less recent
but durable works by Bennett, Evans, Burden, Patrides, Maccallum,
Danielson, and Gardner[3] are contributions to the same inquiry. So,
in another dimension, is Lewalski's inquiry into the rhetoric and
genre of *PL*.[4]

The book is divided into four large chapters.

In chapter 1, I show why the ostensible metaphor of pleading
God's case has to be taken literally in *PL*, with a rigorous eye to
the art of pleading; why, in Milton's legal as well as literary traditions, epic narrative is an especially happy choice of genre for
pleading God's case; why, in Milton's Biblical and theological traditions, a Christian God would tolerate or even welcome being put
on trial; and why, given the libertarian ideals of God's attorney, it
isn't dereliction or incompetence for him to let grist for the prosecution turn up in his narrative.

In chapter 2, after reviewing the notion of freewill elaborated in
PL (especially in *PL* 3), I offer a critical survey of the evolution of
freewill in the West, via key episodes in that evolution accessible to
Milton: the contributions of Aristotle, Plotinus, Augustine, Aquinas, Valla, Pomponazzi, Erasmus, Molina, Arminius, Descartes,
and the author of *Christian Doctrine*; and I go on to argue that the
notion of agency simpliciter—of personhood—is at least as crucially at stake in *PL* as the notion of *free* agency.

In chapter 3, I explain why the task of justifying God's ways calls for an account of Creation (in multiple versions) as well as of the Fall—and above all for an account of Creation as an essentially maternal act: why this account has to be saturated with images of chaos; how, in the Dialogue of Reconciliation, Eve's maternity parallels God's; and how, in the twin images of cosmic feasting and cosmic alchemy, the holiness of matter turns out to be evidence (material evidence?) for the innocence of God on one of the two counts against him.

In chapter 4, I face the dichotomy between the two counts directly. My distinguished predecessors—especially Helen Gardner—have properly diagnosed Satan's terminal disease as obduracy; but here I need to explore the relentless minuteness with which *PL* captures every horror of that disease, because the exquisiteness of that horror—which is destined to go on forever—is a precise measure of the exquisiteness of God's hate, and above all because somehow a plea on God's behalf has—foolishly or bravely—made room for that measure. The same plea also makes room for a notion of infallible freewill that, once again, casts doubt—foolishly or bravely—on the bona fides of the fallible kind, and hence on the Johannine claim that God is love.

I end by arguing for "bravely" and rejecting "foolishly": on the showing of *PL*, even an omnipotent God is barred from achieving contradictions; even God can't intelligibly choose which of two incompatible values (for example, love and justice) has the greater value. Even God must sometimes choose without a reason, and reconcile himself to inconsolable loss. The God of *PL* 11–12 vindicates himself by enduring the ordeal of his own power, and above all by choosing to join us in the ordeal of our weakness. If my concluding argument is correct, the victory celebrated at the end of Milton's masterpiece is not the acquittal of the accused, but the achievement of a hardwon tragic humanism, the ground of the moral adulthood we are invited to share with the God of *PL*.

The humanism celebrated in the finale of *PL* clashes with the currently dominant outlook—call it modernity—that begins its increasingly powerful rise in Milton's day. But who knows if the clash foretells extinction or just eclipse? No matter which, it's always instructive to take a hard last look at pieties once cherished, and now (to all appearances) ripe only for embarrassment or disregard.

MILTON
AND THE DEATH
OF MAN

1

God's Attorney: Narrative as Argument

Given a self-imposed assignment of defending the Judge of the Universe against impeachment on the charge of grossly abusing the power of his office, Milton could have done worse than follow the recipe in a standard Roman textbook for advocates: a plea stands or falls with the advocate's narrative that starts it off, where the facts of the case are set out, and the court is given an idea of what's at stake. The narrative will make points that counter opposing counsel's arguments: facts about the client's past life, reasons why innocence wasn't enough to spare him his current ordeal, and reasons why the charge against him isn't to be believed in the first place. In short, the advocate's narrative is simply the proof drawn out, and the proof is the clincher that goes with it.[1]

It isn't cynical, Quintilian goes on, to require that points made via the advocate's narrative not only *be* the truth but *resemble* it. Before a human judge, the truth wins out only if it beats the lie at the lie's own game.[2] Milton's allegorical version of this commonplace makes credible storytelling a matter of cosmetics:

> For Truth, I know not how, hath this unhappiness fatal to her, ere she can come to the trial and inspection of the Understanding; being to pass through many little wards and limits of the several affections and desires, she cannot shift it, but must put on such colors and attire as those pathetic handmaids of the soul please to lead her in to their queen [viz., the Understanding]. And if she find so much favor with them, they let her pass in her own likeness; if not, they bring her in to the Presence habited and colored like a notorious falsehood. And contrary, when any falsehood comes that way, if they like the errand she brings, they are so artful to counterfeit the very shape and visage of Truth that the Understanding not being able to discern the fucus which these enchantresses with such cunning have laid upon the feature sometimes of Truth, sometimes of Falsehood interchangeably, sentences for the most part one for the other at the first blush, according to the subtle imposture of these

13

sensual mistresses that keep the ports and passages between her and the object.[3]

Milton is talking here about the interior courtroom, of course; but so, in his own way, is Quintilian. The task of his pleader, too, is to enlist the judge's "affections and desires" on behalf of his cause. If he manages to do this at the start, in the forensic narrative, he has a hope of getting those "pathetic handmaids" to let him into the judge's inner chambers. If the pleader just bides his time in the hope of eventually changing an emotional set of mind once established—*mutare habitum animi semel constitutum*—the game is up; the winner, by default, is the Adversary.[4] In the end the courtroom in which an attorney's story wins or loses is the mind of the judge.

The advocate's narrative wins in both venues if the (psychological) "causes" and "reasons" he assigns for what happens don't go against "nature"; in other words, the personality an agent is assigned by the story has to fit what we claim he or she did, and at every stage the judge has to accept that things turned out the way things were promising (or threatening) to turn out—the plot has to be at least as plausible as the plot of a comedy or slice-of-life skit. The forensic storyteller will do well, as he goes along, to scatter "seedling arguments," at least by innuendo: "He was healthy. He drank—and instantly collapsed. Blueness and swelling followed in quick succession."[5] (By this point, we've been invited to draw the speaker's conclusion in the guise of being allowed to draw our own.) In all of this the great narrative virtue isn't just to *say* something true, but somehow *show* it; to work up a sense—an illusion?—of immediacy (*evidentia in narratione*).[6]

So far we've been talking about the easy cases, where the facts favor us, at least "at the first blush." When they don't, it's not merely safe to acknowledge them anyhow, it's obligatory. If we let the Adversary get away with his inflammatory reading of them, we simply sell our own case down the river. Why not turn candor to advantage, by having the same facts lead to *our* reading—*our* inference to causes and reasons hidden in the minds of the agents? In *causae coniecturales*—cases that turn on the best explanation of our common story—we can't afford to give the Adversary a monopoly on the story.[7]

Another tip from Quintilian is in point here: the credibility of the story grows with the moral authority of the teller. A pleader needs to earn that authority by his chosen way of life first of all; but also by his chosen way of speaking: "The graver and holier the *genus orationis*, the more weight it carries in assertion. So especially in the narrative, avoid the slightest hint of trying to be clever; the narrative stage of the defense, more than any other, is where the judge is on his guard. Don't let anything look made up or contrived. Make the judge think, instead, that it all comes out of the cause, not the defender."[8]

As before, this advice translates easily enough into the practise of *Paradise Lost*. If gravity and holiness are wanted, why not the epic voice? And if the point of a forensic style is moral authority, why not relax the ancient rule by letting the epic storyteller be a distinct presence? Why not frame the story of one's client's innocence with a meta-story, about the terrors and glories of pleading his case?

An essential part of the epic enterprise, after all, is precisely to trace a hero's or a people's suffering to some individual "cause": *Musa, mihi causas memora.* "Say first, for Heav'n hides nothing from thy view / Nor the deep tract of Hell, say first *what cause.* . . ." "*What cause* / Mov'd the Creator in his holy rest. . . ." Typically the first visible link in the chain will be a hero's *mênis*—an anger grim and implacable to the point of being uncanny: the "wrauth" of "stern *Achilles*," or the "rage" of "*Turnus* for *Lavinia* disavow'd."

But the uncanniness of the *mênis* itself extends the chain of causes backward beyond events on the human scale, to something like "*Neptune's* ire or *Juno's*." Here is where classical epic is doomed to failure as a defense of divine justice: the Adversary has been given a license to ask his most embarrassing question—in fact the epic narrator has been lured into asking it for him: "Can such furies live in heavenly minds?" The short answer, of course, is no; "all the gentile 'gods' are demons, and the heavens were made by God" (Ps. 95:6)[9]; unlike the Olympian version, the divine "anger" that "brought into this world a world of woe" isn't a passion but an act—a judicial act of supreme rightness: "just rebuke and judgement given." Even where classical epic comes closest to the "great Argument" of Christian epic, the Christian version is "not less but more Heroic": Zeus's plea on his own behalf in *Odyssey* I[10] is valid enough—once it reappears with full authority as the Creator's plea in *Paradise Lost* 3. Or so, at least, Milton needs to argue.

Against the Adversary's charge to the contrary, Milton's narrator hopes to "assert [i.e., vindicate] Eternal Providence / And justify [i.e., show the justice of] the ways of God to men." This isn't an easy brief: "at the first blush" at least, the evidence in the record goes against the accused—that's why the indictment calls for a hearing, and why the narrator prays to be made equal to the challenge of revisiting that record. The core of the "great Argument," in short, *has* to be a narrative—precisely in Quintilian's courtroom sense. The implied setting of the narrative act is a process at law, a *dikë*; in fact, a *theo-dikë*: a process at law with God in the dock— and, for better or worse, with the fallible reader on the bench.[11]

Two cautionary words to start with. In his proem, the narrator prays for the lucidity and loftiness he needs to make his case worthy of "the highth of this great Argument" (*PL* 1.24); it's "*this* great Argument" because he's just finished spelling the "argument" out in a thumbnail summary of the action—the first human disobedience of God and what came of it (*PL* 1.1–3). "Argument," in short, doesn't mean "subject" or "theme" (as annotators tend to claim). It means precisely what it means as a heading of the plot summaries that precede each book of *PL*—namely, "plot." If the narrator had meant no more than "subject," he could and would have said "subject"; the context flags his preferred alternative as the functional equivalent of Latin *argumentum* and Greek *hypothesis*: what serves the purposes of "assertion" and "justification" in *PL* is the story. The story is the defense's explanatory "hypothesis" or theory of what the defendant really did. At *PL* 1.24 at least, "argument" means "showing of grounds for acquittal." From time to time, I will use "great Argument" accordingly in respectful dissent from editorial orthodoxy.

A second cautionary word: the great Argument is not the only story being told in *PL*. We also follow the triumphs and reverses of an epic narrator. The narrator is in awe of what passes before his mind's eye, of the dangers of witnessing it, and of the difficulties of doing it justice. He is (like the author) blind and embattled. Sometimes (unlike the author) he doesn't so much shape the action as endure it—endure it so helplessly that, at one crucial point, he seriously contemplates warning the Tempter's victims of the disaster that has already befallen them. *PL* invites us, in short, to follow the story's telling as well as the story told. I will honor the doubleness of the narrative by treating the narrator as the hero of the Telling—the implied narrative of God's Advocate pleading before the court of justice. With the reader's indulgence, "the Advocate" is what I will be calling him from here on.

THEODICY MADE (UN)EASY

What must the Advocate do to win an acquittal? What does a successful brief look like? Begin at the beginning, with a Terrible Fact: say, the wrath that brought ten thousand woes on the Achaeans, or the disobedience that brought death into the world and all our woe. The problem is to elude the horns of an obvious dilemma: either the Fact is the morally necessary price of some indispensable good—a good not to be bought more cheaply even by an infinitely just and loving and powerful being—or else the infinitely just and loving and powerful being doesn't and can't possibly exist, and the faithful turn out to be wind-up dupes of an absurdity—fools who have said in their hearts, there is a God. Any divine inability to block the Fact short of a *moral* inability—the impossibility of God's blocking it and being *just*—is incriminating. When Dalila justifies her bad behavior by pleading her faith in Dagon, Samson retorts with obvious conviction:

> Gods unable
> To acquit themselves and prosecute their foes
> But by ungodly deeds, the contradiction
> Of their own deity, Gods cannot be:
> Less therefore to be pleas'd, obey'd, or fear'd.
> (*Samson Agonistes* 896–900)

To show that the existence of a particular kind of evil isn't evidence that we're at the mercy of Neptune or Juno, much less of Dagon the fishgod, the Advocate isn't called on to produce God's actual reason for letting the evil exist, much less reasons for every kind of evil in the world. Success with one kind is enough to establish that, given world enough and time, others can yield to a determined effort.[12]

Success here means showing that a scenario involving an infinitely loving, just, and powerful God explains, say, the first disobedience better than competing scenarios—equivalently, that the fact of a first disobedience confirms the existence of such a God.[13] Defeat for the Advocate would be a showing that his scenario makes the disobedience less likely than it is in itself—equivalently, that the fact of disobedience makes the existence of an infinitely loving, just, and powerful God less likely than it is in itself.[14] Imagine, for the sake of argument, that the central idea in the scenario—the thing for which evil is a price worth paying—is freedom: "Loosely, one may say that evil will confirm the existence of God only if it is very probable that God will bring about freedom and very probable that freedom will lead to evil, and not very probable that evil will occur if there is no God. Otherwise evil will be irrelevant or disconfirmatory."[15] If disconfirmatory—to repeat—then the "Yahweh" of Biblical Christianity names, if anything, a demon of terrible power and caprice, one of whose crueller masquerades is the God of the faithful.

"The adoption of the Jahwist's unsophisticated myth [of the Fall] as the official Christian explanation of the existence of evil exposed it [viz., the myth] to all the philosophical difficulties entailed in the reconciliation of a perfect Creator with an imperfect Creation."[16] Quite right—with the crucial exception that if the Genesis narrative had been adopted as a mere myth, much less an unsophisticated one, it would instantly have failed as an explanation. To be an "argument" in Milton's and Quintilian's courtroom sense—a proof suitable for winning one's case—the story has to be (probably) *true*: the appearance of evil should confirm it, and be confirmed by it. That's what it means, in the science jargon of Milton's day, for an explanatory hypothesis to "save appearances" for the client's innocence.[17]

The problem is that the Genesis narrative itself is among the appearances to be saved. As it stands, it's "exposed" to difficulties with a vengeance; it gives the Adversary everything he could want, short of an outright guilty plea. To make it serve the defense, the Advocate-narrator will need to plug the holes as he goes along with a full array of backup theories:

1. a theory of causation and accountability that (a) clears God of complicity in the wrongs and suffering that he could have ruled out in the act of designing human nature; (b) lets the original generation's wrongdoing make accomplices as well as victims of all the generations that follow; (c) lets moral evil be the origin of natural evil—disease, earthquakes, storms, famines, etc.;
2. a theory of justice (and moral agency) that makes it just (a) for God to create a causal order satisfying 1; (b) for him to condemn finite offenders (Adam, Eve, Satan) to infinite punishments; (c) for him to single out, as a paradigm of wrongdoing, an act (of eating) that's wrong only in virtue of being

forbidden; (d) for him to condemn succeeding generations for the acts of the first; (e) for him to accept the sufferings of a scapegoat (the Atonement), no matter how willing the scapegoat, as valid substitute for the punishment of the guilty party; (f) for him to punish a dumb animal (the Serpent) for an offence of which it was merely the instrument;

3. a theory of fairness that makes it fair for God to give the temptees but not the tempter a second chance, even though the temptees were still free and the tempter already in bondage;

4. a theory of infinite mercy that (a) rules third chances out and rules infinite punishments in; (b) allows debts of justice to be forgiven only if an obliging proxy can be found to pay them in full.

Milton takes on the whole brief with the same gallant and unseemly zeal that energizes his defense of regicide—unseemly in this case because God himself, on the poet's showing, despises a *credo quia absurdum* as much as Milton does, and because, measured by his deepest juridical convictions as well as by ours, the current brief is at least as (shall we say) aromatic as the brief for regicide.

And yet—and yet: fortunately for us, the part of 1–4 that continues to matter in a post-Christian age is the part that purports to make sense of man's first disobedience and its "fruit"—that is, to interpret the central action of *Paradise Lost*. If the interpretation fits well enough, divine justice wins its promised rescue from the death of absurdity—but (and this is the part that still matters) only if the idea of a person, a moral individual, gets rescued first. Not that Milton's theory of free will, and of why a just Creator would build it into his favorite creature, proves to fit the story any better than the rest of the brief; but that the Advocate makes us imagine powerfully how deeply unacceptable a poor fit would be.

As in all tragedy, the great argument of *Paradise Lost* draws its energy from the threat of its own failure—the failure of the idea that tragedy struggles to defend from the death of a thousand sneers. It's the idea of agency itself—of being the sort of entity to which acts and sufferings belong; in short, of being a person. That idea is even more fundamental to Milton's humanist project than the equally beleaguered ideas of the justice of God and the freedom of free agents.

Part of what makes ideas like agency and personhood vulnerable is that they're as hard to pin down as to do without. In the second part of this study, I'll try to pin them down, in the form in which they engage the narrator of *Paradise Lost*, by telling a historical and, I hope, true story of my own.

I've been assuming, with Milton, that it makes sense to take these matters seriously—indeed, that the relevant idea of seriousness needs no defense. Villains in Jacobean tragedy have a way of insisting that "there's nothing serious in mortality"—that is, in the existence of mortals; that the labels "fair" and "foul" are ultimately interchangeable; that life signifies nothing. But not to worry; villains are handicapped in this domain—that's what makes them villains. The barest reflection on the nature of the ground of being—the Creator's "let there be"—shows that these nihilistic vaporings are flat wrong—worse than wrong, in fact; absurd. Or does it? Is God an Anarch or an Absurdist after all?

Part of intellectual honesty, I'm afraid, is to take as little as possible for granted. In the remainder of this first part we'll need to consider the seventeenth-century state of a question that threatens to undermine Milton's project even if talk about acts and persons (as opposed to physical objects and what happens to them) turns out to make sense.

Theodicy vs. the *Mysterium Tremendum*

To begin to frame that question historically, we need to appreciate the risk a Christian Advocate of God has reason to know he's taking: not everybody in his tradition thinks theodicy is a good thing; some even suggest that it's very bad.

At a minimum, the Advocate will have noticed the implication of Bildad the Shukhite's reproach to Job: God's will is the standard of justice; to raise a question about that will is to raise a question about the standard. That's why Job's suffering—which Bildad interprets as a judgment of God—can't be undeserved: not only doesn't God "pervert" judgment, he doesn't "pervert"—that is, devalue or disturb[18]—justice itself (Job 8:6, 8:3). The possibility Bildad refuses even to entertain is that God can change the rules of morality at will; if this is even *possible*, then apparently what makes the prevailing rules "moral" is that God happens not to have changed them. (Not everybody finds this possibility frightening, as we'll see a bit further on. Bildad does; so, as we'll also see, does the narrator of *Paradise Lost*.)

At first hearing, the voice from the whirlwind seems to confirm Bildad's nightmare: neither Job nor anybody else is entitled to God's gratitude, so Job has no ground for complaint—even if he's being tormented for nothing: the author of his torment, as of the wealth and health that preceded it, is nobody's debtor and everybody's creditor—the only being with nothing above it, not even moral obligations (41:3).[19]

This takes the ground out from under Job's claim to redress of grievances—but not from under the *notion* of redress of grievance; something frightening about God has come out, but in the end not the black hole that terrifies Bildad. God doesn't say that loans and favors have no obligatory force but the force of God's decree; he simply points out that nobody could conceivably be in a position to make him a loan or do him a favor, and hence to put him under an obligation. What's equally to the point here: this is no refusal to show how God's ways to Job can be just; it's an explanation of why, despite appearances, the issue of justice doesn't arise.

In his brighter moods, anyhow, Job's reply to Bildad's worry is that raising the question of God's justice is an exercise of free speech that honors God, and that God cherishes, just as he loathes the temporizing or flattery ("respect of persons") that Job's comforters go in for (13:7–8); it doesn't occur to them that this is one king who prefers people with the courage to speak frankly in the royal presence (13:15–16)—a king upright men can hope to sue and thus emerge vindicated (23:7). The whole point of Job's complaint is that there *is* an objective standard of justice—a standard that the Judge of the World measures up to, in reality if not appearance.

Elsewhere, Job loses confidence. How can anybody put a stop to God's snatching away the gifts of God (9:12)? How can anybody emerge vindicated from a dispute with God (9:2–3)? Even if Job clears himself, it still won't satisfy this Judge (9:14). Even if Job turns out to be blameless, he's still in the wrong (9:21). In God's courtroom, the same result awaits both the guilty and the innocent (9:22). And isn't Job's petition formally invalid anyhow? His opponent, after all, isn't a fellow human being (9:23).[20] Maybe a process at law would be possible if there were an intercessor[21]—somebody with the standing to arbitrate[22] the issue (9:33).

Meanwhile, far from letting the plaintiff speak without reserve, the accused is intimidating him (9:35). If he did this in person, he would at least be honoring their former intimacy; why has he hidden his face from Job—or (as the ancient translation has it) withdrawn his Presence?[23] Why does he treat Job as an "enemy" (the Hebrew word is, perhaps ironically, cognate with Job's name)[24]—or (to speak with the ancient translation again) why does God shun Job as a murmurer, a slanderer, a blasphemer, a heretic (13:24)?[25] Judges ought to spell out the grounds of their verdicts— not summarily punish or convict (10:2). In a fit of frustrated zeal for due process, Job submits a signed affidavit and demands a similar document[26] from his opponent (31:35).

All of this reads like bitter reproach, but in this tormented text a slight adjustment in the angle of vision changes everything: is Job seriously accusing his judge of unfairness and partiality—or is this harangue designed to cover the lack of legal standing he virtually concedes?

I said a bit earlier that God justifies his ways to Job—but not by giving his reasons for them, only by explaining why God's reasons are beside the point: whatever he does to Job, and whatever the reason, God is under no obligation to do otherwise. Of Job's visitors, Elihu ben Barach'el is apparently saved for last to set the stage for this line of argument: *of course* affliction doesn't imply guilt; the comforters have as little right to accuse Job as Job to accuse his Maker (32:2–3). But to claim that God's justice is unaccountable (33:13) is not to claim that there's no truth of the matter.[27]

Job's mistake here isn't his plea of innocence, it's his readiness to plead innocent by making God out a liar (34:5–6); far be it from God to deal in falsehood (34:10).[28] (Is it significant that "far be it" is a prayer and not an affirmation?) God is no perverter of judgment (34:12). He's the ultimate *teacher* of righteousness,[29] and needs no instruction in fair dealing from Job or anybody else (36:22–23).[30] If there's any bias in the jurisprudence of heaven, it's a bias in favor of the accused; in this court a single advocate is enough to carry the day against nine hundred ninety-nine prosecuting attorneys (33:23).[31]

Part of what God is driving at, in his climactic cross examination of Job, is, indeed, that there's no appeal against God's verdict—no one has the required standing to bring suit: "Do you annul my judgment, clearing yourself at my expense? Can you match God's arm or voice?" (40:8–9). Job is "darkening" God's (royal) counsel[32]— fostering confusion about the protocols of the heavenly court. But coming up against the infinity of his opponent forces Job to acknowledge a deeper difficulty, one that threatens to doom the whole enterprise of theodicy: Job ended up "darkening [God's] counsel" because he failed to understand things that were too "wonderful" for him—too "wonderful" (by implication) for anybody (42:3). Where failing (to understand) is inevitable, trying is foolish.

Job starts out with "a disastrously circumscribed conception of the deity," but not because "[God,] as the omnipotent Creator, finds the merely human notion of justice absurd," much less because a moral view of God is "presumptuous."[33] How does it reassure Job, or us, to be told that "God is just" comes out perfectly true in a language like our own in every respect but the non-moral meaning the new language assigns to "just"? Where did the moral or absurd or merely human sense of "just" come from in the first place if not from the teacher-of-justice par excellence? If anything is being condemned in this passage as presumptuous and absurd, it's Job's expectation that a finite being could follow the reasons of a mind that is not only just but infinite (in the garden variety sense of both "just" and "infinite"); God's *thachlith*—his boundary—is beyond Job's reach (11:4–9) because it outruns that reach forever. Job eventually sees the folly of his demand: only God sees his own reality in the round; for all other beings, being wise about God isn't a matter of comprehension but fear (28:23–27).

This is discouraging testimony—and from an impeccable source. On the other hand, the narrator of *Paradise Lost* is after comprehension. Why *can't* an all-powerful creator confer the required candlepower on his creature's intellect?

Maybe he can but won't. Faith is faith, after all, precisely because its objects are hidden. And what more radical hiding place is there than a contrary appearance—such as the fact that so few get saved, so many damned; or the fact that he makes us necessarily damnable—and does this on purpose? The reason God hides his mercy under eternal wrath, and his justice under inequity, is to give faith its chance to exist![34]

The Advocate will know this argument of Luther's, and Erasmus's reply: Job's God is also the God of the prophets, the God who is so far from standing on his dignity or dodging accountability that he likes to challenge Israel to argue the question of his justice with him point for point.[35] Granted, matters accepted on faith are matters beyond our grasp, but why would that keep a loving God from supplying graspable reasons to accept them?[36] Granted, requests for a divine accounting are sometimes turned down in the

Bible with little evidence of love: "Nay but O man who art thou
that repliest against God? Shall the thing formed say to him that
formed it, Why hast thou made me thus?" (Rom. 9:20). But what's
getting rebuffed here isn't really a *question* at all. It's a snide remark made up to look like one. No wonder it doesn't get an answer—it doesn't deserve any![37]

On the showing of the Advocate's Erasmian tradition, God is
never so much himself as when he lets himself be held to account;
self-revelation is the point of creating the world, of judging it—in
short, of everything God does.[38] So it isn't surprising to find this
God, in *PL* 3, "arguing his own case publicly" and "submitting" it
"to the bar of angelic and human judgment"[39]:

> so will fall
> Hee and his faithless Progenie; whose fault?
> Whose but his own? ingrate, he had of mee
> All he could have.

> *(PL* 3.95–98)

This is the cadence of debate. "Whose fault?" God doesn't say that
in *fact* it's Adam's and Eve's fault; he mocks (via rhetorical question) the *possibility* that the fault was anybody else's. "Ingrate"
isn't an assertion that Adam was ungrateful; it's a vocative missile
aimed at the cringer in the Garden. But why the mockery and the
brickbat—in advance?

These moves are a dry run for a challenge that the speaker foresees and is willing and eager to oblige: to supply a good argument
for the thesis that Adam and Eve can't "justly accuse / Thir maker,
or thir making, or thir Fate." This isn't the performance of a mon-
arch who holds himself above the law. In this king's court, a Father
not only tolerates but cherishes a loving Son's "adversarial 'arguing' ":[40]

> that be from thee farr,
> That farr be from thee, Father, who art Judge
> Of all things made, and judgest onely right.

> *(PL* 3.153–55)

And an "adversarial" posture isn't just a privilege of the royal family. In a celebrated confrontation, God lets a mere man argue (as
the man thinks) against a possible course of action with the same
rash frankness and even the same rash phrase: "That be far from

thee: shall not the Judge of all the earth do right?" (Abraham at Gen. 18:25).

The Judge of all the earth, in short, not only wants to do right but to pay the price of being seen to do it—the price of hearing out and answering people who imagine, and dread, that God might just possibly have it in mind to do something "far from" God. In fact the Miltonic God goes his Biblical counterpart one better by pretending not to understand why Adam might be miserable without a mate of his own kind—just to "embolden" Adam to protest the *unfairness* of comparing God's single bliss with the corresponding state of Adam. "Thus I embold'n'd spake, and freedom us'd / Permissive, and acceptance found" (*PL* 8.434–35). This God goes to ingenious lengths to be argued with, and to argue back.

The dialogue on marriage partners isn't in the commentary tradition. It was made up by the poet, apparently just to develop this side—if it is a side and not, for Milton, the center—of God's character. So are a number of other dialogues that would otherwise be hard to explain.

Example: why invent a lone dissenter to challenge Satan in council? Hardly because Abdiel is "forcing the angels to consider alternative arguments and so to make their choices consciously and freely"; part of the relevant freedom (as we'll see in greater detail later on) is the freedom to be perverse, and turn a deaf ear to the arguments one doesn't like. A better bet is that Abdiel is there to "counter the Satanic debasement of deliberative oratory with a truly heroic, indeed heavenly, model"[41]—though the oratory getting modelled belongs to the courtroom, not the senate, and the person being tried in absentia, as usual in *PL*, is God.

Again, why make up a visit to Adam from a heavenly courier with instructions to tell him (i) that his happiness is "left to his own free will," (ii) that his free will is "mutable" (from good to evil), (iii) that he shouldn't get careless and "swerve," (iv) that Satan has already fallen and is out to seduce Adam to join him (*PL* 5.233-243)? Adam emphatically denies that he was ignorant of his free will to start with; that's the point of his double negative: "nor knew I not / To be both will and deed created free" (*PL* 5.548–49). It would be convenient, to say the least, if these lines could somehow be tortured into saying that thanks to Raphael freedom is now "more clearly defined and known" to Adam.[42] All they say is that his freedom isn't news to him—period.

It would be equally convenient if Adam were getting rescued

from the wrong kind of confidence by hearing about Satan's defection. But the whole point of "nor knew I not" is that Adam is already well aware that he *can* go wrong if he wants. What he's
confident of, at least before hearing of the defection, is that he
won't:

> Yet that we never shall forget to love
> Our maker, and obey him whose command
> Single, is yet so just, my constant thoughts
> Assur'd me, and still assure; though what thou tellst
> Hath past in Heav'n, som doubt within me move.
>
> (*PL* 5.550–54)

Adam's unbroken record of constant thoughts is evidence that he'll
stay the course—or *was* evidence, until nullified by the example of
free agents who failed to stay the course. The result, as he says, is
doubt (in the radical sense of "uncertainty either way"). If we grant
that confidence puts Adam at a disadvantage to his Tempter, then
leaving it intact leaves Adam with an excuse for falling. But why
should we grant this? Adam thought he *wouldn't* fail, not that precautions could be dispensed with because he *couldn't*. In fact, the
doubt treatment turns out to be a failure: "Adam soon repeal'd /
The doubts that in his heart arose" (*PL* 7.59–60). And no harm
done; in *PL*, Adam doesn't fall because he's cocky.

The express point of Raphael's visit is not to keep Adam from
falling, not to make the fall less likely, not to deprive Adam of a
good excuse, but to make quite certain that, at the final accounting,
he doesn't even have a *bad* one: "Least wilfully transgressing he
pretend / Surprisal, unadmonisht, unforewarnd" (*PL* 5.244–45).
The operative word here is "pretend." Without the visit, the transgression would have been just as "wilful"—just as unambiguously
guilty; but Adam would have had a chance at the specious claim
("pretense") that his Creator set a trap for him. Raphael is there to
save the only thing that can be saved from an otherwise total disaster: the credit of his Master (and client). Raphael too is preparing
the defense of God.

To take one last crucial example, why make up a dialogue (*PL*
8.15–38, 90–158)—again with no precedent in the Genesis tradition—in which Adam, in effect, asks Raphael to clear up the scandal of "an apparently irrational and inefficient Ptolemaic
cosmos"—and Raphael "pointedly declines to decide the issue be-

tween Ptolemy and Copernicus"?[43]Actually, Raphael is significantly more forthcoming than "declining" would lead one to
suspect. Given his general mission, he has to be: a just God doesn't
trifle with his creatures by seeming, much less by being, irrational.
Neither the sun nor the earth *appears* to be at the center. Both assumptions are designed to *save* appearances—among other things,
from the taint of irrationality. That's the point of the sample defence Raphael noncommittally provides for each version of the
world system. Raphael may think it's presumptuous (in fact useless) to try to choose between the horns of a God-made dilemma.
But he clearly doesn't think it's presumptuous to do some theodicy
on behalf of both horns; on the contrary, he acts as if he's responding to the call of duty.

THEODICY VS. VOLUNTARISM

In fact, what it is (if anything) for duty to call—for it to be the
case that X "ought" to do Y—is the root of a deeper objection to
the Advocate's project. In the terms that gain currency in the late
Middle Ages, God's "ordained power" defines duties, including the
duty to be just, to which his "absolute power"—the things he could
have ordained instead—can hardly be subject: the call of duty is
nothing but the act of ordaining, a sovereign's call on the compliance of his subjects. This way of spelling out the ground of
"ought"—so-called voluntarism—is all too easy to confuse with
what the voice from the whirlwind has to say about God's not
owing anybody anything: that nobody could conceivably be in a
position to put God under an obligation (Job 41:3). The crucial difference is that on the voluntarist conception there's no such thing
as obligatory force, only the literal force threatened by sovereign
decrees with the backing of sovereign power.
Bildad the Shukhite's reproach to Job, we recall, had been that
God's will is the standard of justice and can't be questioned without
letting anarchy loose on the world (Job 8:6, 8:3). Obviously the
point of linking God's will with the quality of justice is to praise
the will, not the quality. For that praise a price has to be paid: there
has to *be* such a quality; "justice" can't be a blank check, can't be
"will of God" by another name. The price to be paid, in other
words, is a God constrained by a benign necessity, a God whose

glory is that, unlike his creatures both fallen and unfallen, he *can't not be just.*

For the Advocate's intellectual tradition, that price isn't too high—on the contrary; it's a weird kind of piety that insists that God can do anything at all—even keep seven and five from making twelve. God is all-powerful because he can do anything he wills to do, not because he can will anything. It doesn't dishonor God to make him incapable of willing absurdities—moral *or* mathematical; unless, of course, voluntarism turns out to be right.

We need to be careful, at this point, to locate the source of this intellectual threat to theodicy. In particular, sixteenth-century Reform isn't the source. Calvin and Luther may be no friends to the Advocate's project, but they're no more radical than Bildad in freeing God from moral constraint: "Nor do we import the fiction of absolute power, which is as detestable as it is profane. We don't imagine that God is outside the law—not he who is to himself a law; for (as Plato says) human beings cannot do without law, ridden as they are by their lusts; but God's will is not only pure of every defect, it is the supreme measure [*regula*] of perfection, the law of all laws."[44]

The point of Calvin's Platonism is that a standard (say, of willing or acting justly) can't *measure* a quality without *having* it—having it par excellence; that's what it is to be a standard or measure. Ordinary willing or acting gets within reach of justice only by measuring up, more or less, to the prime *example* of justice. That—and not divine despotism—is why talk about justifying God's will only muddles the privileged status of God's will as the *regula* of what is just or lawful. Once we demand that the measure be measured, the justification justified, we blunder over the edge of logic into the sheer drop of an infinite regress.

If this Platonist theme is missed,[45] "law unto oneself" can sound like no law at all, as in this of Luther:

Even if scandalized reprobates fall away by the million, the chosen will remain, and to the ones who ask 'Why did God let Adam fall, and why did he create all of us infected with the same sin, when he could have set Adam aside and created us from another source, or first purged Adam's seed and then created us from it?' the same answer will be given: 'God is he whose will (being matched or surpassed by nothing) has neither a cause nor reason prescribed to it as norm or measure, but is itself the measure of everything. If it had a norm or measure or cause or reason, it could no longer be the will of God. For it isn't because *he* has to, or had to, will a given thing that the thing is right, but, on the contrary, it's because he wills the thing that *it* has to be right.'[46]

Luther's word for "has to" here (*debet*) expresses a metaphoric debt; the studied shifting of the debt from "he" to "it" is the key to the passage: things get to be right by sharing in the rightness of a paradigm, the supremely right will that measures them: they "owe" their rightness to something that is beholden (as the voice from the whirlwind would say) to nothing, least of all a paradigm.

Unhappily for the Advocate, our access to that something is limited:

> In the light of grace it is insoluble how God damns one incapable, by any strength of his own, of anything but sin and guilt. Here the lights of grace and nature together declare that the blame falls not on woeful man but on his wicked God, for nature and grace can reach no other judgment on a God who freely confers an undeserved crown on an impious person, and fails to crown but rather damns another who may happen to be *less* impious, or at any rate not *more*. But the light of glory has something else to declare, and God—whose judgment, in this life, is of a justness beyond our grasp—will be shown in the next to be of a justness no less excellently manifest than just.[47]

Luther goes this far with the Advocate: there *is*, admittedly, a scandal about God, and it must and will be cleared up—but not now, and not by the Advocate.

For voluntarism in cold blood, we have to go, not to the sixteenth-century Reformers, but to a contemporary of the Advocate. Unlike Luther, Hobbes doesn't have to wait for glory to find the hidden reason for God's capricious way with Job and countless other victims: "God may afflict by a right derived from his omnipotence, though sin were not."[48]

Grant, for the sake of argument, that a God who afflicts the undeserving is unjust; it will follow that the Fall is the least of the Advocate's worries: "Although it has been maintained that death entered the world through sin—that is, had Adam not sinned, there would have been no death—it does not follow that had Adam not sinned God could not justly have afflicted him, as God afflicts the other animals, which cannot sin."[49] In short, the suffering of conscious beings is morally indivisible. What happens to dumb animals everywhere and every day is undeserved and atrocious enough to convince Hobbes that if *we* have a right to be spared gratuitous pain, then *they* do. But for him it goes without saying that they don't.[50] So neither do we.

It's *deserved* suffering, in fact, that confuses the underlying issue when desert is thought of as tying God's hands: "The right of God's natural kingship, by which he afflicts those who violate the laws of nature . . . derives . . . from the fact that his power is not to be resisted. In an all-powerful and irresistible nature, kingship and mastership over all human kind inhere naturally. Of the right by which God afflicts and spares whomever he will, the foundation is the power of God, and not, as many have supposed, the sins of men."[51]

Taken on its face, this will strike the Advocate (and perhaps many of us) as outrageous: can Hobbes really mean to claim that a master who can't be stopped has a *right* to hurt his creatures gratuitously— the right somehow conferred by being unstoppable? Can Hobbes really mean to imply that the harder it is to stop an act of wanton hurting—the closer it gets to being unstoppable—the less wrong the hurting is? Is this his bleak vision of the Judge of the World? Equally to the point, is this his bleak vision of justice? Actually, as I'll show a bit further on, it isn't; *his* vision is bleaker.

I remarked early on that the sole authoritative source for the origin of evil—the Genesis account—has the terrible disadvantage, for the Advocate, of giving the Adversary everything he could want, short of an outright guilty plea. In fact, in his forensic narrative, the Advocate himself is daring or foolish enough to emphasize this, by bringing on his opponent to say:

> [Man] by fraud I have seduc'd
> From his Creator, and the more to increase
> Your wonder, with an Apple; he thereat
> Offended, worth your laughter, hath giv'n up
> Both his beloved Man and all his World,
> To Sin and Death a prey, and so to us.
>
> (*PL* 10.485–90)

What's both wonderful and laughable here is presumably the bizarre disproportion between this crime and this punishment. To appease his ruffled vanity, a power-besotted king with a hairtrigger capacity for taking offense is willing to throw his erstwhile favorite to the dogs—over a dietary restriction of breathtaking pettiness.

Or so the Adversary plausibly argues—so plausibly that one has to ask (as we've asked about so many other passages) what this made-up speech is doing in a forensic narrative designed specifically to show that the Adversary's charges are not to be believed. Unless advocacy is the art of selling one's client up the river, only some crucial matter of principle could acquit the Advocate's performance of flat ineptitude. We'll confront this issue of *strategy* here a bit later on. Meanwhile, it's important to see that the Adversary (the name *diabolos* means slanderer) is living up to his name here.

The embarrassment about the dietary law, of course, is that it seems to have no moral *content* at all. Milton's philosophical kinsman, the author of *Christian Doctrine,* carefully explains the legal situation, warts and all:

Man was created in God's image and so contained the whole law of nature as something instinctual and inborn; he needed no instruction in it. So any orders he got in addition, either about the tree of knowledge or about marriage, did *not* belong to the law of nature, but only to the so-called positive law. The law of nature is enough to teach things in accord with right reason, i.e., things good in themselves. By positive law, God—or anybody else vested with just power [*iusta potestate*]—commands or forbids things that, if they hadn't been commanded or forbidden, wouldn't have been good or bad, and so wouldn't have been morally binding on anybody.[52]

In short, eating the fruit of that particular tree is morally wrong, if at all, only by being legally wrong—wrong only after it's forbidden and only *in the sense that* it's forbidden.

We seem to have capitulated totally to voluntarism. With so many fairly unambiguous moral virtues to hold his creatures to—justice, temperance, wisdom, and courage—why does the creator make human destiny turn on high marks in the virtue of perfect Obedience to Naked Commands? Nothing else, it seems, will satisfy him:

One thing at least had to be forbidden or commanded—that thing above all that was in itself neither good nor evil; so that Man's obedience could consist in it. For Man was disposed by his own mind [*suopte ingenio*] to act well, being naturally good and holy. So there was obviously no need to tie him by the chain of a covenant to what he did of his own accord, nor would he have proved his obedience by good works that natural instinct carried him to unbidden. And the bidding of the

Lord or of a magistrate, even with the sanction of reward and punishment, doesn't qualify *ipso facto* as a covenant, but rather an edict [*edictum imperium*].[53]

But look again. Clearly "naked commands" won't do; that's the argument on Satan's preferred reading, but the argument itself goes like this: sometimes one has a moral *as well as* legal obligation to obey a magistrate's command. The basis for the obligation isn't a "covenant" or exchange of promises with the magistrate; it's his *iusta potestas*—the justice of his power to command. And what is *that* if not the justice of what gets commanded? To convict God of injustice, the Adversary helps himself to the assumption that apple eating is the same action *after* prohibition as *before*—morallly indifferent throughout. Milton assumes no such thing; he assumes only that apple-eating *would have* been indifferent *if* it hadn't been forbidden.

The difference between before and after is that in the full-blooded Latin sense (compare *dis-ob-audire*),[54] to "disobey" a commander is to *signify* something: one's refusal to "heed" him. A gestural speech act of contempt or repudiation is possible here precisely because, in effect, the apple ban turns a formerly neutral object into a *pignus et monumentum oboedientiae*[55]—a "pledge and sign" of the creature's willingness to "heed." It turns the object, in short, into a means of expression. Value-laden acts of speech can now be brought off by using and misusing

> The only *sign* of our obedience left
> Among so many *signs* of power and rule
> Conferr'd upon us.
>
> (*PL* 4.428–30; italics mine)

It's an unfairly neglected truism that acts aren't counted the same way as apples; distinct acts can partly or totally *overlap*, as when the acts of (say) currying favor, starting a war, and avenging one's brother jointly "consist in" a single act of (say) pulling a trigger or pressing a button. In "the more to increase / Your wonder, with an Apple," Satan tries to palm off on the jury a correct but disastrously misleading description of a portmanteau act: in the language community made up of Adam, Eve, and God, to leave that particular apple alone is also to pay a debt (of thanksgiving) in the only coin available to the debtor. What the payment happens to "consist in" is mischievously beside the point.

It's true that the apple ban is, in Milton's jargon, positive rather than natural—an *edictum imperium* that simply orders a thing to be done rather than tells whether and why it's the right thing to do. But this, all over again, is the point we've just made. As Eve explains to the Serpent:

> God so commanded, and left that Command
> Sole Daughter of his voice; the rest, we live
> Law to ourselves, our Reason is our Law.
>
> (*PL* 9.652–54)

Naturally it's in the Adversary's interest to get us to read this as presupposing that the command is "outside the province of reason" and "not to be understood through rational argument."[56] But all it presupposes is that knowing a moral law is one thing, and knowing that a positive law is moral is quite another. Milton is banking on his readers' familiarity with this old chestnut about positive laws—at least about the ones that deserve to be obeyed.[57]

In the current example, we can know by reason that *if* there's only one way of thanking our benefactor, *then* we ought (all other things being equal) to act accordingly. But knowing this doesn't leave us any the wiser about whether the "if" is satisfied in a given case; for that intelligence we consult what's actually going on—for example, news that a particular gesture or "sign" has been christened into existence by the "daughter" of our benefactor's "voice." What Eve is driving at here, in short, is that the justice of a concrete act, including an act of (positive) lawgiving, depends on *both* laws of reason *and* facts on the ground.[58]

None of this, be it noted, makes the Advocate a closet irrationalist, gratifying as this conclusion would be to Satan (and some modern critics).[59]

And what (for the Advocate and his ilk) would be so Satanic about closet irrationalism? The short answer is: the irrationalist model of justice is a black hole, and black holes don't need Advocates:

One calls the object of one's appetite, whatever it is, 'good for' one. Likewise, one calls a thing one hates or shuns 'bad for' one. And 'worthless' is what one calls a thing scorned. For the terms 'good [for],' 'bad [for],' 'worthless [for]' are interpreted *relatively* to the speaker, there being nothing that is *absolutely* any of these things; and there being no common measure of 'good,' 'bad,' and 'worthless' that derives from the natures of the objects themselves, rather than (in the absence of a civil society) from the nature of the speaker, or (in the presence of a civil society) from the nature of the person who represents the society, or from an established umpire or judge.[60]

What is it to say an action is good but to say it is as I would wish? or as another would have it, or according to the will of the state? that is, according to the law.[61]

The term common to all things desired, in so far as they are desired, is 'good'; and to all things we shun, 'evil.'[62]

The knowledge—i.e., the judgment—of good and evil was forbidden under the name of the fruit of the tree of the knowledge of good and evil, to test Adam's obedience. . . . Therefore God asks Adam, 'hast thou eaten,' etc., as if he were to say, 'thou that owest to me thine obedience, hast thou claimed for thyself a power of passing judgment on acts?' Whereby it is clearly, though allegorically, signified that the deeds of those whose power is supreme are not to be censured or inquired into.[63]

Men's passions are not sins, nor are the resulting deeds sins, so long as the doers see no power to forbid the deeds. For a law can neither be known ungiven, nor be given so long as the giver has not been agreed on.[64]

'Law' properly so called is the commander's voice, so uttered or so written as to be known for his by all those who are obliged to obey.[65]

A while back I asked in mock disbelief if Hobbes can really mean to claim that an unhindered master has a *right* to hurt his creatures on a mere whim. My stopgap answer was that Hobbes's vision of justice isn't so bleak; it's bleaker. The current passages specify the bleakness.

In Hobbes's moral universe, to have a right to do something just *is* to be unforced or unhindered (by a sovereign power), and to incur an obligation to do something just *is* to be forced or hindered (by a sovereign power). To be good *is* to be desired (by a sovereign power), to be evil *is* to be hated (by a sovereign power)—and so on. These equations can hardly be meant to *analyze* ordinary moral notions; what they do is *eliminate* them. In a moral universe entirely populated by blankly arbitrary commands and tabus, the Advocate is out of a job—or (even more pathetically) his job is made easy to the point of absurdity. That is his occupational nightmare. And that is why he can't afford to be an irrationalist, *in* the closet or *out*.

Even Hobbes doesn't quite bring off the intellectual feat of gazing into the black hole without flinching. Here and there his verdict on "good," etc., gets softened by equivocation. Thus the use of "good" to mean the same as "good for this or that person" no more eliminates objective value from the scheme of things than relativism about "big" ("too big for a fly but too small for an elephant") eliminates objective size. Likewise, the claim that law applies only to those who are "obliged to obey" seems to *support* rather than undermine a real distinction between being commanded and being obliged.

Again, while it's overwhelmingly clear that a Hobbist "law of nature" (or "moral virtue") is nothing but a tendency or urge that promotes one's general self-interest,[66] the natural laws or virtues nominated to fill this bill are comfortingly familiar: fairness, justice, gratitude, and a commitment to the Golden Rule;[67] maybe these are no more than kinds of desire validated by nothing more than instinct and fiat—and maybe not: room has been left for the hope that they're more. Again, maybe these laws or virtues are "unchangeable and eternal"[68] merely because human drives have been determined for keeps—or maybe (more comfortingly) because the *opposite* of fairness, etc., won't qualify as a virtue or law of nature no matter *what* the shape of human instinct happens to be.

Hobbes seems to flinch again when it comes to his mythologized vision of the black hole: the pre-contractual human condition of "Warre of every one against every one."[69] Consider this strange admission about the state of nature: "Covenants entered into by fear, in the condition of meer Nature, are obligatory. For example, if I covenant to pay a ransom or service, for my life, to an enemy, I am bound by it."[70] It seems that covenants are also invulnerable to disruptions of the social contract itself: "In Commonwealth, if I be forced to redeem my selfe from a Thiefe by promising him mony, I am bound to pay it, till the civil law discharge me."[71] "Obligatory" and "bound" had better not take their usual Hobbist meaning here—otherwise Hobbes is elaborately informing us that contracts entered into under coercion are coerced.

For a revealing instant, moral obligation (as opposed to sovereign will or command or power) has crept back to haunt a world from which it was exorcised by the official theory—the theory that in the state of nature "nothing can be Unjust"; that "the notions of Right & Wrong, Justice and Injustice have there no place"; that "where there is no common power, there is no Law; where no Law, no Injustice."[72] On the contrary, at least one natural obligation exists independently of any sovereign command that it be honored: "When a covenant is made, then to break it is *unjust*: and the definition of INJUSTICE, is no other than *the not performance of covenant*."[73] On Hobbes's official definition of "unjust" here, calling covenant-breaking unjust boils down to calling it breach of covenant; clearly Hobbes is counting on us to make allowances for this gaffe by silently bringing back the notion of a justice independent of covenanting. By the same token, on pain of infinite regress, the obligation to abide by covenants had better not rest on a covenant.

Not that the Advocate would be particularly appeased by this concession. We've already noticed that the author of *Christian Doctrine* (with whom Milton was obviously much taken) doesn't think that justice is justice only in the presence of a bargain to abide by it. The fallen Adam tries to quibble his way out of his worst trouble precisely by assuming the opposite:

> Did I request thee, Maker, from my Clay
> To mould me Man, did I sollicite thee
> From darkness to promote me, or here place
> In this delicious Garden? as my Will
> Concurr'd not to my being, it were but right
> And equal to reduce me to my dust,
> Desirous to resigne, and render back
> All I receav'd, unable to perform
> Thy terms too hard, by which I was to hold
> The good I sought not. To the loss of that,
> Sufficient penaltie, why hast thou added
> The sense of endless woes? inexplicable
> Thy Justice seems.

(*PL* 10.743–55)

Adam's grievance is that there was *never any covenant*, never any *exchange* of promises; at most, a conditional promise on God's side. The possibility of a reciprocal promise never came up: Adam never consented to his "being" or the "terms" attached to "holding" it. Why does his failure to honor them earn "endless woes"? Why doesn't God simply consider himself released from his one-sided promise, and take back the unearned gift?

But this is all self-serving literalism. Adam conveniently ignores the fact that God is in the habit of calling his promises covenants;[74] the obligation to comply with the "terms" of the "covenant" of nature can't be finessed so easily. First of all, he's wrong about accepting the "terms." He accepted them, all right—by blithely enjoying the "good" that presupposed them:

> yet to say truth, too late
> I thus contest; then should have been refus'd
> Those terms whatever, when they were propos'd;
> Thou [Adam] didst accept them; wilt thou enjoy the good
> Then cavil the conditions?
>
> (*PL* 10.755–59)

But in the end it's irrelevant whether he accepted God's promise or reciprocated it with one of his own; his sin isn't failure to keep his side of a bargain, it's an ultimately vicious form of contempt:

> though God
> Made thee without thy leave, what if thy Son
> Prove disobedient and, reprov'd, retort,
> Wherefore didst thou beget me? I sought it not.
> Wouldst thou admit for his contempt of thee
> This proud excuse?
>
> (*PL* 10.759–64)

Moral obligation isn't a mere artifact of parties to an agreement; the point is obviously important to the Advocate, and to the tradition he's working in. As the Commonwealth Council of State writes to the Dutch during Milton's tenure as Secretary: "States and Commonwealths can exist without covenants, but not without justice."[75]

I think it's clear by this stage that the defense of God is defending more than God, hard as it is to pin down that "more." Earlier I identified it provisionally with the idea of a person. In the current context, let's speak even more provisionally: what's getting defended is the notion that something *matters*—something about God and something about us; that the "mattering" (whatever it turns out to be) refuses to vanish into a black hole. Milton's formulation is, of course, much more eloquent if not much less vague:

> He hath taught us to love and to extol his laws, not only as they are his, but as they are just and good to every wise and sober understanding.

Therefore Abraham, even to the face of God himself, seemed to doubt
of divine justice, if it should swerve from that irradiation wherewith it
had enlightened the mind of man, and bound itself to observe its own
rule. *Wilt thou destroy the righteous with the wicked? that be far from
thee; shall not the Judge of the earth do right?* thereby declaring that
god hath created a righteousness in right itself, against which he cannot
do. So David, Psalm cxix. *The testimonies which thou hast commanded
are righteous and very faithful; thy word is very pure, therefore thy servant loveth it.* Not only then for the Author's sake, but for its own pu-
rity.[76]

A righteousness in right itself—something to be loved for its own
sake and not merely for its Author's; an "irradiation" from which
he will not and indeed cannot "swerve"; something to which its
Author is bound if only because he has bound himself; something
not reducible to a fiat; something from which a fiat will not release
him. It seems that Elihu ben Barach'el's outlook needs the corrective of Abraham's: the Judge of the earth is bound by the central
duty of his office—and he doesn't mind being called to account by
an officer of the court, like his servant Abraham.

On the Advocate's showing, one conspicuous Biblical precedent
for the notion of the moral law's intrinsic "righteousness" is Psalm
119: "The law of the Lord is perfect, converting the soul: the testimony of the lord is sure, making wise the simple. The statutes of
the Lord are right, rejoicing the heart: the commandment of the
Lord is pure, enlightening the eyes" (Ps. 19:7–8). "Thy statutes
have been my songs in the house of my pilgrimage" (Ps.119:54).
"The law of thy mouth is better unto me than thousands of gold and
silver" (Ps. 119:72). "Thy righteousness is an everlasting righteousness, and thy law is the truth" (Ps. 119:142).

The crucial precedent for the Advocate, however, is St. Paul's announcement that God's law is abolished—crucial precisely because
it's a precedent that's so easy to mistake for a dissent. By supplying
potential sinners with "the knowledge of sin" (Rom. 3:20), "the
law worketh wrath" (Rom. 4:15). The "dominions" of sin and law
are coextensive—to be under either is to be under the other (6:14).
One could be forgiven for imagining that law is just sin under a
respectable *nom de guerre.*

Paul quickly moves to head off misunderstanding here, even if
not quickly enough for some of his modern readers:[77] "What shall
we say then? Is the law sin? God forbid" (Rom. 7:7). "The law is

holy, and the commandment is holy, and just and good. Was then that which is good made death unto me? God forbid" (Rom. 7:12-13). It's not the law's fault if (in perverse hands) a guide to doing right is also a guide—worse still, an incentive—to doing wrong. Being "ordained to life" doesn't rule out being used for death; on the contrary: "Sin, taking occasion by the commandment, deceived me, and by it slew me" (Rom. 7:10–11). "Far from heaping contempt on the law, these declarations of Paul's are a powerful tribute to God's kindness [in giving the law]; for they make it very clear that what our wickedness and depravity keep us from enjoying is the blessedness of life that the law opens up to us."[78]

Calvin, our last quoted Pauline commentator, goes on to draw the appropriate conclusion. Paul's divine master, after all, testifies that he didn't come to abolish the law but to fulfill it (Matth. 5:17). What's getting "abolished," in short, can't be the "holy and good" law itself. It's "the harsh and malign demand [Deut. 27:26] that relaxes nothing from the extremity of the law [*summum ius*] and leaves no trespass unpunished."[79] In a word, the faithful are freed by "abolition," not from the law, but from the "rigor" that "keeps our conscience weighed down by the fear of death." Rigor itself is a violation of law—at least in its unwritten form. That's the point of the commonplace of equity jurisprudence underlying Calvin's telltale Latin phrase: *Summum ius summa iniuria est*—"the extreme of justice is the extreme of injustice."

The premise of the equity jurisprudence Calvin is appealing to (it goes back to the *Nicomachean Ethics*[80]) is that the structure of moral obligation—the unwritten law—is too fine-grained to be captured by the generalities of a code, even if the codifier is God's own secretary and even if the generalities can be relied on most of the time. The *Christian Doctrine*—a book more to the Advocate's liking than Calvin's—owes its version of the abolition metaphor to the same premise:

> The Gospel abolishes the Mosaic law altogether. But by this 'abolition' the law is not *actually* abolished—I mean the sum of the law—but achieves its end in that love of God and neighbor which spirit begets on faith. Hence the truth of Christ's vindication of the law: 'Think not that I am come to destroy the law or the prophets. I am not come to destroy but to fulfil' [Matt. 5:17].
>
> It is unthinkable that the sum of the law, as we said—namely love of God and neighbor—should be abolished. God's scribe the Holy Spirit

merely changes the copy, writing the law on the hearts of the faithful, but writing it in such a way that in particular commandments the spirit *sometimes* seems to disagree with the letter of the law, whenever the love of God and neighbor is more rightly served by not keeping the letter.

The works of the faithful *sometimes* deviate from the letter even of Gospel commands, especially when these are of narrow scope.[81]

God is in the details of concrete moral experience, which his written law "sometimes" captures and "sometimes" doesn't. As with Calvin, this is no announcement that the Ten Commandments have lost their validity. It's an inevitable consequence of the humanist belief that moral truths are true not by fiat but by corresponding to moral facts—that there's a "righteousness in right itself" against which even God "cannot do."

If Milton makes common cause with the Dutch theologian Jacob Arminius anywhere, it's in claiming that God himself incurs obligations:

God, simply as God, is morally bound to no one. None the less by an action of his own he can bind *himself*, namely by making a promise or by demanding an action of someone. God is obliged to keep his promise, for he owes it to himself to be unchangeably truthful, whether his promise is absolute or conditional. By demanding an action, he makes himself a debtor for the power and strength without which the action cannot be performed. Otherwise he reaps where he sowed not. It clearly follows that, having granted man free will and its use, God should not, nay could not, hinder the Fall by frustrating that use; that he was obliged to hinder it only by conferring the wherewithal to beware of it.[82]

It's easy enough to predict the Calvinist reaction to "should not, nay could not": who does this Arminius, this Milton, this Advocate think he is? A Calvinist who talked this way would be violently misreading the phrase; Arminius isn't lecturing his maker on ethics. But perhaps we're already on our way to seeing that people in the Advocate's tradition are at least as deeply interested in the answer to the question "Who does he think he is?" as any heckler. Who the Advocate thinks he is, and who he thinks we are, are as much at stake in his forensic narrative as the truth about the judicial temperament of God.

THE SCENE OF THE CRIME

In the Advocate's moral tradition, to act is to bind oneself to answer for the consequences—even if the actor is God. By issuing a command to his creatures, God binds himself twice over. As their maker, he owes them first of all the power to obey; more basically, he owes them the power to *choose* whether to obey or not: a just God won't block the Fall by withholding or withdrawing the power to choose. All God can do to block the Fall (again at the moment of creation) is to pay his second debt, by sending them into the world equipped with the power to make up their minds, backed up with the power to *beware*.

The Advocate too incurs debts: just by taking up the brief for the defense, he owes his client a story that does the job, or at least does no harm. The last thing the story should do is back up the prosecution, by adding to our reasons for suspecting that God defaulted on his debts even before incurring them—in the very act of creation. So how come the story is forever threatening to do just that?[83] It's time to confront this uncomfortable fact, by walking carefully through the scene of the crime.

> He sought them both, but [a] *wish'd* his hap might find
> Eve *separate*, [b] he *wish'd*, but not with *hope*
> Of what so seldom chanc'd, when [c] to his *wish*,
> Beyond his *hope*, *Eve separate* he spies,
> Veiled in a Cloud of Fragrance, where she stood,
> Half spi'd, so thick the Roses bushing round
> About her glow'd, oft stooping to support
> Each flowr of slender stalk, whose head though gay
> Carnation, Purple, Azure, or spect with Gold,
> Hung drooping unsustain'd, them she upstaies
> Gently with Mirtle band, mindless the while,
> Her self, though fairest *unsupported Flowr*,
> *From her best prop so farr, and storm so nigh.*
> (*PL* 9.421–33; italics mine)

(a) "Wish'd . . . separate"; (b) "wish'd . . . not with hope"; (c) "wish . . . beyond his hope . . . separate." After two unsuccessful attempts, the fragments of Satan's puzzle obligingly come together of themselves, apparently by "chance" or "hap": Eve is unexpectedly and vulnerably alone. The Advocate gives us a wonderful little verbal pantomime of serendipity—or folly mocking itself; in an order of things run by Providence, a "hap" isn't a hap. We've already met this kind of perplexing irony—Satan might never have made it out of Chaos:

> All unawares
> Fluttring his pennons vain plumb down he drops
> Ten thousand fadom deep, and to this hour
> Down had been falling, had not by *ill chance*
> The strong rebuff of som tumultuous cloud
> Instinct with Fire and Nitre hurried him
> As many miles aloft.
>
> *(PL* 2.932–38; italics mine)

The teasing here works the same way. In an order of things run by Providence, an "ill" chance isn't chance[84]—but then isn't Providence left "ill" by process of elimination? The Advocate has troubles enough; why make up one?

This doesn't exhaust the awkwardness, for the Advocate's project, of Satan's lucky find. Consider this understandable response to Eve's proplessness: "Eve, being genuinely and designedly the weaker of the human pair, being here more helpless in a very real sense, can justly be seen as 'hapless' [*PL* 9.404] when she is found alone, but God's providence is not called into question since God has made Adam to be her guide and help. The tragedy is more his failure than hers."[85] More Adam's failure than Eve's? On the reader's showing, how is it *her* failing at all? Or on Satan's showing, for that matter; the Serpent is delighted to

> behold alone
> The woman, *opportune to all attempts,*
> Her Husband, for I view far round, not nigh,
> *Whose higher intellectual more I shun.*
>
> *(PL* 9.480–83; italics mine)

If she falls because she's weak and helpless, a friendly harbor (*ob-PORTU-na*) to temptation, easy prey to the Tempter's superior "intellectual," then how does her having been made that way vindicate God's providence? How does punishing her for being that way vindicate God's justice? If Eve is really "hapless" because, as the Advocate says in the rest of the quoted line, she's "much deceav'd," then she's doubly hapless, because she's condemned for acting *in-*

advertently—in a word, she's condemned *unjustly* by the Judge of all the earth; condemned unjustly beyond the possibility of appeal.

"The unsupported flowers are a metaphor of Eve's moral position."[86] Her moral position? We can't have it both ways. If Eve *can't* weather the "storm" without support, she isn't to blame for bending and breaking under it. If she *can*, then why go on about the pathos of her lack of support? And in the Advocate's narrative at least, it looks as if she can.

It makes sense, of course, to wish she hadn't gone off by herself: if she hadn't gone off, she might not have fallen. But it doesn't follow that she fell *because* she went off by herself, any more than Willy Sutton robbed banks because he was born. In fact, we've already been taught (by God himself in *PL* 3) this lesson about how to interpret the causal background of Eve's and Adam's Fall. But then why risk misleading us—maybe even *guarantee* misleading us? The pathos didn't call for it; and if it did, what made a self-indulgent little effect worth putting the Advocate's whole project in jeopardy?

Maybe part of the answer is that the Advocate can't afford to falsify the record on a material point; according to an unimpeachable witness (no less than St. Paul), Eve is the victim of a swindle (*panourgía*, 1 Cor. 11:3). It *is* deception—though somehow a kind of deception that didn't excuse her. The Advocate can't finesse his responsibility for explaining the "somehow" by simply pretending that the problem isn't there. One way of *not* pretending is to build up the Tempter a bit by making his "incarnation" as visually beguiling and unsnakish as possible. Some of the Advocate's primary audience can be counted on to recall the fabled "kinglet" (basilisk) of Cyrene that "doesn't push its body along by flexing intricately like other serpents, but by walking tall and upright in plain view":[87]

> not with indented wave
> Prone on the ground, as since, but on his rear,
> Circular base of rising foulds, that towr'd
> Fould above fould a surging Maze, his Head
> Crested aloft, and Carbuncle his Eyes;
> With burnish'd Neck of verdant Gold, erect
> Amidst his circling Spires, that on the grass
> Floated redundant: pleasing was his shape,
> And lovely, never since of Serpent kind
> Lovelier.
>
> (*PL* 9.497–505)

As it turns out, the snake is visually beguiling only to us; what eventually "turns" Eve's eye to "mark his play" is his "gentle dumb expression" (*PL* 9.527). To block an easy excuse still further, Eve has been given some emblematic clues to danger. Unlike the Minotaur's lair, here is a "maze" that divulges its secrets by "surging" sideways. And the "carbuncle" eyes may be rubies—but they're also demonically blazing coals (*carbunculi* both times). It's also suspicious that the Tempter is reduced to ignoring the Edenic protocol that beasts come into their mistress's presence only if invited:

> more duteous at her *call*
> Then at Circean *call* the Herd disguised.
> Hee boulder now *uncall'd* before her stood.
>
> (*PL* 9.521–23; italics mine)

The Serpent's "boldness" is a last resort; his frantic efforts to attract attention with "many a wanton wreath" (*PL* 9.517) don't do the trick. Eve's "intellectual," in short, isn't too "low" to resist fancy shows. What *is* it finally too low to resist? Apparently not the Serpent's fulsome claim that beauty makes her the "fairest resemblance of thy Maker fair" (*PL* 9.538). The "Maker fair," of course, is unavailable to sight; fairness in him is precisely wisdom—"a ray of the eternal light and an unsullied mirror of the working of God and an image of his goodness" (Wisdom of Solomon 7:26–27). God's birthday present to Eve, in fact, is the lesson that *only* wisdom is fair (*PL* 4.491). It's true we're expressly warned that "into the heart of Eve [the Serpent's] words made way" (*PL* 9.544–46)— words including the argument that her beauty deserves a better public than a menagerie of

> Beholders rude, and shallow to discern
> Half what in thee is fair; one man except,
> Who sees thee?
>
> (*PL* 9.544–46)

Still, virtue and vice in the Advocate's ethical tradition are measured by what goes out, not what comes in. Flattery isn't the bait Eve rises to.

It seems that what makes way into Eve's heart isn't so much what the Serpent said as that he said anything at all. The Tempter's hook is Eve's urge to communicate with the only one of those "beholders rude" that proves articulate. As in all communication, the process can't get off the ground unless one's partners' rationality and truthfulness get the benefit of the doubt: the partners in question may be "rude," but their behavior is "duteous"—they obey their mistress (*PL* 9.522); and to obey "human sense" is, more or less, to have it (*PL* 9.554). As a magnanimous but careful judge, Eve "demurrs"— she's too charitable to abandon the rationality reading out of hand; after all, "in thir looks / Much reason, and in thir actions oft appears" (*PL* 9.558–59). The fruit's effect gives her a chance at last to test the reading—only to *test* it, because the mere effect isn't conclusive: "Thy overpraising leaves in doubt / The vertue of the Fruit" (*PL* 9.615–16).

If there's a danger to Eve in any of this, it's that the benefit of the doubt a fresh interlocutor is entitled to covers *truthfulness* as well as rationality. Assume, with Eve, that the reporter is truthful:

> Amid the Tree now got, where plenty hung
> Tempting so nigh, to pluck and eat my fill
> I spar'd not, for such pleasure till that hour
> At Feed or Fountain never have I found.
> Sated at length, ere long I might perceave
> Strange alteration in me, to degree
> Of Reason in my inward Powers, and Speech
> Wanted not long, though to this shape retain'd.
> Thenceforth to Speculations high or deep
> I turn'd my thoughts, and with capacious mind
> Consider'd all things visible in Heav'n,
> Or Earth, or Middle, all things fair and good.
>
> (*PL* 9.594–605)

The Serpent apparently is under no sentence of eternal death if he eats, so the eating doesn't test whether God will make good his threat of a death sentence. What's getting tested, if anything, is the fruit; Eve has been provided with a royal taster.

So far Eve has been successfully lied to. She's blamelessly "unwarie"; at this stage to be "wary"—to withhold the presumption of truthfulness—is to break a rule of fairness. The Serpent, so far, enjoys the usual prima facie claim on her trust. Provisionally— unwarily?—she lets herself be guided.

Or *is* the unwariness blameless? Consider the hint we're given of what kind of guiding light this is:

> Hope elevates, and joy
> Bright'ns his Crest, as when a wandring Fire,
> Compact of unctuous vapor, which the Night
> Condenses, and the cold invirons round,
> Kindl'd through agitation to a Flame,
> Which oft, they say, some evil Spirit attends,
> Hovering and blasing with delusive Light,
> Misleads th' amaz'd Night-wanderer from his way
> To Boggs and Mires, and oft through Pond or Pool,
> There swallow'd up and lost, from succour farr.
> So glister'd the dire Snake, and into fraud
> Led *Eve* our credulous Mother.
>
> (*PL* 9.633–44)

This light in the forest is a will o' the wisp—in the usual jargon, "foolish fire"—fire that makes a fool of whoever trusts it. But what kind of fool? The blamably self-made kind? The innocently "natural" kind? Is "our credulous Mother" credulous because she *can't* help it, or even though she *can*? It's puzzling, in the same vein, that the Advocate likes his "vapor" image so much he's given it a dry run by having Satan sneak into the Garden "involv'd in rising *Mist*" (*PL* 9.75; my italics). Unfortunately, the puzzle is an embarrassment; Folly is being brought on as an iconographic twin of Wisdom: "I issued from the mouth of the Most High and *as a mist* did cover the earth" (Ecclus. 24:3; italics mine). Is Eve to blame for getting taken in by the closest kind of family resemblance? The Advocate and his client, to put it mildly, don't need these speculations; even if *Eve* turns out not to have been lured into "Boggs and Mires" against her will, *we* have—thanks to the Advocate. Why? Maybe the actual temptation will enlighten us on this point.

Like "som Orator renound / In *Athens* or free Rom" (*PL* 9.670–71), the Tempter begins with an artifice designed to win him a receptive "audience" (674):

> O sacred, Wise, and Wisdom-giving Plant,
> Mother of Science, now I feel thy Power
> Within me cleere, not onely to discern
> Things in thir *Causes*, but to trace the *wayes*
> Of highest Agents, deem'd however wise.
>
> (*PL* 9.679–83; italics mine)

The Serpent doesn't literally *claim* to have received a gift of "science"; he gets himself figuratively *overheard* thanking the giver. The resulting illusion: that Eve is getting shown something rather than merely being told about it. In the process, the speaker manages to honor a distinction dear to the Advocate: "things" have "causes," but "agents" have (freely chosen) "wayes." The Serpent's new wisdom extends to the "highest" agents, so his portfolio significantly overlaps with the Advocate's: to explain, if not justify, the ways of God to men.

The explainer, it turns out, relies not on privileged insight but precisely on "science." The method of discovery is to "trace" the ways of God (so called) by what stands to reason—after all, Eve already knows that "reason is our law" (*PL* 9.654). Thus it stands to reason that evil known—i.e., recognized—is "easier shunn'd" (*PL* 9.699), so to "hurt" somebody for trying to know evil is to be unjust—and "[if] not just, not God; not fear'd then, nor obey'd" (*PL* 9.701). The prohibition, in fact, is simply a bogey—a device for generating "worshippers" by dimming their eyes with "awe" and "ignorance" (*PL* 9.703–5). With their eyes undimmed, they would be "as Gods" themselves, "knowing both good and evil as they know" (*PL* 9.709–10). The threat of death is, in scarecrow disguise, a promise of apotheosis (*PL* 9.713–14).

In fact, God can hardly have created the tree and its power if Eve can enjoy both without his permission (*PL* 9.722–25). Conversely, if God owns the tree and everything else, then Eve's enjoyment of the tree and its power doesn't thwart his will, much less "hurt" him (*PL* 9.725–28)—unless the hurt is envy, the drive to diminish and begrudge; and "can envie dwell / In heavenly breasts?" (*PL* 9.729–30). "No" is clearly the right answer to this devastating question. The speaker's "science" establishes, in short, that any God capable of forbidding the tree isn't God. In the sense of creator, there is no God, only Gods spawned by nature before we arrived on the scene, and exploiting this fact to hoodwink us: "The Gods are first, and that advantage use / On our belief that all from them proceeds" (*PL* 9.718-19).

The heart of Satan's case for God's envy is made up of three flagrantly bad arguments in succession—bad by Eve's lights as well as ours. A brief review of the fallacies: (a) Knowing evil in the relevant sense (of being able to spot it) is precisely what it means to be "Law to ourselves"—as Eve knows she is: "our [moral] Reason is our law" (*PL* 9.654). Satan is equivocating on "knowledge" in the sense of "direct acquaintance"; one doesn't have to eat a rotten apple to know it's rotten. (b) Again, wanting obedience doesn't mean wanting disobedience to be out of the question. (c) Again, one needn't be "hurt" by disobedience to be wronged by it. If Eve gets taken in by this stuff, surely the Tempter's words won "too easy entrance" into her heart (*PL* 9.734; italics mine). She has no excuse; she knows better. She *lets* herself be taken in.

Or does she? The Tempter's words enter her heart because they're "impregn'd / With Reason, *to her seeming*, and with Truth" (*PL* 9.737-38; italics mine). We're generally no more responsible for how things *seem* to us than we are for the weather—though perhaps in this case, if the odd syntax isn't merely odd, the seeming is "hers," is something she's doing to herself.[88] And what do we make of the fact that Satan's language about God's jealous fear is God's own language in the canonical source—language the Advocate eventually does his client the disservice of quoting outright? Adam and Eve need to be barred from Eden because "like one of us Man is become / To know both Good and Evil" (*PL* 11.84–85). And Man mustn't be allowed to improve on the likeness by winning immortality from the other tree (93–98; cf. Gen. 3:22–23).

Maybe it helps here that in the Advocate's version God turns out to be equivocating on "know": the object of the sinners' new knowledge is (a) the good they lost by sinning, and (b) the evil they got (*PL* 11.87).[89] Nothing godlike about the "knowledge" in a guilty conscience—though the equivocation robs "like one of us" of its point (to justify the expulsion). And maybe it also helps that God is made out, in an afterthought, to be equivocating about the danger of the sinners' making themselves immortal:

> Lest therefore his now bolder hand
> Reach also of the Tree of Life, and eat,
> And live for ever, *dream at least* to live
> Forever . . .
>
> (*PL* 11.93–96)

—though the backup motive for expulsion here is pretty feeble; if what's really in prospect is only a dream of rival godhead, why spare the sinners a rude awakening? Above all, why risk even the *appearance* of God's being every bit as jealous and fearful as Satan claims? Why not skate around the canonical embarrassment at this point?

All this while, the Advocate has been preparing us for the moment fast approaching, one of two on which the case for God's justice stands or falls. If everything goes according to plan, we're about to catch Eve in the process of making up her mind and acting—without being made to do either; though a plausible case could be made for her having made up her mind at the start, by not nipping the temptation in the bud. "One needs to be watchful," says the *Imitatio Christi*, "especially at the beginning of a temptation, because the Enemy is the more easily defeated at that stage—if he is not allowed to get through the mind's front door, but is met outside the threshold, as soon as he knocks." "The first thing to come up is the mind's bare thought, then the strong image, afterward the delight and the corrupt motive and the consent."[90] Acquiescing in Step One (or Two or Three or Four) is as much an act of consent as saying a general yes at the end of the sequence.

Eve begins her general yes a little ominously, by miming disrupted conversation as the Serpent had—rhetorically "turning away" from herself; her new interlocutor is the object of her desire: "Great are thy Vertues, doubtless, best of Fruits" (*PL* 9.745). The Serpent had converted Eve's disobedience into an act of courage: God should be proud of her for defying him; she would be showing

> dauntless vertue, whom the pain
> Of Death denounc'd, whatever thing Death be,
> Deterr'd not from atchieving what might lead
> To happier life, knowledge of Good and Evil.
>
> (*PL* 9.694–97)

Eve follows suit by converting prohibition into endorsement:

> His forbidding
> Commends thee more, while it infers the good
> By thee communicated, and our want.
>
> (*PL* 9.753–55).

The "commendation" is backhanded; God's ruling passion is envy. In him, an act of forbidding "infers"—implies—an act of begrudging. But notice that this "inference" goes through only if Eve has already accepted the Serpent's libel—only if she has already shed her faith in God's lovingkindness. And how can she do that unless she has already fallen—already (disastrously) made up her mind? But we've been steadily listening to her thoughts; how did we manage to let the crucial moment get by us?

Grudging or not, a person in authority "forbids us good, forbids us to be wise" (*PL* 9.759); isn't there a duty to comply? Eve's answer: "Such prohibitions bind not." The moral hurdles are now behind us; the remaining hurdle—fear of the consequences—is easily negotiated:

> What fear I then, rather what know to fear
> Under this ignorance of Good and Evil,
> Of God or Death, of Law or Penaltie?
>
> (*PL* 9.773–75)

As a matter of fact, Eve's alleged ignorance of death and penalty is a red herring—though here the real culprit is the (Biblical) testimony the Advocate is committed to making sense of. The death threat fudges the point of God's love test twice over: (a) it makes obedience a counsel of prudence as well as (or instead of) love—with the effect of grossly trivializing love or its divine sponsor; (b) if the threat works the way a threat is supposed to work, then the obedience it induces (*causes*) is unfree as well as unloving. That's why Eve isn't exonerated by ignorance of the danger, only by ignorance of the moral nature of her act—viz., by thinking she's defying tyranny rather than betraying love.

Strangely for somebody so balefully in the dark, Eve has grasped at least one essential point about obedience. It *is* (partly) an intellectual virtue, calling for reliable notions of morality if not prudence—notions to which, if we believe her, Eve doesn't have a clue. The *a priori* road is blocked, it seems. The only way to learn obedience, then, is to get directly acquainted with what's involved in disobedience: "Here grows the Cure of all" (*PL* 9.776). Moments before, Eve had no trouble helping herself to the relevant prudential notion: "How *dies* the Serpent? hee hath eaten and *lives*" (*PL* 9.764; italics mine). As for Eve's newfound ignorance of law and morals, somewhere along the line she apparently mislaid her membership in the species that "live law to ourselves; our Reason is our Law." Either that, or (against all appearances) she has been a beast or baby all along! In short, we are listening to a veteran in the art of lying (in this instance, to herself). Eve is already infected. Once again, the decisive act of will, if any, is well past; somehow or other, our attention was engaged elsewhere at the time.

We're holding the Advocate to an unreasonable standard, of course. Acts of will don't announce themselves by getting observed, but by being the best way of accounting for what *does* get observed. If they were just additional grist for observation, they too would be candidates for an account—and so on to infinity. We have

God's word for it (in *PL* 3) that they're more than just the best way of accounting for the fall—they're the *right* way; but the Advocate's job is to see to it that they pass at least the minimum test of working better than rival accounts. And what we've been noticing, as we walk through the scene of the crime with our nose to the ground, is that the Advocate's job performance is disturbingly uneven. Unfortunately, the fall of Adam simply doubles the discomfort.

After recovering from his initial paralysis, Adam reacts to Eve's fall in two stages. In the first, ominously, conversation is disrupted: Adam breaks only "inward silence," not outward. We get a long aside—his unspoken thoughts:

> (a) How art thou lost, how on a sudden lost,
> Defac'd, deflowrd, and now to Death devote?
> (b) Rather how hast thou yeelded to transgress
> The strict forbiddance?
>
> (*PL* 9.900–903)

The first flinching pass at an assessment runs up against "rather": those participles of victimization won't do—seduction isn't rape. To be (in the morally actionable sense) "defac'd," "deflowrd," "devote," you have to cooperate; no "transgressing" without "yeelding." The third pass, unfortunately, is an exercise in backsliding:

> (c)   som cursed fraud
> Of Enemie hath beguil'd thee, yet unknown,
> And mee with thee hath ruin'd, for with thee
> Certain my resolution is to Die.
>
> (*PL* 9.905–7)

The pair are helpless victims of the same fraud, Eve "beguil'd" and Adam "ruin'd." Ignorance or delusion, contrived by a third party "yet unknown," is Eve's excuse; what's Adam's? What lets the responsibility for his "ruin" or "resolution" be fobbed off on the "enemie"?

> I feel
> The Link of Nature draw me: Flesh of Flesh
> Bone of my bone thou art, and from thy State
> Mine never shall be parted, bliss or woe.
>
> (*PL* 9.913–16; cp. 956–59)

If Adam is telling himself the truth, we may as well forget about spotting the moment of decision. Adam falls by being set in motion, not by deciding to act, or acting. His fall isn't something he *does*, but something that he "feels" as it *happens to* him: the partners are "linked" by their (physical) nature; as one partner falls, the link gets taut and "draws" the other, too, over the edge. On Adam's testimony, he isn't to blame for what he's about to do; something inexorable is *making* him do it. This is testimony against the Advocate's client; is it credible? And again—does it belong in a forensic narrative on behalf of that client? Maybe; to fall, sometimes, may be to become an accomplice in the supreme libel.

Along with the pull on Adam, it seems there's also a push: the inconsolable pain of living on without her (*PL* 9.908–13). Note that Adam's first and last thought here is for what's more agreeable (or at least less painful) to *him*; Eve is "lost," so worrying about *her* is apparently wasted effort. Preferring love of Eve to love of God, in the Augustinian perspective at least, is a maudlin form of idolatry.[91] On the other hand, the corrupt Eve says Adam has given a "glorious trial of exceeding love, / Illustrous evidence" (*PL* 9.961–62). Neither description is quite right here. The first requirement for loving somebody, in the Advocate's tradition at least, is caring about the somebody's welfare. For Adam to be acting out of love, as Eve says, is for him to be acting "for her sake" (*PL* 9.993) and not for his own. What wins out over the love of God here isn't idolatry, isn't chivalry, isn't caring about another. It's just egoism.

So far Adam has broken only "inward silence"—despairingly. What he finally gets around to saying aloud is more cheerful; apparently insincerity is the first gift of the fall. Instead of "defac'd," etc., Eve is "adventrous" (*PL* 9.921); instead of having "transgressed," she has "provok'd" great "peril" (*PL* 9.922). Instead of being "devote" to death for an act of desecration, she stands a chance of being convicted of a lesser charge; the fruit, after all, had already been made "common and unhallow'd" by somebody else (*PL* 9.928–31). Above all, it doesn't stand to reason that a "Creator wise" would "labor" pointlessly, as he has if it now turns out that he created only to be ignominiously forced to "uncreate." By destroying Adam and Eve, God would be handing the Adversary an easy "triumph," by convicting himself of fickleness (9.938–51).

On this last point, of course, Adam is quite right: an infinitely loving God can be depended on to have a loving plan for picking up the pieces; all the more reason not to make things worse by compounding human guilt—especially given the chance to plead credibly, in the Abrahamic mode, for somebody Adam is supposed to care about more than about himself. A whole epoch of debased intellectual currency lies between the Advocate and us, and threatens to obscure the ironic point of all this: in the strict sense anyhow, there is *no love* here, and so no tragic collision of authentic but incompatible "oughts." What there is, is "compliance bad" (*PL* 9.994). Adam's disobedience is (by the Advocate's own lights) unequivocally wrong. It's also deliberate—Adam knows what he's doing: "he scrupl'd not to eat / Against his better judgment, not deceav'd" (*PL* 9.997-98). Here at least the Advocate is home free—if he leaves well enough alone.

But—by this time, predictably—he doesn't leave well enough alone:

> He scrupl'd not to eat
> Against his better judgment, not deceav'd,
> But fondly *overcome* with female charm.
>
> (*PL* 9.997–99; italics mine)

I remarked a while back that, if Adam is right about his inescapable "link" or "bond" with Eve, then the fall isn't something he *does*, but something that *happens to* him—something that comes over him, or (even worse) by which he is "overcome" in spite of himself. This is a revelation the Advocate can afford as little as the other revelations we've had to face on our walk through the scene of the crime.

Of course, "overcome" needn't get Adam off the hook. It's one thing to be (excusably) overcome *tout court* by an impulse, and quite another to be *fondly* overcome—to be (inexcusably) foolish enough to *let* oneself be overcome (see *PL* 9.313). Well, which is it? But maybe the "fondness" itself is as good an excuse as the female charm; maybe Adam was "fond" by his own choice rather than his Maker's. Which is it? Moreover, if Adam is to blame here for "fondly" overriding his better judgment about an infinitely loving God, then how can he be merely "submitting" here to "what *seem'd remediless*" (*PL* 9.919)? How can he be be an innocent dupe of appearances? Or does he somehow choose how things look to him? Is he, like Eve earlier (9.738), a *guilty* dupe, the architect of the "seeming" he's conveniently submitting to? Again, which is it?

More fundamentally: if God is to win his case, we need urgently to catch these people dead to rights, not thwarted at every turn by ambiguities; why—beyond mere ineptitude—is the Advocate going out of his way to trouble our faith? Why hasn't he left well enough alone?

Suppose that, partly by not leaving well enough alone, the Advocate winds up undermining the defense: with his customary gallantry, he faces his challenge and emerges a loser—by standards of philosophy and jurisprudence that he himself clearly takes for granted.[92] Does the intellectual failure of the narrative as plea translate into its aesthetic failure as dramatic mimesis of pleading? Not if the pleader has fought with exemplary force against formidable odds, and especially not if the audience, cast in the uncomfortable role of jury, has a high enough stake in the pleader's success.

But what sort of stake would this be—especially if Milton's primary audience is eked out with the likes of *us*? Even granted the voyeuristic and sacrificial fascinations of courtroom drama, how can post-Christians be powerfully absorbed in the fortunes of this particular defendant? Aren't many of us *dis*interested—to the fatal point of being *un*interested—in whether this or any other attorney manages to get an acquittal for God? I've already sketched the outlines of an answer: not when we're in the *dock* as well as the jurybox.

The Advocate's free will brief is—as a defensive strategy—a thesis of cosmic laissez-faire: God lets us do our worst because he respects *the autonomy of the autonomous moral agent*—respects us *as we would prefer to think of ourselves*. Suppose the failure of the case for God brings with it the failure of the case for the grounds of that respect. Suppose the death of the divine is also the death of the *human*. This latter much-buffeted notion, I've suggested, can be summed up in two truisms even more basic and (in the end) enigmatic than free will, or autonomy: that some beings do things, and have things done to them; that the deeds and sufferings of such beings matter. In the current chapter, I've talked about the threat, inside and outside the faith, to the notion of *mattering*. In the next chapter I turn to the seventeenth-century state of the more basic question—the question of what it is, if anything, to be *somebody acting*.

The Advocate has been fair beyond the call of duty in his dramatization of an adversarial process: in nearly every book of *Paradise Lost* the Adversary gets a chance at the jury. Not only are the proceedings of this forensic narrative haunted by a mighty opposite, the proceedings themselves have a grim double, in the form of a demonic anti-epic about the same issues:

> others more mild,
> Retreated in a silent valley, sing
> With notes Angelical to many a Harp
> Thir own Heroic deeds and hapless fall
> By doom of Battel, and complain that Fate
> Free Vertue should enthrall to Force or Chance.
> Thir song was *partial*, but the harmony
> (What could it less when Spirits immortal sing?)
> Suspended Hell, and took with ravishment
> The thronging audience.
>
> (*PL* 2.546–55; italics mine)

We're conspicuously unfit jurors, as the Advocate is well aware: "We bring not innocence into the world, we bring impurity much rather: that which purifies us is trial, and trial is by what is contrary." What is contrary, in the current case, is a falsehood highly seductive to our delusions of victimhood: God is the secret engineer of our apparent guilt. The Advocate can't leave well enough alone, can't make his song "partial" by erasing all suspicion of this possibility from his version of the available evidence. He can't do this, precisely because his innocent client's behavior *is* suspicious, and because "partiality" is the Adversary's kind of tactic. To be free, for a judge especially, is to be a moral adult; the Advocate gambles on his jurors' freedom. It will be up to them, for better or worse, to decide how Adam is "overcome" and Eve "deceived." "Partiality" in laying out the relevant details is a kind of censorship; and censorship, as we've been reminded elsewhere, is "weakness and cowardice in the wars of truth." In the Advocate's libertarian faith, we have it in us to keep our weakness and cowardice at bay long enough to render judgment. And we have a right to be given the chance.

2

Free Will in *Paradise Lost* and its
Historical Roots

Unfortunately, before it can do any good in a defense of God, the notoriously fuzzy notion of "free will" is going to need a defense of its own—from the Advocate if not from his opponents in the Augustinian camp. In the first part of this two-part chapter, I contrast the Augustinian (or dismissive) attitude to free will with the Advocate's appeal to the notion, and his polemic on its behalf, in *PL* (see rubrics (A) through (D)); the remainder of the chapter is devoted to a pocket history of the development of the notion, from its classical beginnings to the state of the question in the Advocate's own century (see rubric (E), sections 1 to 10). By the time we're done, it will turn out that, in his treatment of what it is to act at all, freely or not, the Advocate stands nearly alone in his tradition (with the author of *Christian Doctrine*, with whose work he seems to have been intimately familiar, and in a crucial respect with Spinoza, whom he anticipates).

(A) THE AUGUSTINIAN ALTERNATIVE

There's this much to be said for the alternative defense-of-God strategy of standard Reform theology: you finesse the free will problem. Admit that the Fall was decreed by God and, at the same time, put the burden on the accuser to prove injustice; on the positive side, claim—with Calvin and many other Augustinians before him—that if the fundamental maxim of justice is "to everything its due," then for a creator to put up with indeterminacies is itself a kind of injustice—an injustice to the fineness of the fine grain of things.

If the building is exquisite—that is, if it is just—then God is in the details; a Fall *not* decreed by him would mean that "God has created the noblest of his creatures with an ambiguous end [*ambiguo fine*]."[1] "God bears witness that he creates light and darkness, that he shapes good and evil [Isaiah 45:7]; that nothing evil happens that he himself did not do [Amos 3:6]. Let [the impious] pray tell us whether God exercises his judgments willingly or unwillingly."[2] Predestination, in short, is simply a consequence of a theory (Augustinian-Boethian) of what it is to create the world. "Ambiguous" futures—domains of maybe and maybe not—are out of the question for divine creation because leaving a blank in creatures' *futures* is leaving a blank in *creatures*.

In a biased creaturely awareness, hemmed in by memory and anticipation, body will seem to be one thing and process another. But in a God's-eye view unblinkered by restriction to single moments, points in time don't divide up into past, present and future any more than points in space; in that uniquely objective awareness, bodies turn out to be made up of their tenselessly coexisting stages, like the nude descending a staircase. The same goes for the body of the world; to create a world is to create a history. That's why the perfect creator of a perfect creation, the God of details, *has* to be the divinity that shapes our ends: "Man falls, then, by God's providence so ordering: but man falls by a vice of man's own making."[3] Somehow God jointly performs Adam's act without performing its depravity. This may be an uncomfortable paradox, but on the current view there's no way out of it.

If there are such things as free acts, the agency in each act will need to be doubled to make room for a silent partner: "By free will one moves oneself to act—but it doesn't necessarily follow that the thing freely acting is its own *first* cause. God is the first cause, moving *both* the causes that operate by nature *and* those that operate by will."[4] Thus far Aquinas on double causation. But here as elsewhere Augustine himself is the most defiantly paradoxical Augustinian of all:

> No human will stands against God when he wills to save it. For to will or not to will is *in the agent's power in such a way* that this power neither hinders nor overcomes the power of God. . . . There is no doubt that God's power to sway human hearts at will is unlimited. . . . Human wills are more in his power than in their own.[5] (Italics mine.)

The Augustinian approach, in short, is to deny that the tension between God's creation of history and the freedom of historical agents amounts to a contradiction.

The approach has the merit of doing justice to the dual intuitions of Augustinians. For side by side with Luther's clear and distinct sense of human bondage, we encounter Descartes' clear and distinct sense of the opposite:

> We reach near enough to this infinite power [of Predestination] to perceive clearly and distinctly that God has it, but fail to grasp it firmly enough to see how it leaves people's free actions undetermined; on the other hand we are so conscious of having the freedom of indeterminacy [*libertas indifferentiae*] that we understand nothing more clearly and completely. [6]

The contrast between Luther's and Descartes' versions of the self-evident is stark enough to suggest that they both overrate the insight to be had by searching for freedom inside oneself—especially if one doesn't quite know what it would be like to find it.

The Advocate might well ask, at this point, why the Augustinians balk at the idea of a free will that's free without qualification—free even of control by God. And here, beyond the gappiness this would introduce into the Creator's flawless architecture, the second favorite Augustinian answer is revealingly desperate: absolute freedom is logically out of the question; an omnipotent God is a God who can't be crossed. Again one may ask (with the Advocate): isn't crossing God precisely the required justification for condemning Adam and Eve to death? And as to the alleged absurdity, does a plausible notion of omnipotence really rule out *any* sort of limit on power? Would God be enfeebled by inability (say) to lie, rape, or self-destruct?

On a plausible notion of omnipotence, in fact, God's power *is* limited—by his will: "As the Psalmist sings [Ps. 135:6], God's majesty can do, and does, what it *wishes* in heaven and earth."[7] Very well, if omnipotence is power to do what one *wishes*, then why can't God wish to keep hands off Adam's and Eve's free choice? Why can't God both wish something to happen and wish to refrain from *making* it happen? How would *that* compromise an omnipotence worthy of God? Something over and above omnipotence is at stake here.

"God's will is self-executing [*efficax*]. It can't be frustrated, since God's will is his natural power itself and, further, is too wise to be deceived."[8] It seems that, simply by virtue of wishing people to do things, the God of the Reformers can't *help* making people do them. So he can't wish them to do things he hasn't made them do. In short, a rational God aware of his own nature can wish his creatures to obey him—but not (on pain of contradiction) of their own free will!

Surprisingly, this Augustinian weapon is compelling enough to beat back a professed friend of free will like Erasmus: "Anyone who fails to hinder something he knows will happen must, in some sense of 'must,' be willing it. This is the point of Paul's remark: 'Who is it that withstands God's will, since God has mercy on whom he wishes, and hardens whom he wishes?' [Rom. 9:19]. For if a king were such that, whatever he wills, he thereby brings to pass, we would say that he does what he wills."[9] (That is, for something to be his will is for it to be his deed.)

Something has gone badly wrong here. Consider Erasmus's reason for thinking God shares the hypothetical king's self-executing will: if God really dislikes *something he knows will happen*, then he'll just keep it from happening. This friend of rational argument invites us to imagine things known to be true turning out to be untrue! Still worse, this friend of free will has talked himself into giving up the core of the Free Will Defense: that the only acts of obedience God punishes are the ones his creatures could have refrained from. What's troubling Erasmus here isn't stupidity. It's failure of nerve at a glimpse of what his theodicy obliges him to give up. The price of a God whose justice is defensible is a God who deliberately gives his creatures the power to disappoint him.

In the end, the defense strategy of the Augustinians is too close to a prosecution strategy to satisfy the Advocate and his tradition. If that strategy manages to vindicate anything, it's not God's justice but a wrongheaded version of his majesty.

In a more characteristic moment, Erasmus invites us to "imagine that it's true *in a sense*, as Augustine writes somewhere,[10] that God works both goods and evils *in us* and rewards his good works *in us* and punishes his bad works *in us*. How wide a window to impiety a public announcement to this effect would open for countless mortals!"[11] God's authorship of sin, in short, would be terrible enough even if it were merely "true in a sense." The moral urgings in scripture would be unmasked as so many taunts:

It would be laughable, after all, to say "choose thou" [Gen. 2:17, Deut. 30:19] to someone with no power to apply himself to both courses—as if one should say to someone halting at a crossroads: 'You see the two

paths, take whichever you wish,' when only one was open to him. . . .
In this passage [Deut. 30:19] you hear the language of proposing, you
hear the language of choosing, you hear the language of dissuading—all
of which language would be out of place if the person addressed weren't
free to do good, but only evil. Failing that, it will be like somebody
saying to a man tied up so as to be capable of extending his arm only to
the left: 'Look at the fine wine you have on your right, and the poison
on your left: reach out your hand in whichever direction you like.'[12]

Even Luther edges close to admitting that predestination is a
scandal to believers in God's justice:

Obviously nothing is more offensive to that faculty of common sense or
natural reason than this: that God, purely by an exercise of his will,
abandons, hardens, and damns human kind—as if he delights in the sins
and torments of the wretched, sins and torments so great, so everlasting;
he who is praised for his great mercy, his bounty, and the rest. This
wicked, this cruel, this unbearable thing it has seemed right to think of
God, this thing that has offended so many men, and so great, down the
centuries. And who would *not* be offended?
    I myself have been offended more than once, even to the abyss, even
to the loss of hope, and to the wish that I had never been created a man;
before I came to know how wholesome was that despair, and how
nearly allied to grace.[13]

Luther's homeopathic remedy for despair of God's love is despair of "that faculty of common sense or natural reason":

The God of Lovingkindness does not deplore the death that he *works* in
his people, he deplores the death he *finds* in them and strives to remove.
For this is the work of the God Proclaimed, to save us by taking away
sin and death. For he sent his Word and healed us [Ps. 108:20]. On the
other hand, the God Hidden in Majesty neither deplores death nor removes it, but works life, death, and all things in all things. For by his
Word at that time, he did not *define* himself, but *reserve* himself free
above all.
    In this life our part is to look to his Word, and to let that unsearchable
Will alone. For of necessity it is his Word that guides us, not that unsearchable Will. Who can be guided by a Will utterly beyond searching
and knowing? It is enough to know of the mere existence of a certain
unsearchable Will in God. As for its object, or end, or extent, these we
are altogether forbidden to inquire into, to long for, to care about, to
touch on, but only to dread and to revere.[14]

By contrast to his revealed "Word," "God himself"[15] (when he's in the mood) is a denier of mercy—a being that scorns to be "defined," holding itself in "reserve" in an upper storey of the great mansion, where it scatters here and there the death of the spirit that the "Word" deplores. Not only is "God himself" a denier of mercy but a denier of justice as defined by human reason. But this should scandalize no one; reason's definitions are mere cleverness—*argutatio*.

Not that Luther sees no point in asking how guilt can be assigned to a will in bondage. On the face of it, the assignment is at odds with "common sense"—with a faculty that God created and (in his public mask at least) emphatically endorses. Maybe the insult to common sense will dissolve on closer examination, if only we draw the right distinction: "The God of Lovingkindness does not deplore the death that he *works* in his people, he deplores the death he *finds* in them and strives to remove." The death God "deplores" is one thing, and the death he inflicts without "deploring" is another—yet, on Luther's showing, the deaths are one and the same!

This is no mystical paradox. It's a vision of universal love in word and deadly caprice in deed. This Jekyll is never anybody but Hyde, even when he's being Jekyll. For the Advocate and his tradition, the Lutheran cure for despair is one of two intolerable things; either it is worse than the disease, or it *is* the disease. The author of *Christian Teaching* spells out our stake in the pending action at law with an even grimmer lucidity: Homer had it right when he brought on Zeus to condemn the sinners who blame their fate for the actions they add to fate.[16] The blind pagan saw a lot farther than some Christians who are so eager to make God the author of all there is that they don't hesitate to make him the author of sin; an effort to give them the lie will amount to an expanded case that God isn't Satan.[17]

(B) FREE WILL IN *Paradise Lost* 3

I began by remarking that, if it's going to serve the Advocate, "free will" needs some defending in its own right—we're still less than luminously clear about what free will is free *from*. But before we go on to take a fresh look at the standard suggestions, it's worth bearing in mind that God himself (in *PL* 3) expects a stiffer challenge than the claim that free will is fuzzy, or even the claim that it makes no sense. The question on the table in the heavenly parliament is *cui bono*—who stands to gain by the alleged gift: what makes the ability to fall a power? Why not a weakness?[18] Why not a bomb disguised as a birthday present?

It's easy to see what the Giver gets out of giving it: without free will, no guilt or innocence; without guilt or innocence, no chance to exercise the virtue of justice. But what's in it for the Receivers? Why wouldn't Satan, Adam, and Eve be better off with a will irrevocably tilted in the right direction? Why, in short, wouldn't they be better off just *having* moral goodness rather than being free to take it or leave it? As it turns out, the Advocate's God *does* expect to benefit from his gift, but not at his creatures' expense:

> Not free, what proof could they have giv'n sincere
> Of true allegiance, constant Faith or Love,
> Where onely what they needs must do appeard,
> Not what they would? what praise could they receive?
> What pleasure I from such obedience paid,
> When Will and Reason (Reason also is choice),
> Useless and vain, of freedom both despoil'd,
> Made passive both, had serv'd necessitie,
> Not mee.
>
> (*PL* 3.103–11)

The obedience that gives God "pleasure," in short, is a proof of faith and love. But unfree beings are capable of neither. Any proof of faith and love available to them is going to be bogus ("insincere").

Being self-sufficient, God has no needs. But he has wishes. And what he wishes of his creatures—the angelic and human ones anyhow—is love. Before it's anything else, *PL* is a tragic love story—a story of unrequited love. Love is something a lover can gain only if he puts himself in a position to lose. So far the God of the Advocate is the God of George Herbert's "Pulley": a world in which God's creatures refuse him their love is a world in which both creator and creatures "should losers be." Foreseeing the worst, God plays the game of creation and loses. There's something shocking in this—for the Augustinians, of course, too shocking to be true.

But this looks very much like one cake the speaker can both have *and* eat. Granted, love doesn't do what it *needs* must do, it does what it *wills* to do. But why not both? Why not make a loving creature that "needs must" *do* the loving thing precisely because it "needs must" *will* it? Erasmus, we recall, misreads Luther as claiming that whatever is done by me, good or ill, is something God does in me whether I want to do it or not. God seems to be reading the Augustinians the same way; in fact the Augustinian God makes me do things—the voluntary ones anyhow—by first making me *will* to do them. Why not be that kind of God? In the last part of this book, I will have to consider this question in more detail, on its own merits. For now, I'm interested in what, if anything, the Advocate's God has to say about it.

We've cut him off in mid-speech. His answer is that the kind of love *he* wishes to inspire is precisely the kind that isn't rigged. A rigged thing is a mechanism. No matter how busy it gets, the things it "does" are just events firing off in the causal chain linking its parts. For a rigged thing to *"do"* things is for them to *happen* to it. In that sense of "passive," a rigged or (causally) necessitated thing is passive. But—and this is apparently the point—the love the speaker desires and cherishes isn't passive. It isn't a domino effect or clockwork process in the economy of the lover. It isn't a passion. It's an act.

The act requirement explains why it isn't enough for love in the speaker's sense to be voluntary and rational. Will and reason are "useless" and "vain" if they're merely rigged up to trigger the choice of what to love. The resulting pseudo-choice is something done *to* the lover rather than *by* him. So we have the rest of the answer to the question of *cui bono*: freedom is what makes events that merely originate in me *belong* to me as my acts—what binds them to me as uniquely and intimately as my body and mind are bound to me. If this seal of ownership is a blessing, then freedom is a blessing. To cherish it, in fact, is to cherish oneself—at least if the Advocate's brief is to be believed.

(C) FREE WILL IN ACTION: THE BIRTH OF SIN

The catch, of course, is that the freedom to give one's love is inseparable from the freedom to withhold and betray it. And in *PL*, which is after all about loss—the same metaphor does duty for both:

> All on a sudden miserable pain
> Surpris'd thee, dim thine eyes, and dizzie swumm

> In darkness, while thy head flames thick and fast
> Threw forth, till on the left side op'ning wide,
> Likest to thee in shape and count'nance bright
> Then shining heav'nly fair, a Goddess arm'd
> Out of thy head I sprung.
>
> (*PL* 2.752–58)

Free will is both father and mother to its own version of Athena. What's more to the point, free will is a creating Spirit that both broods and impregnates (*PL* 1.21–22). The psychological metaphor of "conception" is as archaic, at least in the Advocate's polyglot culture, as a metaphor can be.[19] So is the bisexual metaphor of creation. An act starts out as an idea. The male principle that gets (or begets) the idea is one and the same with the female principle that conceives it. To act freely is to create—*like God*. And for the resulting offspring, no second parent can take the credit or blame—*not even God*.

As metaphors have a way of doing, this turns color treacherously as we look at it. The point, one would have thought, was to *incriminate*; the effect is to *excuse*. Granted, on the current theory of moral genetics nobody but this particular "mother" can take the blame for the birth of this particular "offspring." Still, look again at the childbirth scene being offered here: is it obvious that the blame can fairly be laid on the "mother" either? What we're shown is a birth organ erupting in the throes of a cruelly violent C-section: "Thy head flames thick and fast / Threw forth." It's hard to imagine an act of giving birth more passive and victimlike, less like an act, than this one. Can the sinner really be to blame for something that comes to him as a wrackingly painful surprise, leaving him blind and dizzy?

Of course, the Advocate will want us to remember that all of this is beside the point—the "birth" of an act is only a follow-up or *actus secundus*; what the sinner is really the agent of, and to blame for, is the interior fornication[20] that caused these effects. The essence of an act is the moment of "conception"—the *actus primus*; and this we aren't allowed to see. But still, why trouble us with the effects while hiding the cause? Maybe for reasons of courtroom fairness we've already explored. And maybe the nearest we can get to an image of free will at conception is the image of its reenactment by a sinner already in bondage, cohabiting with his sin:

> familiar grown,
> I pleas'd, and with attractive graces won
> The most averse, thee chiefly, who full oft
> Thy self in me thy perfect image viewing
> Becam'st enamour'd, and such joy thou took'st
> With me in secret, that my womb conceiv'd
> A growing burden.
>
> (*PL* 2.761–67)

In this corrupt tableau, the central figure manages to be both passive and active: the active partner eggs on the passive one by a kind of flattery—by mirroring it in a "perfect image." The result is an auto-erotic parody of an Augustinian idea: free agents start by persuading themselves to consent to a *spontanea cogitatio*.[21] In each case, the persuader is the consenter.

(D) THE DEBATE ON AUTONOMY

God's reason for leaving humanity to its own devices wasn't that human ability [*potentia*] could then be proved (by temptation); from the mere fact of falling, the inability [*impotentia*] to stand doesn't follow now and never did. What God saw fit to test, instead, was human *obedience*—the obedience of a creature with a God-given power to decide for itself [*potens arbitrii sui*], a creature God made master [*dominus*] and (by exercising its will) first beginning [*principium*] of its own actions.[22]

It's a bit unfortunate, as we'll see shortly, that Jacobus Arminius is under the illusion that he can consistently make the temptation in the Garden be a test of (a) Adam's and Eve's free will (b) their character (in particular, their "obedience" or disposition to obey). On the other hand, it's not surprising that a luminary of the Advocate's libertarian tradition like Arminius should favor God's plan to let Adam and Eve be tempted.

What's more surprising—or would be if we hadn't been focussing on a pattern of kindred surprises—is that the Advocate should make up a debate between Adam and Eve in which Eve is all *for* submitting to undergoing a test, and Adam—at the outset anyhow—is all *against* it. The fact that the male supremacist Advocate puts the pro-temptation position in the mouth of the weaker vessel has raised a widespread suspicion that there must be something wrong with it, and that the stronger vessel's eventual capitulation shows that even the strong vessel is pretty weak—maybe even weaker than the weak one.

On the surface, the issue at hand is simple. Adam and Eve have a duty of action as well as omission—what Adam calls an assignment (*PL* 9.231) and Eve (in the remarks we're about to look at) an injunction: the job of taming excess growth in the garden. Eve is clear that the job is both a duty and a pleasure—a "pleasant task enjoin'd" (*PL* 9.207). At the same time, the way she and Adam have been approaching it up to now strikes her as self-defeating; far from letting itself be restrained, the garden makes a joke of their efforts by growing "luxurious by restraint" (*PL* 9.209):

> what we by day
> Lop overgrown, or prune, or prop, or bind,
> One night or two with *wanton* growth *derides*
> Tending to *wild*.
>
> (*PL* 9.209–12; italics mine)

Now, besides being absurd, "enjoining" what can't be done is the pettiest of petty tyrannies. Eve presumes God's innocence: keeping down a riot of fertility won't turn out to be impossible; just hard. The obvious solution is to accomplish more by indulging less:

> For while so near each other thus all day
> Our task we choose, what wonder if so near
> Looks intervene and smiles, or object new
> Casual discourse draw on, which intermits
> Our dayes work brought to little, though begun
> Early, and th'hour of Supper comes unearn'd?
>
> (*PL* 9.220–25)

In his style of deliberation, Adam's ideal of family politics anticipates Aristotle's: a wife is a non-ruling but none the less free citizen of a kind of republic, enjoying adult rights of advice and consent; in the conjugal polity, husbands rule—but rule by rational persuasion.[23] So the "motion" on the table needs to be taken seriously:

> Well hast thou motion'd, well thy thoughts imploy'd
> How we might best fulfil the work which here
> God hath assign'd us, nor of me shalt pass
> Unprais'd; for nothing lovelier can be found

> In Woman, then to studie houshold good,
> And good works in her Husband to promote.
>
> (*PL* 9.229–34)

The good work Eve is promoting here, to repeat, is obedience to a divine command (injunction or "assignment"). "Not unpraised" perhaps understates the value of her intentions, fruitful or not. In fact, Adam seems to have underappreciated them in two other respects: Eve starts out by calling the task a pleasure, and shows no signs of a puritanical urge to transform it into "irksome toil." And if it's really so obvious that the couple's "joynt hands" will keep the wilderness away "with ease," however "wide" they have to walk (*PL* 9.244–46), then why does the Advocate take care to tell us how "much thir work outgrew / The hands dispatch of two Gardning so wide" (*PL* 9.202–03)? Why discredit Adam this way if not to encourage us to look around for whatever it is that's made Adam so poor a listener?

There are worse things than an ill-tended Garden, and they're on Adam's mind. Satan

> seeks to work us woe and shame
> By sly assault; and somewhere nigh at hand
> Watches, no doubt with greedy hope to find
> His wish and best advantage, us asunder,
> Hopeless to circumvent us joyn'd, where each
> To other speedie aid might lend at need.
>
> (*PL* 9.255–60)

If we're "joyn'd," Satan is "hopeless to circumvent us"; if we're "asunder," Satan has a "hope" of carrying off his effort to "withdraw / Our fealtie from God" or from each other (*PL* 9.261–63)—a hope that Adam endorses: Adam and Eve "asunder" offer Satan his "best advantage." Adam isn't simply reporting Satan's "wish" here; for there to be a "hope" is for there to be a chance; for there to be no "hope" is for there to be no chance.

The wish report reading—"hope" or "advantage" in Satan's eyes alone—can serve Adam in a pinch: charged with casting doubt on Eve's unaided capacity for "fealtie," he can always claim a misunderstanding. For further insurance, the "danger"-"dishonor" distinction he winds up with (*PL* 9.267) has a palliative effect; the "fealtie" question is just one item on a long list of worries, including the possibility of violence.

Left to herself, it seems, Eve is at a *dis*advantage—is ill-equipped to avoid being "circumvented" by a "sly assault." What Adam is really worried about, in short—as Eve herself has no trouble understanding—is "that my firm Faith and Love / Can by [Satan's] fraud be shak'n and seduc'd" (*PL* 9.286–87). He applies the same argument (with cosmetic chivalry) to himself: "I from the influence of thy looks receive / Access in every Vertue" (*PL* 3.309–10); but Eve sees through palliatives as shrewdly as she sees through the warning about undefined (physical?) "danger": "[Satan's] violence [toward me] thou fearst not" (*PL* 9.282). If Adam is to be left a leg to stand on, we need to see a petulant Eve quick to take offense. What we're shown instead is "sweet austeer composure." Eve responds with composure but, with some reason, as "one who loves and some unkindness meets" (*PL* 9.271–72). There is no sign here of an "impatient desire to prove herself"[24]; only of a frustrated desire to be trusted.

Adam's backpedalling in reply makes up in velocity for what it lacks in conviction: it seems he *has* been misunderstood after all. He wasn't "diffident" of Eve (*PL* 9.293); he was worried about Satan's *subjective* hope of circumventing her—that and the resulting injury:

> For hee who tempts, though in vain, at least asperses
> The tempted with dishonour foul, suppos'd
> Not incorruptible of Faith, not prooff
> Against temptation.
>
> (*PL* 9.296–99)

Merely by treating Eve *as if* she could be corrupted, Satan succeeds in compromising her honor; apparently, "supposing" Eve corruptible is morally equivalent, as "dishonor," to proving the supposition. An "affront" is a moral injury—no wonder Adam wants to "avert" it (*PL* 9.302).

The argument virtually refutes itself. Eve makes short work of it:

> [Satan's] foul esteem
> Sticks no dishonour on our Front, but turns
> Foul on himself; then wherfore shund or feard
> By us?
>
> (*PL* 9.329–32)

Meanwhile Adam's real worry is as obvious as it is obsessive: a tempter "subtle" enough to seduce angels (*PL* 9.307–08) is more than subtle enough to seduce the likes of Eve. So much for Adam's "healing" claim that he is not "diffident of thee" (*PL* 9.290, 293).

If Adam and Eve are better off together, then they're at a disadvantage apart—a disadvantage in moral acuity or (worse) in will power! In short, the trouble with the theory of collective security is that it undermines the Advocate's defense of God by collapsing into a theory of individual weakness. The first thing the Advocate does after describing the Fall is to give the theory a hasty burial: *neither* sinner taken singly was at a disadvantage—precisely because at the outset *each* sinner's mind is

> with strength entire and free will arm'd,
> Complete to have discover'd and repuls'd
> Whatever wiles of Foe or seeming Friend.
> For still they knew, and ought still t'have remember'd
> The high Injunction not to taste the Fruit,
> Whoever tempted.
>
> (*PL* 10.12–14)

Oddly enough, Adam has just finished hearing from an authoritative source about the duty (not just the possibility) of self-reliance:[25]

> to stand or fall
> Free in thine own Arbitrement it lies.
> Perfet within, *no outward aid require*;
> And all temptation to transgress repel.
>
> (*PL* 8.640–43; italics mine)

Still more oddly, up to this point it seems that the only disputant to have profited from Raphael's message is Eve:

> what is Faith, Love, Vertue unassai'd
> *Alone, without exterior help* sustain'd?
> Let us not then suspect our happie State
> *Left so imperfet* by the Maker wise,
> As not secure to single or combin'd.
>
> (*PL* 9.335–39; italics mine)[26]

I add "up to this point" because now at long last Adam "fervently" renounces his tacit premise that "the Maker wise" left his handiwork disastrously "imperfet."

Not that he stops worrying:

God left free the Will, for what obeys
Reason is free, and Reason he made right,
But bid her well beware, and still erect,
Lest by some fair appearing good surpris'd
She dictate false, and misinform the Will
To do what God expresly hath forbid.

(*PL* 9.351–56)

The things that the Ground of Right tells us to do can't be wrong. Hence the problem: free will obeys reason; reason obeys Right; so how in the world can freedom ever go wrong—for example, how can free will ever disobey God's command not to eat the fruit? Answer: by disobeying God's command to beware of things that look good at first sight. Every act of disobedience begins as an act of inattention. The bedrock of the law is: Beware.

In Adam's view, the best way to beware of temptation is to avoid it—which is "most likelie if from mee / Thou sever not" (*PL* 9.365-66). Unfortunately, "*most* likelie" in this case is not very likely at all: "Trial [i.e., temptation] will come unsought" (*PL* 9.366) if "from me / Thou sever not." The kind of temptation one has a hope of avoiding is the kind that *doesn't* come "unsought"—the solitary kind in which the *force* of a forbidden desire is unopposed by the *force* of social sanctions—in particular, by the force of "shame to be overcome or overreach'd" [*PL* 9.313]). What worries Adam, in short, is *freedom itself*—in particular, the free decision not to beware, followed by the free decision to fall.

Adam has given up trying to argue against freedom. But he hasn't given up distrusting it. He still badly wants Eve to stay—so badly that he takes a fumbling stab at a prohibition of his own:

Wouldst thou approve thy constancie, approve
First thy obedience; th'other who can know,
Not seeing thee attempted, who attest?

(*PL* 9.367–69)

Adam is quite right: no one will be in a position to "attest" Eve's constancy to God unless she's "attempted." And that's precisely the point: getting her to attest her constancy to Adam will effectively block her chance to attest her constancy to God. "Th'other"—that is, constancy to God—"who can know?" Answer: nobody, if Adam has anything to do with it. To repeat: *what worries Adam isn't an outbreak of frailty; it's an outbreak of freedom.*

On the other hand, it occurs to him in these last awkward moments that if Eve obeys him, "thy stay, not free, absents thee more" (*PL* 9.372). Subordinate or not, Eve is a moral adult. Adam recognizes that he has no business denying her the chance to face a critical decision on her own; and no business forcing her to choose between his command—so far lamely defended at best—and the dictate of her own conscience.[27] Staying against her better judgment is worse than not staying at all—it "absents" her more.[28] Adam doesn't add what would be painfully obvious to anybody in the Advocate's intellectual tradition: doing something—anything—against one's better judgment is the classic criterion of *acrasia* or weakness of will; staying against her better judgment absents her not only from him but (morally) from herself as well.

Ordering her to stay is no solution. A good argument in favor of staying would be. But Adam has only bad arguments. We have reached an impasse.

At this critical point, Adam does something remarkable.

He has been arguing badly but desperately against her seeking temptation—desperately enough to toy with the possibility of simply ordering her not to. Now he orders her to follow her own better judgment. She should act against his better judgment if she disagrees with it—if she thinks not seeking temptation "may find us both securer [i.e., less wary] then thus warn'd thou seem'st" (*PL* 9.370–72).[29] In the end, the only obedience he demands of her is free obedience to her own better judgment.[30]

The risk throughout has been that freedom to obey is inseparable from freedom to defy. It's the risk Adam has been recoiling from. Now he's resolved to emulate the inventor of free will by living with the risk:

> Go in thy native innocence, relie
> On what thou hast of vertue, summon all,
> For God towards thee hath done his part, do thine.

Of course he would be living with the risk of Eve's freedom even if he went through with ordering her to stay. But he would also be replacing a test of obedience to God with a test of obedience to himself; instead of emulating God, Adam would be playing God.

It's curious that there are critics who think his failure to do this is a fatal sign of weakness.

Eve meets the attached condition ("if thou think," etc.), and so obeys the order to go,

> forewarn'd
> *Chiefly* by what thy own last reasoning words
> Touch'd only, that our trial, when least sought,
> May find us both perhaps farr *less prepar'd.*
>
> (*PL* 9.378–81; italics mine)

There's no sign of rebelliousness in her speeches—no hint that she would have defied an order to stay (she questions Adam's reason for ordering her to stay [*PL* 9.265], but questioning isn't defiance, and Adam doesn't read it that way[31]); in fact, the narrator is careful to assure us of the opposite: Eve at the end remains "*yet* submiss"—as submissive now *as she has been up to now.*

The real difference is that now Eve has Adam to thank for a clearer idea of what following her better judgment entails. To seek something (e.g., temptation) is to be on the lookout for it; her real peril ("unwariness") starts when she forgets what she's on the lookout for. Adam has invented a Christian commonplace: "Many seek to flee temptations," says the *Imitatio Christi*, "and fall into them the more heavily. By flight alone we cannot win. By patience and true humility we are made stronger than all our enemies." "The proof of the iron is the fire. The proof of the just man is temptation."[32]

The debate on autonomy is relentlessly complicated, and it's easy to misread it. It's wrong, for example, that Adam caves in to a termagant Eve; he doesn't cave in, and she's no termagant. It's wrong that Eve's confidence amounts to an arrogant claim of self-sufficiency; what it amounts to is faith that, as Raphael and Adam say, God has done his part and left it up to Eve to do hers. And it's wrong that a decision that leads to the Fall has to be perverse; on that ground,[33] the gift of free will itself gets convicted of perversity, not to mention the Creation.

It would be easy to misread the debate as the Fall, Phase One, and it would be a great pity.[34] It's a true intellectual collaboration—in the end, more collaboration than debate. Eve weans Adam from the fear of free will, and Adam helps Eve get clear on precisely where the risk of free will lies.

On the other hand, the intellectual collaboration is also an intellectual mess. Neither interlocutor notices that being "less" than ideally "prepar'd" for a deception (*PL* 9.381) diminishes the guilt of falling for it. And neither notices that there's something strange about tracing a *free* choice of sin to unwariness—or even to a free choice of unwariness, whatever that is (we'll need to poke about in this part of the mess a little later, in the historical part of this chapter). The moral of the story can hardly be that poets (alas) aren't philosophers; the Advocate inherits the confusions in his notion of free will from philosophers. And the moral can hardly be that philosophers are stupid; they inherit the confusions they valiantly strive to put right from the perennial wisdom of common sense. Next, a pocket history of the notion—and the confusions.

(E) FREE WILL: A BRIEF HISTORY

1. Aristotle

On Aristotle's showing, a common sense of sorts on the Will is embedded in the silent part of ordinary talk—the part that goes without saying: for an act to be voluntary (*hekoúsion*) is for it to "have its beginning [*arché*] in an agent who knows the details of the act."[35] Doing is never just moving or behaving. Without the inner event or drive (*hormé*; e.g., the mental act of *trying* to move or behave), what a thrown rock or falling man "does" isn't a deed.[36] And in every case of doing something willingly, it's the *hormé* and not the movement or behavior that specifies what's getting done. Exactly which act Oedipus can fairly be accused of at the crossroads—killing his father or getting even with a grizzled bully—will depend on which details of the massacre got picked out by the killer's originating desire-cum-belief.[37] Given a suitable *hormé*, moving and behaving aren't even required for a voluntary act—sometimes just standing there is doing something: it makes respectable sense to attribute "voluntary" suffering to people who accept the suffering or submit to it; to accept or submit is to do something.

In the common sense view that Aristotle is trying to put to rights here, the *hormé* of a voluntary action is naturally wired ("disposed") to comply with the agent's idea of the best available thing to do.[38] In this minimal sense (following one's better judgment), voluntary action is always rational, even when wrong.[39] The will strictly so called (*boúlesis*)—unlike desire (anger or lust)—is simply the appetite for following one's better judgment or "right reason" (*orthòs lógos*),[40] or what passes for these in genuinely bad but free agents.[41]

On the other hand, many of us are neither bad nor good; our moral decisions, among others, sometimes begin with ambivalence. In the ensuing tug of war, either one's urges or one's will may end up yielding to superior force; what isn't forced, but voluntary, is the eventual *resolution* of forces, and along with it the way the system acts as a whole.[42] Moral character is simply the inner hookup (varying from one agent to another) that yields a resolution of forces—one's arrangement or "disposition" (*diáthesis*); or, in a folk metaphor that Aristotle is fond of, the distinctive balance (*rhopê*) of one's will and feelings—one's inclination.[43]

So far the common sense account seems to promise tolerably clear answers to whether this or that act is voluntary. Trouble sets in when we have to classify things people do *against* their better judgment, and things they do because (in their judgment) the other possibilities are even *worse*. How can one be doing voluntarily what strikes one as a bad thing for one to do? (Here the Advocate would be in a position to point out that not even Satan could *will* to do evil without first saying: "Evil, be thou my good!" [*PL* 4.110])

Actually, the trouble with common sense on this score is not that clear answers aren't supplied, but that the ones supplied are inconvenient. To jettison cargo rather than risk drowning, or help robbers rather than condemn hostages to death—to choose the least bad of one's exclusively bad options—is to settle for the closest available approximation to the (nonexistent) greatest good; so by the test we've laid out—compliance with one's better judgment—the resulting action comes out voluntary. Likewise, to get momentarily distracted from a sober to a besotted notion of the best thing for one to do is to follow what is, for the moment at least, one's better judgment; so, by the common sense test once again, an incontinent act also comes out voluntary. Yet we pity people with grim options, and we go easier than we would otherwise on people who do things they later regret. How is common sense to be rescued from incoherence?

In each case Aristotle's justification for leniency is to find a plausible sense in which the agent's better judgment is getting violated after all. To do something bad to prevent worse is not to choose the bad but to have it forced on one by limited options—against one's (ideal) better judgment; the thing one does voluntarily here is not to do bad but to prevent worse.[44] As for incontinence, a better judgment unattended is still there—and still getting acted against; [45] the incontinent mind is alienated from its own knowledge—as if it weren't an individual but a bickering family.[46]

The metaphor of the bickering family comes naturally enough, given Aristotle's habit of treating agency as the operation of parts "disposed" in a system: a chain of mental causes and effects that ends (if all goes well and there are no crazy links) with voluntary movement or behavior. The point here, as usual with Aristotle, is to spell out what common sense doesn't bother to—what goes without saying. It goes without saying that the more thoroughly *like* Jane Doe it is for her to do such and such, the odder it would be to think (absent further information) that Jane Doe is acting against her will; that's what she *would* do in the given circumstances, what she was *disposed* to do, and what her judges (if it comes to that) ought to hold her to account for.[47] The act is a bona fide product of the Jane Doe System.

The disposition test of voluntary action—at least if the point is to locate where the buck stops—is open to an obvious objection: a disposition doesn't dispose *itself*; shouldn't the buck be passed back a step, to the disposer? Or a step before that, to the disposer's disposer? How do we stop the buck from passing all the way back to the First Disposer, with the undoing of the Advocate's whole enterprise? Aristotle's confrontation of the problem is grimly forthright enough to quote in full:

> Consider the argument that everyone seeks the apparent good, and that we aren't in control [*kyrioi*] of how things appear to us—that how the right end appears depends on the kind of person it's appearing to.
>
> Now if there's a sense in which one is responsible for one's own disposition, then there's a sense in which one is responsible for the way things appear to one.
>
> On the other hand, if our dispositions aren't our own doing, then no one is responsible for doing evil. Everyone does evil out of ignorance of the right end, in the belief that by evil means good will come to him; seeking the right end is not one's own choice—one is beholden to one's nature for the eyesight (if you will) to judge well and pick out what is good in fact. To be so nobly endowed by nature really *is* to be 'someone with natural gifts' [*euphyés*]. For that is the greatest and noblest gift— and one that can't be taken or learnt from somebody else.[48]

By the same token, no one who owes his moral insight to nature is responsible for doing good.[49]

So much for the problem. Aristotle's solution is twofold. (1) Give up the assumption that things are willingly sought only if they appear good to the seeker. Granted, whether they look good depends on the looker's nature; what's voluntary (if anything) is whether the looker accepts or rejects what looks good.[50] (2) Recognize that a disposition is something we can choose to acquire or discard: "One's actions in particular situations are what make one this or that kind of person. This is obvious from people in training for any contest or exploit: they're continually practicing. Only somebody senseless could escape knowing that dispositions grow out of particular actions."[51] Coming to be a particular kind of person takes drill. And so—*if one chooses*—does becoming still another kind of person. For us to be free is for the choice to be up to us.

That mysterious phrase "up to us" (*eph' hemîn*) is Aristotle's. Precisely what it means—in his jargon or ours—is hard to say. But think of the clown duet in *Waiting for Godot*:

> *Vladimir.* Question of temperament.
> *Estragon.* Of character.
> *Vladimir.* Nothing you can do about it.
> *Estragon.* No use struggling.
> *Vladimir.* One is what one is.
> *Estragon.* No use wriggling.
> *Vladimir.* The essential doesn't change.

On the view we have before us, the clowns' self-serving despair is a tissue of confusions. One's temperament isn't one's essence; being what one is, when character is in "question," is compatible with coming to be what one isn't: "Being [e.g.] morally good is up to us (*eph' hemîn*)—and being morally bad likewise. For where doing something is up to us, not doing it is, too; and where *No* is up to us, so is *Yes*."[52]

My disposition doesn't explain my voluntary acts by being what made me do them. *Nothing* made me do them—that's what makes them fundamentally voluntary: I was in a position to have done something else. Whether or not they were to happen was up to me and me alone.[53] On this view of will, there *is* such a thing as willing what one judges to be evil. It's the thing Satan does when he asks evil to be his good—at the moment of utterance at least, he knows very well by its real name which of the two opposites he's *freely* addressing (and embracing).

Side by side with the notion of will as rational appetite, in short, is the notion of will as no appetite (or disposition) at all—simply as the power to have acted otherwise. These two notions, as they stand, don't fit together; unfortunately, common sense *seems* (to Aristotle and many others) to commit us to both. No wonder we find him inflicting on himself and his lecture audience this embarrassing piece of choplogic: (a) Doing what one wants is acting voluntarily even if it's against one's rational calculation—against what one thinks is one's best course of action.[54] But (b) everything one does voluntarily, one does willingly; and what one does willingly, one believes is best to do. So (c) things one wants to do in spite of believing them bad to do (hence in spite of willing not to do them), are both voluntary and involuntary![55]

The "could have done otherwise" rule may seem to fail miserably in a certain kind of situation. Suppose Eve willingly refrains from eating the apple—and also that her system has been helpfully wired up to collapse at the first stirring of an attempt to eat.[56] Given the safety device, we have a case—not inconceivable after all—of Eve doing something willingly that she couldn't *not* have done! But the exception is bogus. The actuality we're asked to conceive of is Eve *trying to refrain and succeeding*. But the alternative possibility the safety device limits her to is Eve *trying not to refrain and failing*; in other words, precisely a case of doing otherwise. On Aristotle's view of doing, the inner trying—the *hormé*—is crucial; the story of doing can't be told from the outside.

Maybe we can get closer to discrediting the "could have done otherwise" rule by revising the story a little: suppose that Eve willingly ate the apple, but that *if* she had changed her mind God would have intervened by "disposing" her mind to cause her hand to bring the apple to her mouth, etc., etc. Here, at least, she eats willingly and yet couldn't have done otherwise? But once again the "could have" we've been limited to is the same *behavior*, not the same *act*. What's getting illustrated, on the contrary, is precisely the voluntary agent's power to do otherwise—an aborted attempt to refrain is as much of an act as a successful attempt to eat.

Unfortunately something else is getting illustrated too: for Eve to eat willingly, the possibility of an alternative *hormé*—even one that pops into one's head out of nowhere and causes the right behavior—isn't enough. It isn't enough for Eve's *mind* to be capable of

changing—Eve has to be *doing* the changing. The real act, whatever it is, isn't the relevant chain of mind and body events at all, not
even if the chain starts with an uncaused link—the *hormé*—inside
the presumptive agent's mind. The *hormé* is just one more thing
that *happens to* Eve; we need to be told what makes it something
she *does*. Side by side with the horizontal question of how the deed
is (or is not) causally articulated, we have the vertical question of
how it belongs to the doer.

In the end Aristotle exhausts the resources of common sense or
intuition or what is nowadays called folk psychology. The rest is
almost, but not quite, silence. It comes to just this: if my behavior,
its inner cause, and its external effects are ingredients in something
I *did*, then I myself—not parts of me, not their arrangement—am
related to the behavior, the inner cause, etc., in a special way. For
that way Aristotle supplies no clearer account than a metaphor: the
doer is the *kyrios* of the deed—the bearer of *authority* for what got
done. Eventually the authority metaphor reappears (or is rein-
vented) in the jargon of Roman law: the person responsible for
something is its *auctor*. Later still it becomes a staple of Rabbinical
Hebrew probably familiar to the Advocate: everyone has been given
the authority (*rᵉshuth*), says the Aristotelian Maimonides, for deciding which road to turn down, good or evil.[57] The metaphor gives us
a self that officially presides over the contest of its options as an
umpire (Latin *arbiter*—hence *liberum arbitrium* "free will").

One arguable reaction to all of this is dismissal. Out of ideas? Try
a metaphor. But the disreputably moral notion of AGENT is no worse
off in this respect than the respectably scientific notion of CAUSE; it
too has eluded analytical capture and at last report is still at large.
In fact, there's an instructive irony in the fact that CAUSE makes its
debut on the stage of Western thought in the *metaphorical* disguise
of a special case of agency—transferred from persons to events: a
cause is an event one can justifiably "accuse" (Lat. *ac-*caus-are*)
of its effect (cf. Gk. *aiti-âsthai*, "hold responsible"). When a notion
is basic, we pass up the wild goose chase of hunting for an analysis
for it and make do with a metaphor. Could it be that the trouble
with AGENT is not so much that it's inexplicable as that it's basic?

We don't end up quite empty-handed; the inglorious payoff of
Aristotle's pattern-setting search for an account of agency does
have something to tell us about what, beyond the defense of God,
is at stake here for the Advocate's tradition: on the common-sense
account, an agent doesn't "act" in the collective sense in which an

army "fights" or a team "plays" or a bee swarm "swarms" or (even) a clock "tells the hour"; whatever else it is, a *kyrios*—the "lord" of an act—is the radically individual subject of whatever (if anything) agency turns out to be; and presumably also the subject of whatever else turns out to be true of a *person*.

Elsewhere Aristotle seems to think that personhood isn't very deeply rooted in the structure of things, that PERSON has as little hope of being a free-standing category as CITIZEN or FOOT.[58] Not here. What's at stake here, in short, is a vision or fantasy of personhood as a fundamental part of the scheme of things. If sense can be made of the *kyrios* of agency, then maybe a coherent story can be told of what it is, if anything, to deserve to be accused or exonerated, punished or rewarded, hated or loved—what it is to be human.

2. *Plotinus*

Aristotle does common sense the great favor of rigorously spelling out a truism. As elsewhere, he acquaints common sense with what it already knows, or thinks it knows, about free will: to be the *kyrios* of what one does is to do it without having to. "Without having to" is the point of the matching truism that doing something of one's own free will is having it in one's power to do otherwise: the laws of nature combined with the facts rule out neither alternative— free acts transcend causality.

For Plotinus and Alexandrian Platonism, this transcendence drastically shrinks the domain of free agency; after all, everything outside the inner trying—outside the act of will itself—is at the mercy of the laws of physics, beginning with physiology. Countless facts of the latter kind—most of them well beyond one's control—are what turn an attempt to move into a motion. The world outside, including one's body, may be rigged so as to change an attempt at doing otherwise into an act of doing the same. Only withdrawal from motion into contemplation lets the mind be its own master.[59] In that state of rest, if anywhere, we get to do or be (same thing at this level) what's really "up to us"[60]; if "state of rest" is the right name for the pure activeness or "actuality" (*enérgeia*) of a mind released from matter[61] or "necessity" or "chance."[62] In the Alexandrian view, the whole scheme of things branches downward from a single incomprehensible source; becoming one's own master (*kyrios hautoû*) is a process of going back up (*anábasis*), through oneself, to the root of things.[63]

Plotinus retreats into mysticism partly out of despair: in the end, whether an attempted action gets aborted or brought off is up to luck and the laws of nature; it seems nothing is up to us—nothing, that is, except for the inner trying.

No doubt this last point deserves better than the short shrift Plotinus gives it: the inner trying *is* something that happens in the world; and, whenever nature and circumstances let it succeed, the trying simply falls into place as the *arché* of some tangible result or other. The launching of the arrow, if its flight path lets it, becomes a shooting of the quarry. The real question, as before, is what it is for either the launching or the shooting (or the trying, for that matter) to be the archer's act, rather than a sequence of things that happen to his mind and body and surroundings. Plotinus's non-solution is to locate the "real" archer and his "real" act outside the world of cause and effect altogether, hidden at its "root."

What's in hiding up there (the reality tree is inverted) is what Plotinus, and the rest of our cast of characters, are trying hardest to find. In the end the worry about WILL and ACT translates into a worry about SELF. The Plotinian self as agent, unfortunately, turns up outside the world looking in at the inert sufferings of a double fettered in feet and manacled in hands,

> A soul hung up, as 'twere, in chains
> Of Nerves, and Arteries, and Veins.
> Tortur'd, besides each other part,
> In a vain Head and double Heart.[64]

A few paragraphs back, I remarked that Plotinus drastically shrinks the domain of free agency. If the point of agency talk is to settle practical issues of responsibility, even "drastically shrink" is an understatement; what Plotinus does to that domain is eliminate it.

3. Aquinas

The Advocate is a Christian. Clearly no Christian, Augustinian or otherwise, can welcome the Plotinian solution to the problem of free will. As usual, getting kicked upstairs is no promotion; denying the self an active role in the world is denying it altogether:

> A substance owes its individuality simply to being itself. [Instances of] qualities owe theirs to . . . some substance or other. . . . But a still

more specific and perfect kind of individuality is found in *rational* substances—the ones that have sovereignty [*dominium*] over their acts, and that not only are (like others) *made* to act, but act by themselves. Individuals [in this sense] are things in which actions occur. This is why, among substances in general, the rational individuals are assigned a specific name: 'person.'[65]

Because even in separation the soul doesn't lose the natural attribute of joining with something else to form a unity, the soul isn't properly called an individual—i.e., *hypostasis* or primary substance—any more than a hand is, or any other part of a human being. And so the soul answers neither to the definition nor to the name of 'person.'[66]

A person is an agent par excellence: I act, therefore I am. And "I" here doesn't name the mind or soul. It doesn't name the body. Least of all does it name the body-mind *pair*. What it names instead is the *individual they add up to*. (The analogy to numerical sums is very close. Add a pair of numbers and you get still a third—a single number, not the number pair you started with or *any* pair.) The act belongs, says Aquinas, not to a set or sequence or system, but to an individual—an individual that exists (acts) only in the world, not in a metaphysical halfway house for disembodied souls, much less in a cloudcuckooland for abstractions à la Plotinus.

There's something strange and interesting about this individualism that will come into sharper focus when we get around to seeing what Milton makes of it. The thing to notice at this stage is that Aquinas inherits Aristotle's vacillation between two clashing accounts of inner "trying."

On one account, acts have causes, like all other natural events—one ultimate cause, in fact: the Will (Aristotle's *boúlesis*, Aquinas' *voluntas*); that is, the ("higher") disposition (urge) to follow one's better judgment: "A lower urge isn't strong enough to move us without the consent of the higher. This is the point of Aristotle's doctrine[67] that the higher urge moves the lower as the outer sphere [of the heavens] moves the inner."[68] "Aristotle remarks that when we form a judgment by taking counsel, our desire is to follow the counsel. This is how choosing itself comes to be called a kind of judging; hence the name *liberum arbitrium* [*arbitrium* = verdict by an umpire or *arbiter*]."[69] The power to act freely, on this account, is the power to choose (*vis electiva*; *prohaíresis*)—in particular, to choose the best means for the ends we have in view; in short, freedom is reason in action. As the Father tells the Son in the Advocate's narrative, reason isn't only thinking, "reason also is *choice*" (*PL* 3.108; italics mine).

On the other account Aquinas inherits from Aristotle, doing act A freely is doing A without being made to by anything, including one's disposition: "Free will isn't determinately disposed to choosing either well or badly. So it can't be a disposition; what remains is that it's a power"[70]—the power to do otherwise than one actually does.

Aquinas tries at one point to reconcile the two accounts: a rational agent isn't "determinately disposed" precisely because a rational agent goes by anticipated outcomes, and the outcome of any course of action is always indeterminate.[71] But the argument has a telltale desperation about it: among possible outcomes, some are generally more likely than others; rationality is going to be free only in case of a tie—which isn't free enough to tally with the second account. The point being ignored with desperate ingenuity here is that, on the second account, an essential part of freedom is freedom to act badly—freedom to go against reason.

In the end, Aquinas's tactics have nothing to offer the Advocate or his tradition; the underlying strategy is Augustinian: "God's causality, as first agent, extends to all beings"[72]—free agents included: "That which is *by* free will is *from* predestination."[73] Within the totally scripted scenario, free will plays a totally scripted role.[74] Aquinas's libertarian readers, in short, can take comfort in the assurance that free will is determined by nothing—but God's eternal decree. The comfort is pretty cold. For genuine forerunners, the Advocate will need to find candidates elsewhere.

4. Erasmus

One obvious candidate is Erasmus, Luther's opponent in the most conspicuous Reformation debate on the subject—humanist man of letters, magisterial scholar and interpreter of classical texts, champion of Gospel liberty, and (maybe less happily for present purposes) master of ironies. Two ironies in particular will engage us here. It's at least mildly ironic, to start with, that libertarian Erasmus shares predestinarian Aquinas's (unexamined?) tolerance of incompatible ideals of will.

On the one hand, we're given causal indeterminacy (*arbitrium*) or freedom proper: the "orthodox" believe that we have it in our power (*arbitrium*, that is) to "apply our will [*voluntas*] to grace, or turn it away."[75] *Arbitrium* is what "applies" *voluntas*. In the hierarchy of freedoms, *arbitrium* comes out on top. In fact, "will" had better be used to refer, not to rational appetite, but to appetite in general: " 'Free will' [*arbitrium*] is the term for the kind of will that is capable of turning either this way or that. Given the residue of sinfulness in us, maybe this kind of will leans more [*propensior est*] toward evil than good. But no one is forced toward evil, unless he agrees."[76] Where evil is freely chosen, "evil propensity" is a pseudo-explanation; free choice is not driven by disposition or propensity, by a rigged necessity or likelihood, but by no cause at all.

On the other hand, Erasmus offers autonomy—the disposition to follow one's better judgment or "right reason." In the end indeterminacy (alias "freedom") is a weakness that the autonomous will sloughs off as it grows into its real state of mastery:

> [i] *If he so willed, Adam was able to turn away from good and swerve toward bad.* The angels were created in the same condition, before Lucifer and his comrades deserted their creator. In the ones who fell, the will was too far gone in corruption to be able to turn back to better things. In the ones who kept standing, the will was [ii] *strengthened to the point of not even being capable, any longer, of swerving toward ungodliness.*[77]

Clearly "freedom" is the ideal required by the Advocate's forensic narrative: the Fall can't be allowed to be something the perpetrators can't help; it can't be allowed to be a *necessity*. But here we run up against a second and fatal irony: in Erasmus's (Scholastic) philosophical dictionary an event is "necessary" not only when it has to happen come what may but when it has to happen only given another prior event. Unfortunately, Erasmus manages to persuade himself that the latter "necessity" is harmless:

> It's possible to assume that human affairs exhibit a kind of necessity that doesn't rule out free will. . . . In this connection the technical Scholastic treatment [Erasmus's guide here] concedes the necessity of the 'consequence' ['*If* God foreknows and hence wills Judas's betrayal of his master, *then* Judas will betray his master'] and rejects the necessity of the 'consequent' ['Judas will betray his master'].[78]

The trouble is that the supposedly harmless "consequence-necessity" is none other than logical entailment by another name: for the betrayal to happen by "consequence-necessity" is for the conditions that guarantee it to have been met—God's foreknowledge and (above all) God's will. What good does it do Judas's actual free will that "Judas will betray his master," unlike "Twice two is four," comes out false in some possible worlds? Thanks to "consequence-necessity," "Judas will betray his master" comes out true in all the possible worlds in which "God wills Judas to betray his master" also comes out true—including the one we're in.

With enemies like Erasmus, Luther doesn't need friends.

5. *Arminius and Molina*

The Advocate will find still a third possible genealogy equally disappointing: Arminius and Molina, the two leading heirs to Erasmus's libertarianism—on the Reformation and Roman side, respectively—manage to reenact their master's performance.

For Arminius the beginning of the end comes with a harmless distinction out of Augustine, as harmless as the distinction Erasmus reaches for: grace is either "efficacious" or "sufficient." The reason why God foreknows rejections of the Holy Spirit with certainty is that people who aren't persuaded "efficaciously" just *won't* respond favorably to being persuaded "sufficiently" even though they *can*.[79] Arminius's distinction is not merely as harmless as the one Erasmus reaches for; it's the same one: "efficacious" grace is the kind "without which a person will actually not believe or be converted."[80] For "efficacious grace" to be "fit" for conversion is for it to *guarantee* conversion—uniquely.

In short, "efficacious grace" is both necessary and sufficient for conversion and "sufficient grace" is neither. So again we have "consequence-necessity": rejection of the wrong kind of grace is guaranteed by lack of the right kind. What good does free will do the damned if they "can" accept "sufficient" grace in this Pickwickian sense of "can"—that is, if they accept "sufficient" grace in all and only the possible futures in which the grace they enjoy is not only "sufficient" but also "efficacious"?

As it happens, possible futures or "orders of affairs" are the basic terms in which Luis de Molina, Arminius's Papist counterpart, makes much the same case for free will: people predestined to be saved "will freely cooperate with God's gifts and aids so as to arrive at everlasting life *in this order of affairs that he decided to create*."[81] But God can choose to create any one of a range of possible futures in which a sinner tries to cooperate with God's help and succeeds.[82] The particular help and cooperation involved vary freely from one such future to another, so there's no causal law linking divine help and human cooperation. In the sense of natural cause anyhow, human acts aren't caused—by an act of God or by anything else.

But that doesn't mean they aren't caused, and by an act of God at that. In Molina, as in Erasmus and Arminius, God *does* something: wills into existence a particular one among those optional futures—say a future that contains Jane Doe's act of "freely" accepting grace. The *effect* of God's act—given the contents of this particular future—is that Jane Doe eventually does the right thing. The cause and effect being described here aren't covered by a law of nature, so Molina can play Humpty Dumpty by limiting the application of "cause" and "effect" to the ones that *are* covered. And he can argue that the foreknowledge that guides God isn't absolute certainty about what sinners will do but simply an innocuous "middle knowledge"—conditional certainty about what they will do *if* God chooses to will into existence a particular future.[83] What we end up with is causation all the same.[84]

Humpty Dumpty arguments take after their patron; they start off audaciously and come to a bad end. I've remarked that with enemies like Erasmus, Luther doesn't need friends. And now it turns out that with friends like Erasmus, Arminius, and Molina, the Advocate doesn't need friends like Humpty Dumpty.

These are cheap shots, coming as they do from somebody with nothing to lose in the wars of faith. But there's an important moral to be drawn from the fact that the cheap shots hit home. We've met the moral before, but it's worth reminding ourselves of it here: Augustinians in the libertarian vein aren't simply putting on an act. They're trying in good faith to do justice to what I called, in the previous section, dual intuitions: the sense that among the things that simply happen to me are my so-called deeds, and the contrasting sense that at least occasionally the deeds are really mine and really deeds—that somehow I was in charge of them.

Even Calvin needs, grudgingly, to make room for the latter idea, or at least for the same ill-fated indeterminacy formula:

> In the state of moral wholeness they started with, human beings had the power of free will—the power to achieve everlasting life if they so willed. Here it's irrelevant to raise the issue of God's hidden predestination: the issue before us isn't what can and can't happen, but what human nature is like.

Adam, then, had it in his power to stand if he so willed, since it was only by his own will that he fell. But his will could bend either way [*in utramque partem flexibilis erat*]—Adam wasn't granted the constancy to persevere. That's why he fell so easily.[85]

Calvin, being Calvin, can't resist spoiling the claim (as well as undermining the Advocate's kind of enterprise) by turning the blessing of "flexibility" into the curse of inconstancy—the reason why Adam fell, indeed the reason why Adam had no trouble falling. And in Snark-like fashion, predestination is ruled irrelevant by naked assertion. It's rather like Johnson's dogs walking on their hind legs: what's interesting isn't that the attempt to accommodate free will is well done, but that it's done at all.

6. *Descartes vs. Hobbes*

For our purposes, the most interesting case of libertarian twinges in an Augustinian is Descartes. His performance brings together the Aristotelian, Neo-Platonic, and Augustinian strands of our story— and above all, if considered along with Hobbes's ostensible counterattack, it nicely reflects the state of play in the Advocate's own period.

One theme that runs through the whole Western dialogue on free will from the start is the poignant narrowness of the domain of this alleged power—the domain believers and would-be believers are prepared to claim for it. For Plotinus, the domain is not of this world. For the others, the writ of free will hardly runs further than the beleaguered inner trying that Erasmus sees behind his favorite Pauline and Patristic metaphors:

Where [St. Paul's] 'contest' is,[86] there is the will's trying [*conatus voluntarius*], there is the danger of quitting and losing the prize. . . . I have difficulty reconciling 'contest,' 'garland,''just judge,' and the talk of reward and competition with the unqualified necessity of all things, with a will that acts not at all but only suffers.[87]

Thanks to his notorious body-mind "dualism," Descartes seems to agree emphatically: "If there's anything in our absolute power it's our thoughts—namely the thoughts that come from rational appetite (*volonté*) and free will (*libre arbitre*). . . . Our free will has no absolute jurisdiction at all over any bodily thing."[88] The metaphor in "jurisdiction" is probably worth taking seriously. It's an ancient variant of Aristotle's notion that free agency is a kind of authority: to be free is to preside over one's inner courtroom, applying its law to current cases; to be, as the Romans say, *sui iuris*—subject to one's own law; or, as the Greeks say, "autonomous"—subject to a law (of moral reason) that is somehow not imposed from outside.

As it stands, of course, this won't do; the freedom we're shown is an incorruptible officer of the court, and the freedom we're on the trail of wouldn't be freedom if it weren't capable of taking bribes. Descartes is aware of the inconvenience: "It's always open to us to call off the pursuit of an obvious good or the recognition of an obvious truth—just so long as we think bearing witness to our free will this way is a *good thing*."[89] Unfortunately, the bribe for abandoning one judgment of the good is another; free will continues to be an inner compulsion to be reasonable: "The more numerous the reasons I'm *driven* by, the more *freely* I'm *carried along* toward something; because at that point, surely, our will moves itself more easily and impetuously."[90] "We're not only *free when ignorance of what's right makes us indeterminate* [i.e., capable of going either way], but especially when a clear perception [of what's right] is driving us [*impellit*] to pursue what we pursue."[91]

The passives here are symptomatic: it seems that acting freely is a case of getting pushed or pulled in the right direction, presumably thanks to having the right disposition. To be free, as Augustine says, is to be drawn to the Truth[92]—or (Descartes adds in effect) to a reasonable facsimile. It's equally symptomatic that the kind of freedom that interests us—indeterminacy or *libertas indifferentiae*—makes its appearance here as a kind of groping in a moral darkness that may or may not be of our own making. The Advocate can hardly welcome this analysis; it turns the great Fall that brought death into the world and all our woe into a great Pratfall. Descartes owes us a story about why we're to blame for groping, or for being in the dark in the first place.

Apparently this is it:

When something morally suitable to us is clearly in sight it's very hard—even impossible, in my view—to stop desire in its tracks. But the nature of the soul is to pay barely a moment's attention to any one object, so the moment our attention is distracted from the reasons that ground our knowledge that the object is morally suitable to us—the moment when all that we remember is that the object struck us as desirable—it becomes possible for us to represent to our minds still other reasons: reasons for doubting the object and suspending judgment about it; maybe even reasons for flatly rejecting it.[93]

Given a clear view, we would be incapable of wrongdoing for as long as the wrongness was in sight. Hence the dictum that every sinner is ignorant—*omnis peccans est ignorans*. . . . Given human inability to pay perfect attention to duty all the time, paying attention at all is a good deed, resulting in a will that follows reason too firmly to be even slightly indeterminate.[94]

The built-in shortness of the human attention span guarantees that sooner or later we'll be out of touch with our own better judgment; that's when the so-called freedom of indeterminacy takes over, and when we're taken in by a lesser or bogus good. I say "so-called" because the tendency to get distracted from one's better judgment is a disposition—in fact, the disposition Aristotle worried about under the name "incontinence." If there's indeterminacy in the "sooner or later," we're its victims, not its masters. Descartes reminds us, a little unhelpfully, that we have a duty to pay attention to our duty. But what if this duty in turn eludes our chronically wandering minds? The answer is obvious: it's incumbent on us to pay attention to our duty to pay attention to our duty—and so on (absurdly) world without end. If the resulting infinite regress of duties and attentions is a joke, it's a joke on all of us.

Even if Descartes's free will were outside the natural order, it wouldn't escape an order that is infinitely wider and more inexorable than nature—the same one the ingenious Molina works so hard to domesticate:

Before God sent us into this world, he knew all the future inclinations of our will to the last detail; it was he who put them inside us. It was also he who arranged [*qui a disposé*] everything outside us, so that our senses would meet such and such objects at such and such times—a meeting that, as he knew, would be the occasion for our free will to determine us to such and such. And he wished the will to do so—but by so wishing he didn't wish to *constrain* the will to do so.[95]

On Descartes's own showing, fulfilling this last wish will be a neat trick. How is the prearranged "occasion" expected to trigger the will's prearranged "inclinations" if not by causing them to go off? What are the "inclinations" pre-set for if not to go off on contact with the right "occasion"? Otherwise, why bring them up? How does the implied causation qualify as "indeterminate"? We've already heard the celebrated rationalist's answer: a finite mind can't remotely hope to fathom the contrivances of a mind that's infinite; it's enough for us (or ought to be) that "we're so conscious of having the freedom of indeterminacy that we understand nothing more clearly and completely."[96]

Again an Augustinian attempt to build up a notion of free will bears a suspicious resemblance to demolition. Descartes seems to be happily unaware of the failure, but he's as well aware as the Advocate of what failure would *mean*:

A supreme perfection of the human creature is that it acts voluntarily—that is, freely; by acting freely it is, in a special sense, the author of its acts. That's why it earns praise. No praise is coming to automata for accurately going through the motions they've been designed to go through; automata are accurate by necessity. The praise goes to their maker, for making them accurate—and for doing this not by necessity but of his own free will.[97]

Descartes is a determinist friendly to Aristotle's psychology of "dispositions" or "habits"; a predestinarian convinced that the world is an expression of God's will through and through; a rationalist with little respect for the notion of a power to decide whether to disobey reason. How can he turn around, not once but often, and celebrate that very power—and the clear and distinct idea he thinks we have of it—as the "supreme perfection" of the species? One might almost imagine that he vehemently disagrees with Hobbes on this issue. With so much else to quarrel with Hobbes about, why carry on the *illusion* of a quarrel?

I think the quarrel isn't illusory, and isn't really over free will. The indeterminacy Descartes defines out of existence shares no more than the *label* of "free will" with the "supreme perfection" he really means to celebrate. Hobbes's threat here is his dismissal of that "perfection," not his war against indeterminacy, and not even his materialism.

Hobbes agrees, in fact, on the essential point that Will in the strict sense is the disposition to act on one's better judgment—though here we're supplied with an explicit account of how better judgments get arrived at:

When animals alternate between seeking and avoiding one and the same thing according to the pleasure or harm they think it will bring them, we have (a) an alternation of seekings and avoidings, paired with (b) a series of thoughts [*cogitationes*], the so-called DELIBERATION. . . . Once the deliberation is over with, the last act in the process is the so-called act of WILL—positive if it's a seeking, negative if it's an avoidance. . . .

In short, 'freedom' in the sense of exemption from necessity applies to neither brute will nor human. But if by 'freedom' we understand, not a power of *willing*, but a power of *doing* what one wills, then in that sense, at least, freedom can be conceded to both kinds of animal.[98]

As Hobbes explains more pungently to the equestrian Marquis of Newcastle: "Your Lordship's own experience furnishes you with proof enough, that horses, dogs, and other beasts do demur oftentimes upon the way they are to take, the horse retiring from some strange figure that he sees and coming on again to avoid the spur. And what else doth a man that deliberateth, but one while proceed toward action, another while retire from it as the hope of greater good draws him or the fear of greater evil draws him away?"[99]

The account differs from Descartes's on two important points, of course: Hobbes's rationality is a matter of prudence rather than conscience, and he extends rationality to the non-human animals Descartes writes off as automata. (Another way of putting this latter point is that he extends rationality to the non-human automata!) But neither difference, important as it is, affects the issue of how Will operates. For Hobbes, deliberation is a sequence of "thoughts" about pros and cons—in short, a cost-benefit calculation that ends in a better (or best) judgment. Given that judgment, says Hobbes, voluntary action *necessarily* goes right—that's what makes it voluntary.

So far, Descartes speaks the same necessitarian language: "A clear view of the right thing for us to do results in our doing it without fail and with no indeterminacy at all, as in the earthly life of Jesus Christ."[100] It's true that Hobbes has no use for the supposedly common sense premise that necessity and praise don't mix:

What is it else to *praise*, but to say a thing is good? Good, I say, for me, or for somebody else, or for the state and commonwealth? And what is it to say an action is good but to say it is as I would wish? or as another would have it, or according to the will of the state? that is, according to the law. Does my Lord [Bishop Bramhall] think that no action can please me, or him, or the commonwealth, that should proceed from necessity? . . . It was a very great praise in my opinion that Velleius Paterculus gives Cato, where he says that he was good by *nature, et quia aliter esse non potuit* [i.e., 'and because otherwise (i.e., without his goodness) he couldn't exist'].[101]

On the other hand, what the Roman historian praises in Cato looks indistinguishable from what Descartes praises in Jesus Christ.

Hobbes complains that Descartes "assumes the freedom of the will without proof, against the opinion of the Calvinists,"[102] and of course the complaint is on the mark: "I've assumed nothing but what all of us experience in ourselves—what, by the light of nature, we know best. However large the number of people who look at God's foreordaining and can't understand how our freedom can co-exist with it, none who simply look at themselves fail to learn by experience that the voluntary and the free are one and the same."[103] How is it that necessity disqualifies Descartes's automaton from praise—but not his Christ? Or is necessity a false clue? Are we being invited to look for a deeper or (at least) more interesting difference between automata and agents? I think so. I also think the Advocate issues a similar invitation. But to say exactly what's *in* the invitation will need to await further developments.

7. *The* Christian Doctrine

Our pocket history of free will speculation concludes with another seventeenth-century text. This one will be of special interest to the Advocate: it seems to have been written by his favorite theologian (let's call him "the Theologian" for short). At a later stage we'll be in a position to make a somewhat more impressive claim for the text. For present purposes, it will be serving as our lone example of an authentically non-Augustinian approach—no decree of the Fall hidden in the fine print, à la Erasmus and Co. As a bonus of sorts, the old familiar split between *voluntas* and *arbitrium* comes back in a clearer form than ever—clear enough to help us to a useful diagnosis.

First, *voluntas*: in the Theologian's account, too, the kernel of free agency is an inner "trying"—the kind that grows out of "zeal" for "acting well." Again we're sternly warned against misreading: the "zeal" isn't an inner "disposition" (*propensio*); the agent isn't *made* to act well the way the fire is *made* to burn—"determinately."[104] We're also warned against reading "determinacy" into Scripture. When true believers are described as having been "ordered" for true belief (Acts 13:48), "ordered" doesn't mean "destined." It means "more disposed, as it were" (*quasi dispositior*), than others.[105] We need to guard against the standard theology jargon too: grace is "efficacious" when the right person *lets* it be. It's a call, not a hex:

> Some of the soil [viz., of human nature (see Matt. 13)] is stony, some brambly, some good after a fashion, at least in comparison with the stony and brambly soil—even when it hasn't yet been given the seed. ... What accounts for the possibility of being worthy before the hearing of the good news, if not the fact of being 'ordered' [Acts 13:48]—that is, of being spiritually well attuned and disposed—to everlasting life?[106]

> [Jesus' words about a sin against the Spirit that 'shall not' be forgiven (Matt. 12:31)] clearly refer to the greatest enlightenment we receive from Him through the Holy Spirit—the last enlightenment; whoever resists it has exhausted his chances of holiness.[107]

And as if these precautions weren't enough, we need to steer clear of the pitfalls in ordinary grammar, which is also liable to misreading. "Ordered," "disposed," etc., don't require something or somebody to do the "ordering" and "disposing." In fact, "passives don't always denote outside interference; thus to call someone 'abandoned to vices' and 'inclined to this or that' is to attribute the abandon or inclination exclusively to the person's own cast of mind [*suopte solum ingenio*]."[108]

By this time, we hardly need to be warned against the warning. For one thing, the "bad" metaphor is too close for comfort to the "good" one: soil is clearly no more to blame than fire for doing its thing—the thing it's made to do; whether or not the passive in "made" implies a maker, clearly neither the soil nor the fire nor the person's *ingenium* makes *itself*. On the contrary, even the Theologian tells us to look in people's nature—including their *ingenium*—for the cause of their acts of (self-)making. He also tells us in effect that many are called by their *ingenium* but few are chosen: among the many disposed to belief, the few that actually believe are the ones who were "*more* disposed"; presumably dispositions vary in causal force, and in a conflict "more" prevails. Why appeal to a "zeal *for* acting well" if not to cite the *cause* of the acting?

Since the Theologian is no more aware of trouble here than Aristotle was, we get no reply from him to objections like these. But the reply of common sense is obvious enough, and deserves at least a passing acknowledgement: "If I know you well, I may be able to predict what action you will take in response to a certain set of conditions; it does not follow that you are not free with respect to that action"—that is, free from "causal laws" that "determine" that "[you] will perform the action, or that [you] won't."[109] Well, barring a wild coincidence, why *doesn't* it follow? When people get to "know me" well enough to say how I'm likely to respond in a given situation, what is it about me that have they gotten to "know" if not my emotional makeup—my *naturalis indoles*, as the Theologian would say?[110] Suppose the likelihood they arrive at falls well short of certainty; suppose it barely justifies a wager: won't the dice still be loaded—loaded *causally*—in favor of some outcomes rather than others? If so, my will isn't free enough to deprive me of an excuse when I go wrong.

Which brings us straight to *arbitrium*. My habits excuse what I do (*ex-*caus-ant*) only if they *cause* it; only if they're my "inner propensity"—my clockwork—going off on cue. I'm to blame only for the rules or habits I choose *without* a cause:

> Surely the purpose of asserting the justice of God, especially in his calling to us, is far better served this way: grant human nature a measure of free will, if not in works at least in attempts (*conatus*)—the good ones rather than the morally indifferent ones; a measure of free will, that is, left over from the original state, or restored to human nature for the Caller's sake. . . . If God bends human will toward moral good or evil as he wills, then rewards the good and punishes the bad—this is the source of every grievance lodged against the justice of God.[111]

> In the end all of us are equipped with enough reason to resist corrupt emotions—lest anybody impudently or resentfully put the cause on natural corruption.[112]

Reason is strong enough to resist emotions. What it can't resist, when we have a mind to overrule it, is us. Without the freedom to overrule it, in fact, the "choice" of reason is meaningless. Without the freedom to break my promise, my oaths and covenants are meaningless.[113] Without the freedom to defile love, so is my love.[114] "Where [causal] necessity is imposed, everything commendable in duty done sickens—no, melts away; free will dominated and loomed over by a decree of fate cannot be free."[115] So far, the author of *Christian Doctrine* is in full agreement with the God the

Father who speaks up in his own defense in the Advocate's forensic narrative (*PL* 3).

Less happily, both are also in agreement with Iago. Remember his annoyance at being told that will power is a matter of the right disposition or "virtue":

> Virtue? A fig! 'Tis in ourselves that we are thus or thus. Our bodies are our gardens, to the which our wills are gardeners; so that if we will plant nettles or sow lettuce, set hyssop and weed up thyme, supply it with one gender of herbs or distract it with many—either to have it sterile with idleness or manur'd with industry—why, the power and corrigible authority of this lies in our wills. If the balance of our lives had not one scale of reason to poise another of sensuality, the blood and baseness of our natures would conduct us to most preposterous conclusions. But we have reason to cool our raging motions, our carnal stings, our unbitted lusts.[116]

Maybe Roderigo's nauseating lovesickness is a "lust of the blood," but that doesn't excuse it; it's also a "permission of the will."

Revealingly, Iago's two crucial metaphors here also appeal to the Advocate. Gabriel invites Satan to compare the respective outcomes of choosing resistance and cooperation as weighed out by the constellation Libra:

> look up,
> And read thy Lot in yon celestial Sign
> Where thou art weigh'd, and shown how light, how weak,
> If thou resist. The Fiend look'd up, and knew
> His mounted scale aloft: nor more; but fled
> Murmuring.
>
> (*PL* 4.1010–15)

As it turns out, the prudent option carries more weight for the prudently *disposed* Satan. Like Libra, Satan himself is simply a passive weighing device. The whole process of rational decision works automatically—and that's why (with the aid of God the Father) Gabriel counts on it to *cause* Satan to cooperate. There's no room in the system for free will—for a "power and corrigible [i.e., corrective] authority"—to make the final decision on whether to go by the result of measurement. In the ancient metaphor, rational or prudential thinking is a kind of weighing—*ponderatio, examinatio, pensatio*, etc. Like Iago, the Advocate makes his point by letting will be the master and not the servant of the scales: the Fall wasn't mechanically "necessitated" by a torque ("moment") or "impulse"; with no decisive weight in either direction, the sinner's free will was "to her *own* [act of] inclining left / In even scale" (*PL* 10.44–47; italics mine).

In the parallel metaphor, also ancient, the mind is a garden up for "cultivation" or "education" (training-up like a plant). Alternatively, thanks to an allegorical reading of the Song of Songs (4:12), the *soul* is the garden—in Milton's beloved Spenser, an enclosed garden tricked out by the Witch Acrasia (Incontinence) to simulate Eden. Again the Advocate makes the same point as Iago by letting the will be the gardener rather than the garden.

In Iago's version, Existence precedes Essence—self chooses character. The figurative garden in *PL* has already been planted (like the literal one) with wanton growths, and there's a "reformative" job to do. (Again the Latinate metaphor is useful: rational or prudential thinking [imputing, computing, reputing, etc.] is *putatio*, "pruning.") In the final chapter of this book we'll have to discuss this family of *PL* metaphors in far greater detail. For the time being, the thing to notice is that in *PL* the figurative garden, at least, is its own gardener.

Disturbed by his "transporting" passion for Eve, the unfallen Adam has a passing suspicion that "Nature fail'd in mee, and left some part / Not proof enough such object to sustain" (*PL* 8.534–35). He's quickly put right: "Accuse not nature, she hath don her part, / Do thou but thine" (*PL* 8.561–62). Raphael's point, of course, is that to accuse nature here would be to accuse the *God* of nature—unjustly; the whole point of making the inner garden wild is, once again, to challenge the tenant to tame it. (Again, this wildness will have to be revisited in the final chapter.)

Pruning gives form to the formless. The form that emerges from the figurative kind—on the Advocate's and Iago's account—is one's own character. As moral agents at least, Satan and Adam and Eve are self-created. That's the irony—more horrific than tragic—of Satan's craziest boast:

> We know no time when we were not as now;
> Know none before us, self-begot, self-rais'd
> By our own quick'ning power, when fatal course
> Had circl'd his full Orb, the birth mature
> Of this our native Heav'n, Ethereal sons.

> Our puissance is our own, *our own right hand*
> *Shall teach us highest deeds.*
>
> (*PL* 5.859–65; italics mine)

Maybe the Advocate recalls how the old epic of *The Birth of Sin* brings on the same speaker to "persuade himself" that "he was born by his own strength, that he took from himself the stuff by which he first began to be, that he came to be his own issue, with no First."[117] The equivalent speech in *PL* is the same kind of craziness—except for the figurative part, which is true: the "teacher" of a free act is the hand that performs it and nothing else.

A few paragraphs ago I remarked that the author of *Christian Doctrine* is in full agreement on free will with God the Father in *PL* 3—but that, "less happily," both are also in agreement with Iago. The "unhappiness" is that, on the indeterminacy model of free will, to choose the kind of person I'm going to be is to start out, at least, as no kind of person. The *arbitrium* self—existence before essence—is hardly there at all:

> For when my outward action doth demonstrate
> The native act and figure of my heart
> In compliment extern, 'tis not long after
> But I will wear my heart upon my sleeve
> For daws to peck at: *I am not what I am.*[118]

Iago starts out by boasting that what he really is, the "figure" of his heart, is a well-kept secret. But the point of his crazy parting shot is to scoff at the notion of interiority, the notion that there's a secret in there for him to keep. In his case, the answer to the question "What are you?" will only deliver the improvisation of the moment; it can never deliver *him*. His heart has no face.

If free will is will freed from being causally determined even by character, then it seems the agent of that will is a vacuum on legs. Is this kind of will a power? Is this power a gift? Is this the gift that gives love and honor their chance to exist? (Again, we reserve the final chapter to give these questions the serious attention they deserve.)

Both *voluntas* and *arbitrium*, each in its own way, account for what goes on inside a moral agent. Taken together, they allow us to imagine that there are reasons—but no causes—for what people do of their own free will. *Voluntas* provides the notion of reason as a motive force, *arbitrium* provides the notion of choice unforced by motive. No wonder neither Milton nor his predecessors get around to noticing that the composite picture, like an Escher drawing, is incoherent; or that neither answer to the question of cause begins to address the vertical question we caught a glimpse of while trying to sum up Aristotle's contribution: how something going on inside me, determinate or not, gets to be something over which I am "sovereign" (*kyrios*).

End of diagnosis. But not the end of what the author of *Christian Doctrine* has to say about things that also worry the Advocate—things as deeply worrying as the obstacles to justifying the ways of God to men; not the least being the referent of "I"—the niche in the structure of a sentient or active being where Iago and Satan find only a black hole.

8. Foreknowledge

There's one item of unfinished business to attend to first. Troublesome as indeterminacy is, it earns its keep by clearing God of secretly promoting the act he means to punish. But it's a commonplace of the Advocate's tradition that God is still open to a charge of injustice at the other end: what if God's freedom experiment is compromised by the *bare fact* that he knows how it will turn out? What if certain knowledge of a future event, all by itself, just *means* necessity? Then providing the judge with an alibi isn't enough; the punishment he visits on the helpless victims of a bare fact is still a gross miscarriage of justice.

The standard reply (Boethius's) is well known to the Advocate:

> A lot of things happen as we look on—like the things charioteers do in driving and steering their chariots. Does it follow [from our looking on] that some sort of necessity forces any of those things to happen? Hardly! . . . If things lack necessity *as* they happen, then they also lacked it beforehand, when they were just *going* to happen. It's clear, then, that there are future events whose outcomes are totally free of necessity. For I don't think anybody will say that things happening now *weren't* going to happen beforehand.[119]

Boethius's strategy here is to demystify the backward-looking use of the future tense: "I don't think that anybody will say"—that is, that anybody is dotty enough to say—"that things happening now *weren't* going to happen beforehand." This is the most unthreaten-

ing of truisms, not scary news. Futurity isn't a kind of freedom that
the coming event gets cruelly deprived of by eventually happening,
much less by having been foreseen; the only state that the past or
future tense ascribes to events is occurrence before or after or at the
time of thinking or talking about them:[120] thus knowing the chariot
race *is going to* happen is just knowing that the time of the race is
later than the time of the knowing. The race may or may not be
bound to happen—but it isn't bound by the banal fact that if it's
happening now, then (by the laws of grammar, not fate) it was
going to happen a million years ago.

The charioteer careening before us might not have been careening before us. By the same token, the future winner of the race,
whoever he turns out to be, might not have been the future winner.
If things that are going to happen are free not to happen, then (says
Boethius) "it's obvious that their outcomes, *foreknown or not*, are
free. Just as current knowledge imports no necessity into current
events, advance knowledge imports no necessity into future
events."[121]

Not surprisingly, God the Father is in full agreement—at least as
the Advocate tells it:

> if I foreknew,
> Foreknowledge had no influence on their fault,
> Which had no less prov'd certain unforeknown.
>
> (*PL* 3.117–19)

Here our verbal habits can trip us up. In God the Father's jargon, a
"certainty" is certified by what eventually "prove" to be the facts
of the matter. Elsewhere a "certainty" is certified by having a cause
that guarantees its occurrence. Confuse the two "certains" and we
get the nonsense question of how there can be certainty about
things "of uncertain outcome" (*quae incerti sunt exitus*), like
which option a free agent will choose.[122] The answer to the nonsense question is that God doesn't forecast free acts the way doctors
forecast diseases and sailors storms, by spotting their causes.[123]
They have no causes, and neither does God's absolutely direct
knowledge of them, at least in Milton's Boethian view.[124]

In short, two tempting glosses of "certain" in God's claim that
the fall "had no less prov'd certain unforeknown" (*PL* 3.119) are
ruled out by what the speaker has said so far:

1. Whatever it means for the future fall to be certain even in the absence of someone to be certain *of* it, we've already been assured that it doesn't mean that the fall is *necessary* (*PL* 3.110), much less *decreed* (*PL* 3.115).
2. As for the hypothetically absent foreknowledge, we've already been told that, whether the object is in the past or present or future, knowledge has no *(causal) "influence"* on it (*PL* 3.118).

"Had no less prov'd certain unforeknown" is a different way of putting the same thing: to subtract foreknowledge of the fall from the sum of certain (i.e., actual)[125] facts is not to subtract the fall along with it, as it would be if the foreknowledge were the cause and the fall merely its effect. *Fore*knowledge in general is no more the cause of its object than is knowledge of the present or past; the futurity of what gets known is irrelevant.

The Boethian point about the irrelevance of the future tense spells out what "certain" means here, and why it doesn't mean "necessary." Grammatical tense, to repeat, is a system of relative dating tailored to the convenience of a creature confined (from moment to moment) to a momentary point of view: no event is intrinsically past, present, or future, but merely by virtue of occurring (respectively) *before*, *at*, or *after* the relevant act of thinking or speaking. For example, it's true at the moment that the fall "will happen" if and only if the date of the fall is later than the date of this utterance.

It's easy for a creature limited to an egocentric point of view to swallow its metaphors whole, and to imagine that, until a future event "arrives" at the present, the event is uncertain—uncertain in itself, and not merely in the sense that someone is uncertain *of* it. The future event (as we say) is "yet to be"; for it to escape the blur of "yet"—to achieve the status of a fact—is for it to reach the egocentric present moment. In literal fact, of course, the only moment it will ever be at is the moment it's at already: the fixed or "certain" position it occupies in the order of actual moments and events. In this sense, a future event is not one jot less "certain"— less fixed in the order of moments—than a past event. It doesn't *come* to be certain; it merely *proves* to have been (objectively) certain even when we weren't (subjectively) certain *of* it.[126]

By the same token, past events are not one jot less contingent— non-necessary—than future ones. We say, of course, that what's done can't be undone, but this doesn't mean that what's done couldn't have been otherwise; all it means is that it's logically absurd for what's done to be both done and not done. By the same token, what will be, will be—not because the future is fated, but simply because, like the past, it too is immune from logical absurdity. What will be, will be—but could have been otherwise.

In short, once the cobwebs of grammatical and egocentric illusion are swept away, past and future events turn out to be on a par— equally "certain" and equally free of necessity. If there's no reason to balk at the possibility of knowing the past without causing it, the same goes for the future.

Maybe it's too much to say categorically that "certain" in "had no less prov'd certain unforeknown" doesn't undermine the disclaimer of necessity. What's central to the poet's method is that a weaker claim serves him as well or better: the speaker hasn't undermined himself, let us say—*provided* we give him the benefit of the doubt; *provided* we (a) go on the rebuttable assumption that he's neither deceptive nor inept, and (b) look for a non-subversive English meaning of "certain." The prosecution, of course, will refuse to oblige: the notion of a *certain* future is just the recently rejected notion of a *necessary* future by another name; in which case God is being represented by his blundering advocate as a charlatan in the manner of Belial, caught in the act of trying to make the worse appear the better reason.

But the way of the prosecution is one thing, and the way of the jury quite another. Defended by an English attorney in an English court, the accused is, at the very least, entitled to the common-law presumption of innocence—though it's useful to remember that the presumption of *speaker* innocence is none other than what modern linguists, with good reason, like to call the (hermeneutic) rule of *charity*; charity, after all, or the loss of it, is what Milton's poem is all about.

Which brings us to what's really crucial about foreknowledge in the strategy of the Advocate's forensic narrative.

Among modern readers, God the Father's personality in *PL* has a terrible press; but modern readers aren't on *PL*'s agenda—not unless they're willing to play fair by going along with the narrative and its premises, and by counting these a failure only if the God they deliver is unjust or unloving. But here we run into an embarrassment: it doesn't take a theologically illiterate modern reader to have trouble with the foreknowledge premise; it seems to deliver a

2: FREE WILL IN *PARADISE LOST* AND ITS HISTORICAL ROOTS 101

just God only at the price of casting him as the ultimate hypocrite. Isn't the point of a command or warning (like the elaborate warning issued through Raphael) *to get compliance*? God the Father knows all along that his command and warning won't get compliance. So it seems that he knows all along that they're pointless. Isn't that enough to qualify them as the *ne plus ultra* of hypocrisy?

If "get" means "cause" here, then the libertarian answer—the Advocate's answer—has to be that the point of God's command and warning is *not* to get compliance. Given their source, the command and warning are *reasons* to comply; and reasons (for free actions, at least) aren't causes. The point of the warning is not to cause compliance but to make the option of compliance as clear, and so as free, as possible. Still, the outcome of the free will experiment is known in advance; why not just abort the experiment? The question desperately looks away from the strict implication of "know": if the experiment is aborted, then its outcome *wasn't*—as the question asked us to assume—fore*known* after all. The question, in short, is purest Mickey Mouse. Fudging the Advocate's premises is no way to play fair with them.

Like the "factual" premises of interesting science fiction, *PL*'s theological premises challenge the moral imagination to survive in a climate that's as hostile as it is bizarre; survival in that kind of climate means keeping one's wits about one; in particular staying awake to the tricky difference between (a) a finite mind with the power of aborting a future possibility (b) an infinite mind powerless—on pain of absurdity—to abort a future fact. Coming from a finite mind, the warning of God mediated by Raphael *would* be hypocrisy in full gloat. The mind involved is infinite, unfortunately; and the warning is a love that knows too much for its own (or anyone else's) good, with no choice but to watch the tragic farce play itself out.

The Advocate knows the ordeal he's putting the Jury through. He puts himself through it first:

> O for that warning voice, which he who saw
> Th' Apocalypse heard cry in Heaven aloud,
> Then when the Dragon, put to second rout,
> Came furious down to be reveng'd on men,
> *Wo to th' inhabitants on Earth!* that now,
> While time was, our first Parents had bin warn'd
> The coming of thir secret foe, and scap'd,
> Haply so scap'd his mortal snare.

(*PL* 4.1–8)

The "woe to" idiom is a giveaway of tragic confusion: the closest to a warning that hindsight (the poor man's foreknowledge) can come is a lament.

No wonder Raphael's errand raises suspicions of hypocrisy—suspicions the Advocate could have kept from coming to the surface by simply not making the episode up; it isn't mandated by Genesis. But that, as we've seen often enough, is not his way. Fairness to the adversarial system of justice requires that crucial issues be raised, not swept under the rug. If there's such a thing as a poetics of fairness, *PL* is its masterpiece.

9. Individualism

We're ready to join Milton and assorted others in search of the *kyrios*—the doer of deeds. We should be prepared for a disagreeable surprise: if Iago can be trusted, we'll find a black hole where the doer ought to be.

To begin with, consider Eve inching toward her point of no return, as

> the hour of Noon drew on, and wak'd
> An eager appetite, rais'd by the smell
> So savorie of that Fruit, which with desire,
> Inclinable now grown to touch or taste,
> Sollicited her longing eye.
>
> (*PL* 9.739–743)

A bit later, "her rash hand in evil hour / Forth reaching, to the Fruit, she pluck'd, she eat" (*PL* 9.780–81).

What's a little bizarre about the description is that we aren't given Eve in action; we're given *parts* of Eve—her mind and body—in *inter*-action. To simplify a bit, we have:

(a) Depletion (imminence of lunchtime) + savory smell => eager appetite.

(b) Eager appetite + longing eye => desire to touch or taste the fruit.

(c) Desire to touch or taste the fruit => movements associated with reaching, plucking, and eating.

But we've already noticed that this is too simple to be right. Will *any* old kind of causal link do in (c)? Imagine (*per absurdum*) a series of spasms linking the desire and the movements that fulfil it; would spasm-causation do? Clearly the kind of causation we need is the kind that results in *Eve's* doing the moving, not just in her (mental *or* physical) parts being in motion.

Actually the same goes for Eve's desire: it's a fact about *her*, not about (mental *or* physical) *parts* of her. That's the felicity of picturing the whole-part relation as a sum; the sum of, say, 7 and 5 is a unit, not a pair consisting of 7 and 5. For the same reason, a whole is one and not many; unlike the set of its n parts, it isn't n-fold. So there's nothing surprising about its turning out to have properties all its own. On the commonsense view of PERSON, at least, the sum of a person's parts has properties that aren't just relations among the parts; doing is one such property, thinking is another. As the owner of such properties, a person is undivided; in Milton's Boethian jargon, to enjoy "personhood" (*personalitas*), a thing must be uniquely "individual" (*individuum* = undivided, and in fact indivisible).[127]

For Milton the fundamental texts on *personalitas*—on what it is to be a bodily whole that irreducibly thinks and acts—are two passages the Advocate fuses in his paraphrase of Genesis:

> he form'd thee, *Adam*, thee O Man
> Dust of the ground, and in thy nostrils breath'd
> The breath of Life; in his own Image hee
> Created thee, in the Image of God
> Express, and thou becam'st a living Soul.
>
> (*PL* 7.524–28)

The fusion makes it clear that this "breath of life" isn't ordinary air. It's the figurative kind that the ancient Aramaic paraphrase describes as "speaking"[128]—the intelligent "spirit" that qualifies dust to be a likeness of God. If the Targum is right,[129] to breathe this breath is to "live" by (inward or outward) speech—that is, by thought. Above all, "breath," "spirit," "soul" in this sense makes things likenesses of God by turning them, bodily, into itself. In the end soul or spirit (Heb. *nephesh*) isn't something Adam takes in, but something he comes to be.

The point of the Genesis passages, according to the author of *Christian Doctrine*, is that

> the human animal [i.e., as person] is essentially and strictly one and individual, not double and divisible, not made up of two natures of di-

verse and distinct kinds, not (as the common view has it) a composite welded together out of a soul and a body; on the contrary, the whole man is a soul and the whole soul is a man—that is, a body or substance—individual, alive, sentient, rational. 'Living breath' [Gen. 2:7] wasn't part of God's essence, it wasn't even the soul; but a kind of spirit or power originating in God, and infused into an organic body. Man himself—I repeat, himself; man as an entirety—is described in so many words as having become a 'living soul.'[130]

Almost everyone agrees that form—which is what the human soul is—is drawn forth out of the potentiality of matter.[131]

I think Aristotle's dictum is as true as can be: . . . the entire soul [as the form or activity of the body] inheres in the body as a whole.[132]

As applied to the strange thing God made of red earth on the Sixth Day, "soul" has two coherent uses. One use is to name Adam himself—the human body taken as an individual thing, not as a collection of undetached parts.[133] The other use of "soul" is to name what the individual does—does *literally*, rather than by being credited with the leaderless performance of its parts. (Contrast a person walking with an automaton "walking.") As an earlier supporter of the same kind of materialism says (the supporter's subject is mental acts, but the principle applies to acts in general): "It happens that the act of understanding inheres in matter, but it doesn't inhere in some part of the body or other; rather understanding inheres in the body as a whole. It's of the whole body, taken as grammatical subject, that the act is predicated.[134] The act isn't in some organ or other, because then the organ would be doing the acting."[135]

This is the nub of Milton's quarrel with mechanistic accounts of PERSON: on Milton's account, even when any given act of the whole is precisely correlated with a particular interaction of the parts, the act is one thing and the interaction is another; the individual is an ineliminable part of the story.[136] On a mechanistic account, the individual gets explained away; the "I" in "I act" is no more an invitation to look for something or someone to do the acting than the "it" in "it's raining" is an invitation to look for something or someone to do the raining.

Free agency is in notoriously deep trouble if the notion of uncoerced and uncaused action turns out to be empty. But it's in even deeper trouble if the notion of the moral *individual* turns out to be empty. It's hard to have moral acts, free or enslaved, without moral agents. Without acts and agents, the Advocate is facing what, for his tradition, is the ultimate defeat: he loses his case not because his plea is false but because it makes no sense at all—not because the scheme of things is unjust but because the notion of a just scheme of things is absurd.

We've already met up with Hobbes—along with a lot of others—as an enemy of free will. But the threat his kind of materialism poses to the Advocate's enterprise doesn't stop there—far from it. The real threat is deeper and more devastating. Consider this version of the birth of doing—inner "trying":

> (a) If vital motion [in the heart] is *hindered* by sense-generated motion, the vital motion will be restored by a flexing of body parts as spirits are pushed, now into these muscles, now into those, until the trouble is as far as possible wholly removed. (b) If vital motion is *eased* by sense-generated motion, the parts of the organ will be disposed to direct the spirits in such a way that the easing is maintained and increased. In animal motion, this is the 'first trying' (*conatus primus*).[137]

To try to seek or shun isn't to be an individual, much less an agent, at all; it's to be a collection of body parts cooperating in *conatus primus*.

No doubt the *conatus* process is bound by natural law, by a sort of necessity that rules out free will; but the unique threat of mechanized psychology to the Advocate's whole enterprise isn't the trite old threat of determinism. If Hobbes is right, so-called deeds can be accounted for very nicely, thank you, without counting in doers. More than that: if the account makes good sense, then doers don't. Compared with the quest for a doer, a wild goose chase looks respectable.

Here Hobbes is willing to toss a sop to his nemesis:

> It's quite certain that the knowledge that I exist depends on the knowledge that I think, as [M. Descartes] himself has rightly taught us. But where does the knowledge that I think come from? Certainly from nowhere else but this, that we can't conceive of any act at all without a subject of its own, as dancing without a dancer, knowing without a knower, thinking without a thinker—and this seems to imply that the subject of thinking is something bodily. For act-subjects, whatever act it may be, seem to make sense only as falling under the concept of body or matter.[138]

The idea of myself arises, with respect to my body, from seeing. With respect to my mind, there *is* no idea. Instead we infer the existence of something inside the human body to supply the animal motion that senses and moves; and this something we call *mind*.[139]

What Hobbes gives with one hand he takes with the other: sensing and moving are "animal motions"—transactions of body parts. As for the associated proof of "my" existence, it's a proof in name only; there's a particular collection of body parts whose identity with "me" Hobbes already takes for granted. What goes for sensing and moving also goes for thinking:

> Now what do we say if it happens that reasoning is nothing but the linking of names or designations by the verb 'is'—so that what we infer by reason isn't about the nature of things but about their designations? (Here it doesn't matter whether or not the linking of names follows arbitrary agreements about their meanings.) If this is as true as it is possible, then reasoning will depend on names, names on mental images, and perhaps (if I'm right) mental images on the movement of bodily organs. *So mind is nothing but movement in parts of an organic body*.[140]

Descartes gets a bit more credit than he deserves for his celebrated claim that "being capable of thinking is incompatible with the nature of body."[141] If this is the test of Cartesianism, many an Augustinian is a Cartesian in good standing; Calvin, for example: "Man is made up of two substances. Neither is so thoroughly mixed with the other as to lose its own distinctive nature. Soul isn't body. Body isn't soul. Consequently things are said of soul that simply don't apply to body, and vice versa. And things are said of man as a whole that don't make sense if applied to body alone or soul alone."[142] (That last sentence obviously cries out for comment—but comment will need to be saved till the end of this section.) The world didn't have to await Descartes to savor the delights of "dualism."

What's more interesting, at least for our current purposes, isn't Descartes's "dualism" but the individualism on which it partly rests. Take his reply to Hobbes's suggestion that thinking is "movement in parts of an organic body":

> Reasoning *does* involve linking—not of names but of what the names mean; I'm amazed that the contrary thesis could enter anyone's mind. Who doubts that a Frenchman and a German can entertain the same

reasoning about the same things, even though the words that occur to them are entirely different? And doesn't the philosopher [viz., Hobbes] condemn *himself*, when he talks of our arbitrary agreements about the meanings of words? If he admits that there's something the words mean, why doesn't he want our reasonings to be about this something instead of just about words?[143]

The crazy "contrary thesis," in short, is that "parts of the brain work together to form thoughts."[144] Thoughts in this sense— linkable signs in the brain—are like characters on a page; without a reader to read them—a party to the agreements that give them a meaning—they mean anything and nothing:

Under the name 'thought' I include everything that's 'in' us in the sense that our consciousness of it is direct, not through a medium [i.e., a representation]. Thus all acts of willing, understanding, and sensing are thoughts. I added 'not through a medium' to rule out the results of acts of willing, etc.; voluntary movement, for example, begins with thought, but isn't itself a thought.

Under the name 'idea' I understand the *form* of an act of thinking—the thing I'm perceiving without a medium when I'm conscious of my thinking; so that it's impossible for me to express something in words, understanding what I say, without proving by this very fact of understanding that I have 'in' me the idea of what the words mean. Thus in my usage 'idea' doesn't denote mental images exclusively. In fact, 'idea' doesn't denote mental images at all, as things stored in the body—i.e., as things represented in some part of the brain; but only as things that 'inform' a mind that turns to the part of the brain in question.[145]

The bare existence of brain signs—concerted motions of brain parts—gives us only the *means* of thinking, not the *thinker*. It gives us what goes on inside the thinker as he thinks, not the agent of thought or his act. Even Hobbes finds it hard to avoid drawing the means-agent distinction whenever he needs to give his theory some minimal plausibility: sometimes it's not a theory of willing, but merely of "what goes on inside a person *as* the person wills something."[146] The "as" reports a coincidence between two separate kinds of event, a brain process and the act of a person.

Hobbes can, of course, claim that his "as" is merely a stand-in for an "equals" sign; that he's speaking with the vulgar while thinking with the learned. Among Hobbes's intellectual heirs, pedagogy is still the excuse of choice for using the fiction of brain-owners or brain-users or irreducible brain-wholes or "thinkers" to help the laity grasp the bogglingly complicated reality of brain-part interaction. Some modern examples (with "when" and "while" doing the work of "as"): "the same part of the brain people use *when* they speak or think words"; "[Broca's area is] activated *when* people . . . silently talk to themselves"; "brain activity *while* a person is having a given experience";[147] "the brain does not yet know it is seeing an apple"; "the brain has a way of knowing where objects are in space"; "the brain decides that it has an apple in its visual field"; "it is easy to be fooled by one's own brain."[148]

A more recent variant of the same pedagogy applies thinker talk to the myriad brain parts themselves: they're just mini-people, quasi-understanders engaged in quasi-understanding. Thus a modern Hobbes descendant wonders what to do about the regrettable fact that "people haven't learned how to imagine such a system. They just can't imagine how understanding can be a property that emerges from lots of distributed quasi-understanding in a large system. They certainly can't if they don't try, but how could they be helped along on this difficult exercise? Is it '*cheating*' to think of the software as composed of homunculi who *quasi-understand*, or is that just the right crutch to help the imagination make sense of astronomical complexity?"[149]

Descartes's answer is, in effect: right on the first try; it *is* cheating. What else can we call the tactic of ruling a notion out of court as a pack of nonsense, and then bringing the alleged nonsense back, with "quasi" attached, to make sense of its preferred replacement? That's no pedagogical crutch; that's the last refuge of a desperate argument.

At this point, Descartes slips from individualism into "dualism": to reach the *agent* of thought, we have to reach beyond body parts—and hence beyond the body. Milton agrees with all of this except the "hence"; what becomes a living soul—a mind—is precisely Adam's body. A more conventional thinker like John Donne weakens some celebrated words of praise by yielding to misgivings: "One might *almost* say, her body thought"; the fact that our bodies "are ours" seems to have convinced him that "they're not we."[150] Milton labors under no such inhibition; in his reading of Adam's creation, the resulting individual is precisely a body that thinks.

The notion of a thinking body admittedly looks very odd; that oddity is the will o' the wisp that, from a Miltonic point of view, lures Descartes and his fellow dualists into the bog. Descartes really does owe Gassendi and the rest of us a reason to agree that nothing can conceivably have both mental and physical properties—that nothing can conceivably be both a body and a mind. If something can, then we have at least one perfectly harmless reason for the oddity of "her body thought"—or "her mind was five feet tall" for that matter: reports don't usually pick out their subjects by the wrong hat. The oddity of "her body thought" is precisely the oddity of "the surgeon led his troops to victory" (where the general is also a surgeon), or "the barber ably represented his client in court" (the barber moonlights as a lawyer). We can also see why it makes no particle of difference whether the accused laid violent hands on his victim's body or his victim's "person."

10. A Seventeenth-Century Foil: Spinoza

We haven't quite got to the bottom of Milton's individualism. We're brought within sight of it by this talk of things having material *properties* rather than being made of matter; materiality, like mentality, on this view, is just another sharable feature—it doesn't seem to be playing its traditional (individuating) role:

An individual being can't possibly share its essence with anything else—the essence by which it is what it is, and by which it differs from all other things."[151]

A single thing has a single essence—subsistence or (equivalently) substantial essence. If you assign two subsistences or persons to one essence, you contradict yourself."[152]

[Things] just don't differ numerically without differing in essence. Theologians wake up. Now if things that differ numerically differ by essence, not matter, then they must differ in their forms—not the ones they share, but forms of their own. Thus the rational soul is the form of man in general; Socrates' soul is a form of his own [*forma propria*]. A thing's own form makes it what it is—gives it its unique being. Given that the essence of an individual is partly shared and partly peculiar to that individual, matter accounts for what it shares and form for what it doesn't.[153]

The writer is rejecting the traditional answer to an old question: what is the "essence" of an individual thing, say, Socrates? What remains when you imagine him stripped not only of the properties he shares (or can share) with others but also the unsharable properties that could have belonged to somebody else instead? What trait picks him out not only in actual fact but in any circumstances in which he could exist? Being a "substrate" or a chunk of matter won't fill the bill; it's just another shared property calling for still another "substrate" to "individuate" it. What we're looking for, to repeat, is Socrates' "very own form" (*propria forma*), the "Socrateity" that belongs, and could belong, only to him. Unfortunately, the closest we can come to cornering this particular wild goose is to point in its general direction. The revealingly desperate Scholastic word for "very own form" is "thisness" (*haecceitas*).

We've run up against a problem for the Advocate's individualist program, and more generally the notion of PERSON we've been surveying.

It seems there's a kind of whole—perhaps, my cat—some of whose mental and physical properties (e.g., her raising of her foreleg) can't be understood in terms of her parts (e.g., the foreleg's rising). Her act of foreleg raising isn't true of her foreleg but only of her—true of her at every point in the space she occupies at the relevant time. So far, so good.

The problem is: how, in principle, to draw the boundaries of a distinct cat? At first blush, the solution might seem a trivial matter of common sense. Surely the boundaries of my cat are defined by the laws of nature regarding cats. Unfortunately, this truism runs afoul of the embarrassing fact that what counts as a cat law depends on what counts as a cat boundary, trapping us in a vicious circle. Still, a non-circular *general* rule for defining the individual wholes suggests itself—roughly: draw boundaries so as to result in the most manageable—that is the simplest—system of laws describing individuals and their relations. But then, it seems inescapable that, beyond the "reasonable" or "convenient," there's no real fact of the matter about defining individuals.

Probed to the quick, common sense turns out to be merely common fiat. The guide here and in all similar cases—*including persons*—isn't fact, only convenience. So why not rest content, as Spinoza will urge, with the only non-optional and hence *real* individual: nature (or God) as a whole? What I conveniently think of as my cat's foreleg-raising is really a sequence of facts about the whole of nature as it "unfolds" itself at a conveniently specified sequence of times and places.

The result is a reassuring gain in clarity and stability. The attributes of the nature of things stay the same, just get "unfolded" or manifested variously from place to place and moment to moment. An eternal individual isn't even notionally destructible; it doesn't even notionally break up into finite parts. The gain is cheap at the price: reconciling ourselves to the fact that we and the other optional individuals aren't even *parts* of the only real individual, just ways in which its eternal attributes are locally expressed. We don't amount to so much as an adjective ("attribute") in the biography of nature (or God); the most we can aspire to is an adverb ("mode").[154] And what goes for finite body goes for finite mind: there's only one basic individual available to be the thinker of our thoughts, and it isn't any of us.[155]

What's interesting here, for our purposes, is that this is where Spinoza *ends up*. Where he *starts* is with the same general vision of body, mind, and individuality as the Advocate's. Mind and body are one and the same thing under different aspects; choice and appetite are mental and physical "expressions" of the same event.[156] Essences come one to a customer: "Two or more things with the same nature or attribute are an impossibility."[157] Yet the universe has room for only one individual. How does the Advocate's individualist project avoid a similar shipwreck? What, short of inattention, keeps him from detecting the reef?

Consider the Advocate's idea of creation:

> Boundless the Deep, because I am who fill
> Infinitude, nor vacuous the space.
> Though I uncircumscrib'd *myself retire*,
> And put not forth my goodness, which is free
> To act or not, Necessitie and Chance
> Approach not mee, and what I will is Fate.
>
> (*PL* 7.168–73; italics added)

In this version, creation happens when the creator finally decides, in total freedom, to stop "retiring" himself, that is, stop *withholding* himself. "Self" can't mean presence in this context. To be God is to be everywhere always, even in the places soon to be jointly occupied by creatures. Not only is God everywhere but so is his goodness, which is as essential to him as his omnipresence; the difference is that before creation the goodness is there *without being "put forth."* In God's parlance, before creation, his "goodness" (or "self") is "retired." God creates, in short, by *imparting* rather than "retiring" the part of himself that he calls "goodness." By being co-present with him somewhere or other, the creature gets to *share* it, and so to be (derivatively) good itself.

This move doesn't solve the individuation problem, but it rules out Spinoza's one-individual solution. Maybe a finite individual is *no more* than part of the individual-par-excellence, but it's also *no less*. One thing it's not is a tenuously real "mode" of God's "attributes." Moreover, in this version of creation, finite doesn't mean finished. Though no finite thinking creature can hope for the perfect unity of the master individual, each such creature has a "unitie defective" (*PL* 8.425) of its own, an individuality that the master can foster to the point of full personhood (participation in dialogue with himself):

> [thou]
> Canst raise thy Creature to what highth thou wilt
> Of Union or Communion, deifi'd.
>
> (*PL* 8.429–31)

It seems the Advocate's basic individuals are these defective unities, bodies that think:

> *My self* I then perus'd, and *Limb by Limb*
> Survey'd, and sometimes went, and sometimes ran
> With supple joints, as lively vigour led:
> But who I was, or where, or from what cause,
> Knew not.
>
> (*PL* 8.267–71; italics added)

Adam knows *what* he is. He's the body under his "perusal" and control. But this body, by the same token, is what does the perusing and controlling. It's a body that manages to transcend the status of a system of limbs and joints.

Anatomy can't prompt Adam here. One can't know *who* one is by way of an inventory of "every particle and utensil labelled to [one's] will." Better to resort to Belial's method of specifying the personhood that survives the loss of his free will: "*this* intellectual being"; "*those* thoughts that wander through eternity" (*PL* 2.147–48). Even a denier of free will as implacable as Calvin dimly feels the need to insist that the whole person somehow transcends its parts: "Things are said of soul that simply don't apply to body, and vice versa. And things are said of man as a whole that don't make sense if applied to body alone or soul alone." This faith that persons are part of the basic furniture of reality began its long dying while *Paradise Lost* was being born. It's a faith of which, with the current triumph of materialism, we seem to be on the verge of seeing the last.

3

The Creator Defended

On the Adversary's reading, the action of *PL* 9 clinches the first part of the case against God:

> [Adam] by fraud I have seduc'd
> From his Creator, and the more to increase
> Your wonder, with an Apple; [God] thereat
> Offended, worth your laughter, hath giv'n up
> Both his beloved Man and all his World,
> To Sin and Death a prey.
>
> (*PL* 10.485–90)

We've already[1] had occasion to admire (and puzzle over) the force and marksmanship of Satan's argument here. A little "fraud" went a long way. The stupidity of the Fall was a "wonder," thanks to Adam's genius for gullibility—but whose fault was *that*? Now the Judge of All the World has put on a demonstration of his judicial temper by letting himself be "offended" to the point of making a capital offense out of a crime inspired by fraud in one of nature's fools. Never mind the fundamental maxim of judicial fairness, that extreme justice is extreme injustice;[2] leave misgivings about special circumstances to *lower* courts. The ferocious impartiality of this highest of courts has no truck with respect of persons; it's willing and eager to visit the extreme of justice on "[God's] beloved Man" and "all [God's] World" besides. Meanwhile, it can't fail to "increase your wonder" that the world-historical object at the center of the crime was—an apple!

Coming from the Judge of All the World, or any judge, the performance is embarrassing enough. Coming from the Creator, not to mention a *wise* Creator, it is (in Adam's timid phrase) "not well conceav'd":

> Nor can I think that God, Creator wise,
> Though threatning, will in earnest so destroy

114

> Us his prime Creatures, dignifi'd so high,
> Set over all his Works, which in our Fall,
> For us created, needs with us must fall,
> Dependent made; so God shall uncreate,
> Be frustrate, do, undo, and labor lose,
> Not well conceav'd of God, who though his Power
> Creation could repeat, yet would be loath
> Us to abolish, least the Adversary
> Triumph and say, Fickle their State whom God
> Most favors, who can please him long?
>
> (*PL* 9.938–49)

Which brings us to the second part of the case against God.

A being essentially creative—creative through and through—doesn't betray itself (not to mention its creatures) by stooping to uncreation. The motto of the supreme artisan is *nihil frustra*—nothing in vain. The last thing we would expect such an artisan to do is resign himself to being "frustrate," least of all by stooping to the "fickleness" of junking a creature he started by "dignifying so high." In short, to the charge of dereliction aimed at the Judge, add a charge of professional incompetence aimed at the Creator.

In fact, if Satan is right, the notion of CREATION itself makes no sense, at least as an explanation for the non-emptiness of the universe:

> strange point and new!
> Doctrin which we would know whence learnt: who saw
> When this creation was? rememberest thou
> Thy making, while the Maker gave thee being?
> We know no time when we were not as now;
> Know none before us, self-begot, self-rais'd
> By our own quick'ning power, when fatal course
> Had circl'd his full Orb, the birth mature
> Of this our native Heav'n, Ethereal Sons.
>
> (*PL* 5.853–63)

In "self-begot, self-rais'd," Satan isn't claiming that he literally existed before he existed; he's a better logician than *that*. The point is rather that the creation hypothesis is unmotivated and unnecessary—a whisker ripe for Ockham's razor. Natural things don't need a maker. They simply grow out of suitable matter—angels, for example, out of the ether. That's the point of dubbing the angels

ether's "sons." The metaphor of self-begetting merely elaborates
on the same basic idea: generation out of the ether is spontaneous
and (hence) *self*-reinforcing, like the "quickening" and "maturing"
of a seed or embryo. It seems that matter itself just has a "quick'n-
ing power," a power obedient to its own laws or "fatal course" of
development. It's even conceivable (to Satan at least) that space itself is the creative principle, by an abhorrence of its own emptiness:
"Space may produce new Worlds" (*PL* 1.650). To think otherwise
is to let oneself be sold a bill of goods. As Satan tells Eve later, we
have to choose here between swallowing what we're told and looking for ourselves—between dogma and experience:

> The Gods are first, and that advantage use
> On our belief, that all from them proceeds;
> I question it, for this fair Earth, I see,
> Warm'd by the Sun, producing every kind,
> Them nothing.
>
> (*PL* 9.718–22)

Eventually Eve makes Satan's vulgar empiricism her own:

> Experience, next to thee I owe,
> Best guide; not following thee, I had remain'd
> In ignorance, thou open'st Wisdoms way,
> And givst access, though secret she retire.
>
> (*PL* 9.807–10)

For all the loyalist angel's more orthodox talk of God's commanding this or that, Raphael's version of Genesis falls back repeatedly
on the idea of spontaneous generation:

> The Earth was form'd, but in the Womb as yet
> Of Waters, Embryon immature involv'd,
> Appear'd not, over all the face of Earth
> Main Ocean flow'd, not idle, but, with warm
> Prolific humour soft'ning all her Globe,
> Fermented the great Mother to conceave.
>
> (7.276–81)

> The Earth obey'd, and strait
> Op'ning her fertil Womb teem'd at a birth
> Innumerous living Creatures, perfet formes,
> Limb'd and full grown.
>
> (7.453–56)

The command that earth "obeys" here is God's—at least if we believe the God-appointed storyteller; but *figurative* laws don't require a literal lawgiver. The laws of nature are just ways that the "powers" of matter make chunks of matter interact; spelling out how, in fact, is precisely what it is for such laws to explain. Why go on to explain the explanation? Why pretend not to know that natural "law" is a metaphor? Science isn't the point, surely; could the point be the propagation of an official myth?

To an innocent eye, the usual inference from laws to lawgiver— the argument from design—is compromised by hints of pointlessness in the alleged design; for example, why the immense cosmic light show to serve the pathetic little ball at the center? Hasn't the master architect labored "in vain" after all? The tempter glances at this embarrassment in his insinuating dream serenade to Eve:

> now reignes
> Full Orb'd the Moon, and with more pleasing light
> Shadowie sets off the face of things; *in vain*,
> If none regard.
>
> > (*PL* 5.41–44; italics added)

But Eve needs no prompting to put a naive version of the qualm to Adam: "Wherefore all night long shine these [stars]? For whom / This glorious sight, when sleep hath shut all eyes?" (*PL* 4.657–58). Adam rushes to the rescue with a passable explanation, but by the time Raphael has told his story of civil war in heaven, Adam himself has worked out a sophisticated but recognizable version of the same query:

> reasoning I oft admire,
> How Nature wise and frugal could commit
> Such disproportions, with superfluous hand
> So many nobler Bodies to create,
> Greater so manifold to this one use,
> For aught appeers, and on thir Orbs impose
> Such restless revolution day by day
> Repeated, while the sedentarie Earth,
> That better might with farr less compass move,
> Serv'd by more noble then her self, attains
> Her end without least motion, and receaves,
> As Tribute such a sumless journey brought
> Of incorporeal speed, her warmth and light.
>
> > (*PL* 7.25–37)

Clearly the stakes are as high as the language is gingerly: the great creating "Nature" on trial here is *God*;[3] the question before the court is whether *God* is really "wise" and "frugal." Raphael's answer, in effect, is that the "disproportions" in question aren't in the appearances themselves, but in Adam's theoretical effort to *save* appearances (i.e., posit connections to account for them). The risk that such efforts run isn't sin, only folly; sometimes there isn't a best explanation at all—sometimes the appearances testify only to the Maker's range of options, or freedom of choice:

> [God] his Fabric of the Heav'ns
> Hath left to thir disputes, perhaps to move
> His laughter at thir quaint Opinions wide
> Hereafter, when they come to model Heav'n
> And calculate the Starrs, how they will weild
> The mightie frame, how build, unbuild, contrive
> To save appearances.
>
> (*PL* 8.76–82)

Raphael declines to violate the creator's secret about "whether Heav'n move or Earth" (*PL* 8.70). Gratifying Adam's curiosity would be countereducational; the fact of the matter about what God chose to put at the center "imports not" (*PL* 8.71). The important question is whether *either* option would convict the architect of "disproportion " and call his "frugality" and "wisdom" in question.[4] The answer, of course, is no, and the question is important because, if Raphael had sidestepped it, the ways of God would have gone scandalously unjustified. Raphael, in short, is going about his Master's business—the part of the business he shares with the Advocate.

In fact, the Advocate's conduct of the joint business is open to a charge of disproportion: in his forensic narrative the story of the Fall is told once; the story of the creation is told and retold, at various removes and in various perspectives, like a gem being turned over slowly under a jeweller's loop; not to mention the vistas of the newborn creation we get to peer at over Satan's shoulder or (perhaps) through his eyes, vistas that bring him at least once as close to repentance as the damned can be brought. Of course, the disproportion is a figment if creation is relevant—intricately relevant—to the Advocate's brief.

Inquiring into that relevance is the next order of business. The

rest of this chapter is devoted to a study of *PL*'s creation stories—
the primal act of loving kindness as the hatching of an egg, as the
emergence of a universe made of light, as the taming of infinity, as
a confusion already pregnant with order, as the creator's sharing of
her substance ("her," be it noted, is not a misprint), as a work in
progress in which creatures themselves play a part, as a work in
progress in which a fallen Eve (of all creatures) plays an unexpected part, and as the alchemy of God. If I'm right about the Advocate's Great Argument, the jurors can't be spared a course of
reflections on the *first* week if they're to come to a decent apprecia-
tion of the terrible but ambiguous thing that happened a week later.

PROEM TO *PARADISE LOST* 1

The Advocate begins with an epic invocation, and a historical
analogy that goes as follows:

As Moses's second-hand knowledge of the Creation is authenticated by God's first-hand knowledge of the Creation, so the Advocate's second-hand knowledge of the Fall is authenticated by God's
first-hand knowledge of the Fall.

Moses could not have taught Israel "how the Heav'ns and Earth /
Rose out of Chaos" (*PL* 1.9–10) without the instruction of the spirit
of God, who (after all) was present at the Creation. By the same
token, the Advocate won't be able to teach his audience about the
Fall without the instruction of the Spirit of God, who (after all) was
present at the Fall. "Instruct me, for thou know'st. Thou . . . wast
present"—where? At the Fall, obviously; the logic of the analogy
demands it. But if that's what logic demands, logic is in for a frus-
tration; the historian of the Fall, like the historian of Creation, relies
on his Eyewitness Informant's presence at—*the Creation all over
again*!

> Instruct me, for thou know'st; Thou from the first
> Wast present, and with mighty wings outspread
> Dove-like satst brooding on the vast Abyss
> And mad'st it pregnant.
>
> (*PL*. 1.19–22)

Did we get the analogy wrong the first time around? If so, we're now in a position to correct it at the cost of replacing a term:

As Moses's second-hand knowledge of the Creation is authenticated by God's first-hand knowledge of the Creation, so the Advocate's second-hand knowledge of the Fall is authenticated by God's first-hand knowledge of *the Creation.*

But the cost isn't trifling. Now we're stuck with the claim that to understand any event through and through is to understand the first event of all. Has the Advocate begun his attempt at a Free Will Defense of God's justice by blundering into an endorsement of determinism?

What saves us, of course, is a single word: much virtue in "from." The Spirit can testify first-hand to the Fall because it has been present *from* the first, and hence present at the Fall. It seems the analogy goes just as we thought it did, and the Great Argument hasn't been repudiated in advance after all. Yet why run the risk of making it seem otherwise? We've already been reminded (in the part about Moses) of "how the Heav'ns and Earth / Rose out of Chaos" (*PL* 1.9–10); why distract us with this elaborate reprise? And the reprise is elaborate. A closer look is in order.

According to the Hebrew text of Genesis 1:2, the earth was a riot and tumult, darkness was on the face of the deep, and the Spirit of God hovered[5] over the face of the waters. To the early Rabbinic commentators, "hover" suggests a brooding dove keeping close watch over her young.[6] At the equivalent stage of world generation in the Orphic literature, we get a chaos-egg hatched by a bisexual divinity.[7] So in the Advocate's culturally hybrid—Jewish-Hellenic—metaphorical language, the Spirit-Dove becomes a male principle impregnating or fertilizing the deep, and at the same time a female principle hatching it.

Aristotle remarks that a moral agent is the begetter of his deeds.[8] For the Advocate, God is father *and* mother of his first deed—and especially the mother. The cosmic bird spreads her wings protectively over her inchoate young: "Keep me as the apple of the eye; hide me under the shadow of thy wings" (Ps. 17:9). "I will hide in thy tabernacle forever; I will trust in the covert of thy wings" (Ps. 61:4). In the Advocate's first pass at understanding the Creation (and thereby somehow understanding the Fall), the voice of the penitential Psalmist mingles with that of the prophet of Sinai: the

Creation is the first exercise of a kind of love that pre-dates, and makes, its object, and then sees it through to maturity. In the Psalms, the metaphor for it is the outspread wings of the mother bird.

PARADISE LOST 3, PROEM

The voice from the whirlwind humbles Job with an unanswerable (and ambiguous) question: "On what road (in what manner) does light dwell (exist)?" (Job 38:19). The Advocate, too, is at a loss to spell out the manner of existence of the "holy light" he's trying to invoke at the outset of *PL* 3. (1) Is it the firstborn "offspring of heaven" (*PL* 3:1), presumably God the Son? (2) Is it the uncreated home or shrine, "coeternal" with God,[9] where God the Father "dwelt" from eternity (*PL* 3:2–6), in which case light itself is the *ultimate* dwelling place, and the whirlwind's question of where it dwells is a *trick* question (like the location of the universe)? (3) Is it the "stream" of ether summoned by God's voice ("Let there be light") the day before he parted the waters of the heavens from the waters of the deep (Gen. 1:3–8)? A conflation of the last two possiblities gets extended treatment in *PL* 3:

> hear'st thou rather pure Ethereal stream,
> Whose fountain who shall tell? before the Sun,
> Before the Heav'ns thou wert, and at the voice
> Of God, as with a Mantle didst invest
> The rising world of waters dark and deep,
> Won from the void and formless infinite.
>
> (*PL* 3.7–12)

Imitatio Christi (to take one illustrious example) carefully distinguishes the "perpetual light" it prays to from "all created lights"; God's is "transcendent."[10] The light creation story in *PL* 3 belongs to an alternative tradition. The original deep was formless—naked of form. The light that comes to "mantle" it is precisely the Wisdom celebrated in Jewish Wisdom literature:

I issued from the mouth of the Most High and as a mist did cover the earth. I dwelt on high and my seat was upon a pillar of cloud. I alone encircled the sphere of heaven and in the depth of the abyss did I walk about.

(*LXX* Wisdom of ben Sirach 24:3–5)

This conflation has at least one crucial attraction: invoking *outward*, or material, light—light as a mantle or mist or stream (of ether)—captures a genuine unity; outward light, inward light, and "wisdom" are (somehow) one and the same thing:[11]

> So much the rather, thou Celestial light
> Shine inward, and the mind through all her powers
> Irradiate, there plant eyes, all mist from thence
> Purge and disperse, that I may see and tell
> Of things invisible to mortal sight.
>
> (*PL* 3.51–55)

The blind Advocate, in short, has a second (interior) "entrance" for "wisdom at one entrance quite shut out" (*PL* 3.50). Again the identification of light with wisdom parallels the conception of Wisdom in the Apocrypha:

> [Wisdom] is a ray of everlasting light, and an unstained mirror of the working of God, and an image of his goodness. And though she is one, she can do all things, and though she abides in herself, she renews all the world; even passing according to the generations into hallowed souls, she prepares the friends of God and his prophets.
>
> (*LXX* Wisdom of Solomon 7:26–27)

In the ancient Rabbinic version of the newly fashioned Adam's transformation into a living soul, the living soul becomes a kind of lamp—"a spirit that speaks, to light up [Adam's] eyes and incline his ears."[12] The Advocate begins by telling us that God is light (*PL* 3.3); if so, it seems God creates some things out of his own substance—the inwardly "speaking" things. The voices of light silently affirm his "wisdom" against the Adversary's scoffing charge to the contrary.

THE URIEL EPISODE: INFINITY (*PARADISE LOST* 3)

Masquerading as a tourist at the border of Eden, Satan draws out the sentinel Uriel (Heb. "fire, or light, of God")—one of seven such military "eyes" or "lamps" mentioned in the Bible (*PL* 3.654, 650, Zech. 4:10, Rev. 4:5). Uriel turns out to have relevant testimony:

> I saw when at his Word the formless Mass,
> This worlds material mould, came to a heap:
> Confusion heard his voice, and wild uproar
> Stood rul'd, stood vast infinitude confin'd;
> Till at his second bidding darkness fled,
> Light shon, and order from disorder sprung.
>
> (*PL* 3.708–13)

This privileged experience of the Creator's "wisdom infinite" (*PL* 3.706) takes us back one stage. It now appears that "Let there be light" was only the first *recorded* command in the process of creation. Without being "bidden" to shed its "infinitude" and come to a "heap," the raw material of the universe couldn't take on "light" (i.e., order). Infinity is endlessness, and "end" is two-ways ambiguous: purpose and limit. The purposelessness of mass had to yield to the limitlessness of wisdom. The first "infinitude" is "confusion," the second is "order."

PARADISE LOST 2: THE CHAOS EPISODE

Even on Uriel's showing, to be "confused" is to be ripe for order, not to resist it; matter not yet assigned an "end" is ready to "hear" the assigning "voice." We've had a look at a "universe . . . created evil" (*PL* 2.602–3), and this isn't it.[13] To be uncreated, but ready to serve creation, is to be

> a dark
> Illimitable Ocean without bound,
> Without dimension, where length, breadth, and highth,
> And time and place are lost, where eldest Night
> And Chaos, Ancestors of Nature, hold
> Eternal *Anarchie*, and by confusion stand.
>
> (*PL* 2.891–97)

Nature, apparently, can't be rightly understood unless we understand her "Ancestors"—that is, the primitive state of matter we get to look at over Satan's shoulder as he struggles toward the newly created universe. As a description of this ocean, in fact, "unformed" proves to be as misleading as "confused."

The formlessness, or "anarchie," or absence of limit, isn't absolute; Nature's "Ancestors" take after their granddaughter. Even in the Chaos world, there are precise limits to how far primitive matter can be divided, and into what: elementary particles come in "clanns" (*PL* 2.901) distinguished by temperature, solidity, weight, shape, and speed (*PL* 2.898, 902)[14]. If the mark of the Creator is to be the source of form, the Creator signals his presence even in a world in which he chooses not to create. In that kind of world, in spite of its rudimentary structure, "*Chance* governs all" (*PL* 2.910). The "embryon atoms" (*PL* 2.900) skirmish blindly, like Rebecca's unborn children (Gen. 25:22)—a metaphor that is clearly central to what the Advocate is getting at here: the material "womb of Nature" (*PL* 2.911) is helpless to give birth to its "pregnant causes" (*PL* 2.913). So matter in Chaos is not only a Rebecca but an Alcmena, forever in the throes of motherhood (*materia* < *mater*; word origins come in for serious play here). Left to its own devices, this "pregnancy" will never come to term.

In short, in its allegorical dimension Chaos is a thought experiment—an experiment with a crucial bearing on the idea of creation. As an alternative theory of how *our* world began (the "dark ocean" world doesn't seem to have had a beginning), the atheist version of materialism appeals to a likelihood remote to the point of invisibility: that armies of blind particles moving at random will somehow manage to "ordain" the physical universe (*PL* 2.915–16).[15] In effect, the Chaos episode functions as a *reductio ad absurdum*.[16]

The classic atomist rejoinder to the *reductio* is to insist, with Satan, that the world just evolves out of an infinite run of random atom couplings, *given an infinite supply of atoms*.[17] (To see the unhelpfulness of the infinity suggestion as it stands, think of the proverbial typing monkeys: the possible runs of typed characters are infinitely many, like the letters in each run; infinitely many such possible runs don't contain an occurrence of Shakespeare's works.[18])

It's curious and (from the Advocate's point of view) telling that the rejoinder doesn't even convince its inventors. The classic atomists are hard put to explain anything, including the world, without invoking the notion of a "covenant of nature"[19]: the elementary particles obey laws that define their causal *powers*[20]—laws that don't set down what does and doesn't happen, but what can and can't.[21] The causal "covenant" is solemnly "ratified."[22] It's a "deeply clinging boundary marker."[23] It guarantees the "rationality" of the natural "order."[24] A boundary marker put in by whom?

A covenant solemnly ratified by whom? Reflecting whose rationality?

Obviously the atheist can't mean these ideas literally. Yet he seems to be at a loss when it comes to spelling out what *else* he means by them. By default at least, the theist meaning—cosmic law with a cosmic legislator—is the only meaning the atheist has to his name. The law talk is as indispensable as it is embarrassing. It's a short and easy step to the theist atomism of the Advocate's Chaos, in which embryonic laws of particle behavior are already in place, though not yet enough laws for a world to begin.

In short, the Advocate gets unexpected support from the opposition. That's why he can cheerfully offer us a recognizably Lucretian Chaos. Eliminate a lawgiver—a Creator—from your cosmogony, and what's left is the "Anarch" (*PL* 2.988), the lord not only of *No Rule* but of *No Beginning* (*arché* both times—serious play with word origins again).[25] Even the blindest of the fallen angels knows nonsense when he sees it: a world (here imagined as yet to come) in which "everlasting Fate shall yeild / To fickle Chance, and *Chaos* judge the strife" (*PL* 2.232–33).

If Chaos *does* decide the outcomes, of course, then there aren't any; by his kind of "decision" he "more imbroils the strife by which he reigns" (*PL* 2.908–9). But the whole point of the allegory is that in the strict sense of "reigns" (imposing an order) he reigns nowhere, not even in the realm he claims to be defending against God's "encroachment" (*PL* 2.1001). He's an impostor—that is, the theory of world-creation he embodies is an illusion. One fairly obvious piece of humbug is the "dark Pavilion" over his throne (*PL* 2.960), a shameless imitation of the tent of darkness in which God "resides" (Ps. 18:12, *PL* 2.263–68). Chaos lives up to his title of *anarch*; he's the *non-ruler* of his alleged domain. The real ruler here is the ruler everywhere else.

Against this background, the Advocate allows himself a moment of telling irony. Half way on the flight through Chaos, the Tempter is sucked helplessly into a nosedive. Will he fall indefinitely? Will he pull out of it and reach Eden to do his worst? In this neighborhood, we're asked to suppose, the umpire of such questions is "ill chance":

> all unawares
> Fluttring his pennons vain plumb down he drops
> Ten thousand fadoms deep, and to this hour

> Down had been falling, had not by ill chance
> The strong rebuff of som tumultuous cloud
> Instinct with Fire and Nitre hurri'd him
> As many miles aloft.
>
> (*PL* 2.932–38)

The culprit was a "vacuitie"—a pocket of emptiness (*PL* 2.932). Empty of *what*? Presumably, empty of atom "clans" to buoy Satan up. But not—in the Advocate's view at least—empty of the Ground of all being: "I am who fill / Infinitude, nor vacuous the space" (*PL* 7.168–69). "Vacuities" are never what they seem to be.

The point of the irony in the mock diagnosis of "ill chance" is that, pending a good reason to think otherwise, the tenant of all spaces, empty or full, isn't ill and isn't chance: "Necessitie and Chance / Approach not mee, and what I will is Fate" (*PL* 7.172–73). There's a bit more to this irony: "ill chance" saves Satan by using a blast ("rebuff") of gunpowder ("nitre") to thrust him back out of the "vacuitie" pocket. He is, in short, no more self-propulsive than the cannon balls he shot at the angels of light in the war he's just lost (*PL* 6.512); in fact, he's degenerated into a missile himself—aimed by his enemy. The secret master of Chaos is also a master of irony.

On the other hand, if we can't (on the Advocate's showing) have a cosmos without a Creator, we can't have a cosmos without a Chaos either; Chaos is the Creator's "eternal store" (*PL* 7.226). Equivalently, the "Night" whose "wide womb" coincides with Chaos is as "uncreated" (*PL* 2.150) and "eternal" (*PL* 3.18) as the "holy light" God "dwells" in "from Eternitie" (*PL* 3.4–5).

The figurative language, again, is Jewish-Hellenic. An Orphic hymn invokes Night as no less than the mother of nature—and the Advocate later virtually identifies a tag from the same well-known creation myth: "to the *Orphean* lyre / I sung of *Chaos* and *Eternal Night*" (*PL* 3.17–18). Living in the dark, Mammon takes comfort in the fact that God often chooses to "reside" in "the Majesty of darkness" (*PL* 2.263–68; compare Chaos's bogus "Pavilion" [*PL* 2.960]). Later we hear of the "cave within the mount of God" (*PL* 6.4–5); unsurprisingly, the Demiurge in the Orphic *Theogony* also has a cave. In that work, the body, or materiality, of the Demiurge contains everything, and it seems that the Advocate—in a suitably figurative sense—agrees: a thing of darkness that the Creator has had in him all along is waiting to shed its "infinitude" and become a cosmos.[26]

All this doesn't quite exhaust the polemical force of Chaos—a particle collection *personified*—as an "Arbiter" who relies on free will (*liberum arbitrium*) to "decide" things. In classical atomism, "decision" in an agent is a special case of "decision" in a chaos—a collection of randomly moving particles. For particle movement to be random is for it to be free in the only relevant sense of "free": not covered by any law, including laws of cause and effect.[27] Every such movement is a tiny "swerve" [28] from the path dictated by causal laws. In a word, atom-swerves defy *necessity*—both from without and (what's worse) from within.[29]

Randomness freedom is as close as atomism comes to free agency. Unfortunately, that's not very close. A collective atom-swerve may not be something that happens to an agent by *necessity*, but it is something that happens to an agent all the same—not something the agent *does*. In fact, the agent talk here is quite empty; the only agent in evidence is a weather zone. Agents, in all but name, are a casualty of the atomist account of free agency—along with their innocence and guilt. In the context of the Great Argument, the price of this account of freedom isn't just high. It's fatal.

There's a parallel here to what the Chaos episode has to say about the atomistic attempt to account for the world. The beginning of voluntary movement, in that account, is a "creation" of the unassisted "heart."[30] But as with the world, so with the act: a creator is precisely what that account supposes it can do without, or replace (once again) with the Lord of No Beginning.

On the other hand, the Advocate's creation isn't out of nothing. If his Creator can't do without Chaos, we shouldn't be surprised if his Free Agent can't either.

CHAOS ALIVE AND WELL IN THE GARDEN

The slope leading up to the unfallen Eden is "grottesque and wild," with "hairy sides" (*PL* 4.136, 135); also "savage" (*PL* 4.172). Inside, the vines are "luxuriant" (*PL* 4.260); the whole garden, in fact, is "luxurious" (*PL* 9.209). (*Luxuria* is lechery; does one of the seven deadly sins have an Edenic twin?) Brooks roll on with "mazie errour" (*PL* 4.239), the tenants entertain themselves with seemly "dalliance" (*PL* 4.338; "dalliance" is lewd play—or is this another twin?), the still uncorrupted serpent is "sly" and "insinuating" and gives proof of "guile" (*PL* 4.347–49), the growth of the arbors is "wanton" enough to "mock" the gardeners' swamped efforts at "reform" (*PL* 4.625–29), "unsightly" and "unsmooth" blossoms and gums lie strewn about (*PL* 630–31). For the sake of "fruitless embraces," "pamper'd" boughs "reach" too "far" (*PL* 5.213–15).

Unfortunately for the Advocate, the Fall has had its prurient way with all these words; if we're not careful to retrieve the innocent readings, we're liable to think we're listening to Marvell's moral demagogue in "The Mower against Gardens," with his self-serving harangue about hot doings among the plants in the "green seraglio." Still, the innocent readings aren't always easy to come by. How is it innocent to "mock" efforts to reform one's excesses? How is it innocent to be pampered? to overreach? Granted that one can't have too much of at least some good things, can fruitless embraces be among them? For that matter, how can excess be innocent if it cries aloud for "checking" (*PL* 5.214), "pruning" (*PL* 4.438), "lopping" (*PL* 4.629), "riddance" (*PL* 4.632)? Can there be good riddance to a *good* excess?

The answer seems to be: yes—if somehow riddance is what the excess is *for*, and if there's something else, in turn, that the *riddance* is for. But what could the riddance be for? Can Adam's and Eve's cutting back an excess be better than God's simply keeping it from happening? The question answers itself. It seems that pruning, outward and inward, is the human creature's "daily work of body or mind / appointed, which declares his Dignitie" (*PL* 4.618–19)— "daily" because the Creator has guaranteed that the work will need to be done over and over again:

> Nature multiplies
> Her fertil growth, and by disburd'ning grows
> More fruitful.
>
> (*PL* 5.318–20)

> the work under our labour grows,
> Luxurious by restraint; what we by day
> Lop overgrown, or prune, or prop, or bind,
> One night or two with wanton growth derides,
> Tending to wild.
>
> (*PL* 9.208–12)

In short, the riotous lushness of the inner and outer gardens is not only good in itself—"Nature boon" (*PL* 4.242), "wild above [not just outside of] Rule or Art; enormous bliss" (*PL* 4.297)—it's also (and especially) good as a means. As a means, it's a chance to practice

> an art
> Which does mend Nature—change it rather, but
> The art itself is Nature.[31]

As an art of conduct, the challenge to mastery is to "govern well thy appetite" (*PL* 7.546); appetite, in all its exuberance, is one of the things to be pruned—shaped into coherence and proportion. Appetite in the garden before the fall could no more come disciplined in advance than the flowers could come prearranged by the Creator's "nice art" into "beds and curious knots" (*PL* 4.241–42). The whole point of letting the Tempter slip through the hedge, for the Advocate as for the author of *Areopagitica*, is that

> when God gave [Adam] reason, he gave him freedom to choose, for reason is but choosing, he had been else a mere artificial Adam, such an Adam as he is in the motions. We ourselves esteem not of that obedience, or love, or gift, which is of force. God therefore left him free, set before him a provoking object, ever almost in his eyes; herein consisted his merit, herein the right of his reward, the praise of his abstinence. *Wherefore did he create passions within us*, pleasures round about us, but that *these, rightly tempered, are the very ingredients of virtue*?[32]

The Creator of overgrowth also created noisy "passions"— affective overgrowth; without passions, no "provocation," and "provocation" ([etymologically] = "challenge") is the whole point. One otherwise canny interpreter of Edenic wildness in *PL* speaks of it as a "threat."[33] But a provocation is a dare, not a threat. And by this Provoker's express intention in *PL* 3, this particular dare is an opportunity—the very ingredient of virtue.

Classical ethics makes much of *sophrosynë*—the innately rational personality; *encráteia*—the morally agonistic personality—gets praised for winning the struggle for rationality, and demoted to a non-virtue for having to struggle in the first place.[34] In the Advocate's Pauline ethics, by contrast, "every man that striveth for the mastery is temperate in all things. Now [the worldly strivers] do it [viz., exercise temperance] to obtain a corruptible crown, but we an incorruptible" (1 Cor. 9:25). The temperateness in the Greek text is precisely *encráteia*: victory, in the internal *agón* or marathon, over one's own urges. In the metaphoric language of the garden, the equivalent of subduing the urges is pruning them—or lopping or checking or ridding.[35]

One of the urges built into Adam from the beginning worries him enough to come out in the form of something nervously confided to the departing Raphael. With one exception, the pleasure of the garden "works in the mind no change, / Nor vehement desire" (*PL* 8.525–26). When it comes to Eve's beauty, however,

> Farr otherwise, transported I behold,
> Transported touch; here passion first I felt,
> Commotion strange, in all enjoyments else
> Superior and unmov'd, here onely weak
> Against the charm of Beauties powerful glance.
> Or *Nature fail'd* in mee, and left some part
> *Not* proof *enough* such Object to sustain,
> Or from my side subducting, took perhaps
> *More than enough*; at least on her bestow'd
> *Too much* of Ornament, *in outward shew*
> *Elaborate, of inward less exact.*

(PL 8.529–39)

Adam has already had occasion to wonder euphemistically "how Nature wise and frugal could commit . . . disproportions" (*PL* 7.25–37); but here the suspicion of architectural "disproportion" is more subversive. It goes to the Creator's justice as well as his wisdom: by giving one creature too much of a necessary good and another creature not enough, or by giving either creature too much of a marginal good and not enough of a fundamental good, the Creator would be making a farce of distributive justice. Still worse, given the impending loss of paradise, if the ill-equipped creature turns out not to be "proof" against a criminally punishable temptation, then retributive justice is due to die in a kangaroo court. In short, the "failure" of Nature—that is, of the Creator's artisanship ("providence")—would be fatal to the Advocate's case.

In fact, it would be doubly fatal; the evidence of Adam's "weakness" against the "glance" (that is, the dazzle[36]) of Eve's beauty (*PL* 8.533) isn't just what it makes him *feel* ("commotion strange" [*PL* 8.531]) but what it makes him *think*:

> when I approach
> Her loveliness, so absolute she seems
> And in herself compleat, so well to know

> Her own, that what she wills to do or say
> Seems wisest, vertuousest, discreetest, best;
> All higher knowledge in her presence falls
> Degraded, Wisdom in discourse with her
> Looses discountenanc'd, and like folly shews;
> Authority and Reason on her wait,
> As one intended first, not after made
> Occasionally; and to consummate all,
> Greatness of mind and nobleness their seat
> Build in her loveliest, and create an awe
> About her, as a guard Angelic plac't.
>
> (*PL* 8.546–559)

Here, says one critic who succumbs to Adam's suspicion, are "the first signs of the weakness which will eventually lead to Adam's downfall. The whole speech is absolutely central to Milton's presentation of the Fall itself. Adam's confession appears at first to be one of the most original parts of the poem, for although several poets had remarked on his love for Eve none had gone so far as to suggest that he loved her overmuch or in the wrong way"[37]

Fortunately for the Advocate's enterprise, he doesn't "suggest" this either—not in Adam's current speech anyhow. The closest Adam comes to admitting or betraying a moral weakness here is his report that, *against his better judgment*, Eve gives an appearance or "shew" of superior wisdom and knowledge (*PL* 8.549–53); but this is to say precisely that his judgment isn't tied to these appearances.[38] In fact, the point of Raphael's next speech is that what's foolish, if anything, is Adam's fear of getting fooled:

> Accuse not Nature, she hath don her part;
> Do thou but thine, and be not diffident
> Of Wisdom, *she deserts thee not, if thou*
> *Dismiss not her*, when most thou needst her nigh,
> By attributing overmuch to things
> Less excellent, *as thou thyself perceav'st.*
>
> (*PL* 8.561–66)

The danger isn't that he'll get fooled, but that he'll choose to fool himself.

As for Adam's "awe" of Eve and her "greatness of mind" (*PL* 8.557-59), these appearances, at least, aren't deceptive.[39] The Creator *made* Eve "So awful, that with honour thou maist love / Thy mate, who sees when thou art seen least wise" (*PL* 8.577–78); she really is capable of noticing, and alerting him to, his moments of "least" wisdom. (Being smarter and more authoritative doesn't insure Adam against these; which, in turn, insures Eve a right— duty?—of advice and consent. Hierarchy or no hierarchy, the little polity on display here is a republic.)

What *would* be a sign of weakness, says Raphael in effect, is for Adam to value sex with Eve more highly than conjugal "societie" (fellowship)—the "unfeign'd / Union of mind" (*PL* 8.604) that Adam celebrates in a reply that shows that Raphael needn't worry on this score; Adam holds sex worthy of "reverence," but what "delight" him most in his partner are

> those graceful acts,
> Those thousand decencies that daily flow
> From all her words and actions.
>
> (*PL* 8.600–602)

But truthful appearances are no more addictive than deceptive ones; they, too, "subject not" (*PL* 8.607):

> I to thee disclose
> What inward thence I feel, not therefore foil'd,
> Who meet with various objects, from the sense
> Variously representing, yet still free
> Approve the best, and follow what I approve.
>
> (*PL* 8. 607–11)

As usual: without chaos, no creation. There will be moments when we will be "least wise," without quite being foolish. Deceptive appearances and noisy passions are ingredients of sin only when they're also ingredients of moral accomplishment—*only when we know better, or ought to*; and then (on the Advocate's freedom hypothesis at least) it's up to us to follow what we approve, and equally up to us to say, with Ovid's Medea—serious play on the Advocate's part again—"I see the better choice and approve of it; and follow the worse."[40]

Take another candidate for an innate—created—"weakness" that guarantees a creature's "downfall": Eve's enticement by what turns out to be her own image. The play on Ovid here might well suggest "infantile solipsism and self-love"[41]—if one ignored the way the Advocate has pointedly set it up. Like Ovid's Narcissus, Eve thinks (at first) she's looking at somebody else—*until she's told (or shown) otherwise*; in the meantime, the "sympathie and love" (*PL* 4.465) she thinks she's exchanging with the "Shape within the wat'ry gleam" (*PL* 4.461) are neither solipsistic nor self-loving, much less infantile. The same goes for the fact that she starts out preferring the soothing "Shape" to Adam, who frightens her a little: on the Advocate's showing, Eve *does* have reason to think Adam "less winning soft, less amiablie mild" (*PL* 4.479)—*until she's given reason to think otherwise.*

It doesn't quite do justice to this episode, in short, to say that "Eve's untutored feelings, like the natural growth of the plants around her, do not grow in the right direction spontaneously. They have to be 'reformed,' and it is necessary for God to check the 'fruitless embraces' she seeks in her own reflection and lead her to 'wed her Elm.' "[42] The fallacy here, once again, is to think of deceptive appearances and noisy passions as negative—as defects in the scheme of things. Actually the sequel shows that they're no more negative or defective than the "embryons" of Cosmos in the womb of Chaos; in fact, appearance and passion supply the ingredients of moral agency—just as Chaos supplies the ingredients of the act of Creation. Above all, they're not threats that a victimized Eve has to be passively *rescued* from.

God "reforms" and "checks" Eve by persuasion—that is, by supplying her, or having Adam supply her, with the wherewithal to "reform" and "check" *herself*:

> What thou seest,
> What there thou seest, fair Creature, is thy self,
> With thee it comes and goes: but follow me,
> And I will bring thee where no shadow staies
> Thy coming, and thy soft imbraces, hee
> Whose image thou art, him thou shalt enjoy
> Inseparably thine, to him shalt bear
> Multitudes like thy self, and thence be call'd
> Mother of human Race.
>
> (*PL* 4.467-69)[43]

> Whom fli'st thou? whom thou fli'st, of him thou art,
> His flesh, his bone; to give thee being I lent
> Out of my side to thee, neerest my heart
> Substantial life, to have thee by my side
> Henceforth an individual solace dear;

> Part of my Soul I seek thee, and thee claim
> My other half.
>
> (*PL* 4.482–88)

In each case Eve responds to persuasion by dismissing (or reforming or checking or lopping or ridding) a contrary impulse:

> What could I doe,
> But follow straight, invisibly thus led?"
>
> (*PL* 4.475–76)

> I yeilded, and from that time see
> How beauty is excelled by manly grace,
> And wisdom, which alone is truly fair.
>
> (*PL* 4.489–91)

"What could I doe" would be a disclaimer of responsibility if it weren't for "invisibly thus led"—led, that is, by rational persuasion. Eve is given an opportunity to be the author of her own rational acts of "following" and "yeilding"; otherwise she gets no praise for either, and (more to the point, given the sequel) no blame. The wildness of the mental garden, meanwhile, is no more malign than the wildness of Eden. In fact, the Creator seems to have provided for a spree of inner wildness in the off-hours of reason:

> Yet evil whence? *in thee can harbour none,*
> *Created pure.* But know that in the Soul
> Are many lesser Faculties that serve
> Reason as chief; among these Fansie next
> Her office holds; of all external things,
> Which the five watchful Senses represent,
> She forms Imaginations, Aerie shapes,
> Which Reason joyning or disjoyning, frames
> All what we affirm, or what deny, and call
> Our knowledge or opinion; then retires
> Into her private Cell when nature rests.
> Oft in her absence mimic Fansie wakes
> To imitate her; but misjoyning shapes,
> *Wild work* produces oft.
>
> (*PL* 5.99–112; italics added)

It happens that Adam's rhetorical question "Yet evil whence" is on the wrong track; this particular interlude of "wild work" is born of malice. But Adam is quite right that, generated by chance or by malice,

> Evil into the mind of God or Man
> May come and go, *so unapprov'd*, and leave
> No spot or blame behind.
>
> > (*PL* 5.117–19; italics added)

Satan has the power to make his victim dream that she is losing a battle with her desires: "I, methought, / Could not but taste" (*PL* 5.85–86). What he can't do, on pain of logical absurdity, is manufacture his victim's free consent. The closest he comes to this is to make her think she must have consented; the dream cuts to an image of the aftermath of consent ("forthwith up to the Clouds / With him I flew" [*PL* 5.86–87]). The proviso in "so unapprov'd" is crucial here: so long as the dreamer withholds her approval, she's a mere witness to the dream crime—no more "spotted" than God, who witnesses every crime. Without approval, no complicity. Far from leaving a spot behind, urges ripe for pruning are a moral opportunity.

> To fight with bad motions of the mind, to spurn the devil's insinuations, is the seal of virtue and of great merit. So do not be dismayed by fantasies from without, whatever matter they bring with them.
>
> Nor is it an illusion that now and then you are carried away into a sudden excess, and instantly turn back to the heart's accustomed follies; those follies are things you suffer against your will rather than things you do. So long as they displease you, so long as you resist them, it is a merit, not a perdition.[44]

In this reassuring aside from *Imitatio Christi*, what goes for "bad motions" goes double for "follies"—"motions" that are not bad but simply anarchic:[45] without Chaos, no creation.[46]

Creation Out of Oneself

Adam launches Raphael on his narrative of the Creation by asking a loaded question:

> *what cause*
> *Mov'd* the Creator in his holy Rest
> Through all Eternitie so late to build
> In *Chaos*.
>
> (*PL* 7.90–93; italics added)

The question is loaded in the same way as the one the Advocate begins his forensic narrative by putting to his Muse:

> *what cause*
> *Mov'd* our Grand Parents in that happy State,
> Favour'd of Heav'n so highly, to fall off
> From thir Creator.
>
> (*PL* 1.28–31)

If an act is caused, then it isn't free. In particular, if the act of creation isn't free, then what becomes of the claim with which the Creator introduces the Work of Six Days, that "Necessitie and Chance / Approach not mee, and what I will is fate" (*PL* 7.172–73)?

We've already noticed the Advocate's high-risk libertarian strategy of making his own case while leaving in plain view the makings of the case for the prosecution. The prosecution is not only entitled to those makings, it's welcome to them; they're specious anyhow. Obviously our "Grand Parents" wouldn't have (freely) fallen to temptation if they hadn't been tempted in the first place. On this harmless reading of "caused" (= "occasioned"), there's nothing scandalous about asking what "caused" free agents to "fall off / From thir Creator." What would be scandalous would be to think that the Fall followed the Temptation in obedience to a law of nature. In this sense of cause ("necessitated"), what free acts are free of is, precisely, causation.

The trouble is that the resulting standard of freedom is strict enough for a creature, but not for a Creator—at least for *this* Creator. By offering an occasion, the tempter may not cause the tempted to fall, but he surely causes them to *decide* whether or not to fall. Making this decision is something the objects of temptation clearly do. Just as clearly, an act of deciding—*freely* deciding as it turns out—results from the act of tempting. The tricky point here is that even *this* much dependency on somebody else's initiatives compromises the freedom of the supremely free Agent of Western theology.

God's answer to (say) the defection of Satan has to be an answer in name only—an initiative in disguise. It has to express a law of God's nature. That's why "Necessitie and Chance / Approach not mee" *PL* 7.172–73); God's acts are not only independent of any other being, they're non-arbitrary—they're not the capricious "new Laws" that the Adversary tries to pin on God as evidence that the divine form of government is tyranny (*PL* 5.679–83). This fixture of the Christian God concept is Plato's legacy to Christian doctrine, via Plotinus' eloquent treatise on the freedom of God.[47]

Given God's omnipotence, the standard for his freedom is even stricter than that. We might imagine that Raphael could satisfy Adam by spelling out the *purpose* of creation. But an omnipotent being needn't resort to any particular means to achieve its ends; in fact, it can dispense with means altogether, and simply *will* its ends. To account for the act of Creation, final causes make no more sense than efficient ones.

That's why Raphael's implied answer to Adam's question (in the Creator's own words) is more grist for the prosecution; it almost seems as if God created the world to teach Satan a lesson:

> But least his heart exalt him in the harm
> Already done, to have dispeopl'd Heav'n,
> My damage fondly deem'd, I can repair
> That detriment, if such it be to lose
> Self-lost, and in a moment will create
> Another World.
>
> (*PL* 7.150–55)

On the inevitable first-glance reading, God's world-making makes a mockery of his omnipotence by being a means to an end, as well as a response to an occasion, after all. As if this weren't embarrassing enough, the means doesn't even match the end—thereby making a mockery of God's wisdom into the bargain. On the one hand, we're told that Satan is wrong to think he's "damaged" God by depopulating heaven; beings lost to themselves are no loss to God, so "damage," "detriment," and "loss" (predicated of the fallen angels' removal from Heaven) turn out to be misnomers. On the other hand, if Satan's mistake is to take these terms at face value, then how does it put him right, much less cut him off in mid-gloat ("least his heart exalt him"), to show him that it's easy for God to "repair" the non-detriment, non-damage, and non-loss? How do you *fix* what isn't *broken*? On the first-glance reading, in short, the

Creator stands convicted of feebleness and folly—by his own plea of innocence! It's an inglorious performance. If the defense can't do better than this, we can hardly blame the prosecution for "exalting" itself.

By scrupulously including this kind of evidence, the Advocate, to repeat, plays a high-risk game. But a high-risk game needn't be a losing game. Once again the prosecution is welcome to its evidence as well as (from the libertarian point of view) entitled to it; the reading won't survive a second look.

Adam has asked his question *twice*; he treats the two versions as equivalent, but they aren't. First version:

> Deign to descend now lower, and relate
> What may no less perhaps avail us known,
> How first began this Heav'n which we behold
> Distant so high, with moving fires adorn'd,
> Innumerable, and this which yeelds or fills
> All space, the ambient Air wide interfus'd
> Imbracing round this florid Earth . . .
>
> (*PL* 7.84–90)

The second version, which we've already glanced at, follows immediately:

> what cause
> Mov'd the Creator in his holy Rest
> Through all Eternitie so late to build
> In *Chaos*.
>
> (*PL* 7.90–93)

Adam's first question is about the origin of the universe he's *in*. He knows that it wasn't the first to interrupt God's "holy rest":

> As yet this world was not, and *Chaos* wild
> Reign'd where these Heav'ns now rowl, where Earth now rests
> Upon her Center pois'd, when on a day . . .
>
> (*PL* 5.577–79)

Raphael's history of angelic rebellion and civil war makes it clear that various things (for example, angels and Hell) had already been created while "as yet this world was not." Explaining the existence of *this* world, which is what Raphael obliges Adam by proceeding to do, isn't the same as explaining why anything at all exists besides God—the kernel of Version 2.

Now for the threatened embarrassments of Version 1. It's true that *this* world will serve as God's answer to Satan's defection, and also true that an all-powerful God's answer to a creature's deed can't be merely reactive. But the embarrassments don't follow. Satan's punishment *isn't* merely reactive. On the Advocate's objectivist assumptions about moral principles, that punishment is simply the moral law—the law of God's nature—in action. It is, as required, an initiative in disguise and a reaction in name only. Part of that law is retributive justice, and on the Advocate's showing, the retribution for free will abused is free will forfeited. In Satan's case, getting cured of his robotic malice would be no such retribution—though his character is due for a touch of improvement: evidence of God's cosmic "repair" to "damage fondly deem'd" will keep Satan's heart from "exalting" its owner. But the "fond deeming" itself (the delusional hope and urge to damage God via his creation) is going to be left just where it is; it's part of the punishment.

Which brings us to Version 2, and the main point. For starters, notice that the Creator only seems to say he'll create the new world to humble Satan—only seems to say "least his heart exalt him, I *will* repair"; all he actually says is "least his heart exalt him, I *can* repair." This obviously needs filling in: lest Satan's heart exalt him, *he needs to be shown that* I can "repair" the alleged harm. The world currently on the drawing board will do this, of course—but what something happens to *do* needn't be what it's *for*. In fact, with respect to the newest world we already know otherwise:

> there is a place
> (If ancient and prophetic fame in Heav'n
> Err not), another World, the happy seat
> Of som new Race call'd *Man*, about this time
> To be created like to us, though less
> In power and excellence, but favour'd more
> Of him who rules above, so was his will
> Pronounc'd among the Gods, and by an Oath,
> That shook Heav'ns whole circumference, confirm'd.
>
> (*PL* 2.345–53)[48]

The newest world was in the making well before Satan's rebellion. Indeed, if "favour" toward the Son hadn't provoked the rebellion, "favour" toward the projected "new Race call'd *Man*" might well have done the job instead. I remarked a while back that explaining the existence of *this* world isn't the same as explaining why anything at all exists besides God. Why, as Adam puts it, does God break his eternal sabbath in the first place? But even this world can't be explained by saying what it's for—much less by appealing to some moral imperative or entitlement; being created plainly isn't our due, any more than the "favour" reserved for us once created.

"Favour," it seems, marks the spot that the Advocate's visions of the Ur-Act are all pointing at. In those visions, his project of "justifying" the ways of God to men takes a distinctly Biblical rather than Hellenic form;[49] the merit that guides the relevant kind of "justice" is in the giver and not the given-*to*—rather like Hamlet's notion of "bounty": "Use them after your own honour and dignity. The less they deserve, the more merit is in your bounty."[50] If the Creator of this new world, or its predecessors, has an end in view, the end is the creation itself.

Creation is a labor of love—a labor that its beneficaries don't deserve, aren't entitled to, and (above all) don't cause; in a word, an utterly gratuitous act. That's why it stymies a searcher after *causes*—like Adam, or like the Roman atomist whose contemptuously rhetorical version of Adam's question is designed to reduce the creation idea to absurdity: "When the gods had been at rest so long before, what new fact, what afterthought, could awaken in them a desire to change their former life?"[51] The unsuspected answer, of course, is that the question *begs* a question: the love on display here is a forethought, not an afterthought. It doesn't wait for new facts; it makes them.

Another crucial paradox runs through the Advocate's creation stories, this time a paradox woven into their metaphoric design: the love projected—by the *Father* through the *Son*—is mother love. (The strangeness here is partly tamed by the relevant word origins; the object of the newest creation, after all, is "nature." *Natura* = *processus nascendi*, a universal process of coming to birth, or— more to the point—of being given birth to.) The Aristotelian commonplace we've already glanced at, that moral agency is a kind of parenthood,[52] is in the philosophical neighborhhood of the imagery in play here. But another Aristotelian commonplace gets even closer: the greater the parental "activity" (*enérgeia*) invested in child-making, the greater the love for the child; that's why fathers can't love as deeply as mothers.[53]

The crucial difference from the animal experience, of course, is that childbirth costs an all-powerful birthgiver no effort. But that doesn't mean that it costs the birthgiver nothing at all. What it costs him is his own substance, given without being lost. The Creation the Advocate shows us—repeatedly—is not out of nothing. The source is Chaos, the material "store" laid up in God from eternity (*PL* 7.226); less neutrally, the source is the "womb" that shelters "the world unborn" (*PL* 2.911, 5.181, 7.220); more mystically, the "boundless" Ur-Object known as "the Deep," which makes room for non-basic objects by letting parts of itself be bounded. To be born, apparently, is to come to fill part of the ostensibly empty space—the space between and beyond the warring atoms—that owes its existence to being filled by the God of space.[54] By allowing that co-tenancy, God contrives to "put forth [his] goodness":[55]

> ride forth, and bid the Deep
> Within appointed bounds be Heav'n and Earth,
> Boundless the Deep, because I am who fill
> Infinitude, nor vacuous the space.
> Though I uncircumscrib'd my self retire
> And put not forth my goodness, which is free
> To act or not, Necessitie and Chance
> Approach not mee, and what I will is Fate.
>
> (*PL* 7.166–73)[56]

To be born is also to come to fill part of the time that owes its existence to being filled by the God of time:

> For Time, though in Eternitie, appli'd
> To motion, measures all things durable
> By present, past, and future.
>
> (*PL* 5.580–82)[57]

Space owes its "boundlessness" to God. Apparently he fills it, or makes it, by being (boundlessly) omnipresent;[58] if bodiliness is basically extension, then it seems God is (in an appropriate sense) something bodily, the foundation of the material universe. It isn't hard to imagine the Advocate welcoming, or even making up, the argument in *Christian Doctrine* that, if God is the cause par excellence, then he can't just be (par excellence) the efficient, formal and final cause. He has to be the material cause as well:

For God (I say) not to hoard up this all-inclusive substantial power inside himself, but to send it out, to propagate it, to spread it, to whatever extent and in whatever manner he wishes—*what is this but for him to be supremely powerful and supremely good*? The materiality [in God] is neither bad nor worthless, but good, and the seedbed of every good to be produced thereafter. That materiality was a substance to be quarried from nowhere else than the source of all substance. At first unsorted and disarrayed, God set about to put it in order.[59]

On a superficial reading of *PL* at least, the Advocate is a male supremacist.[60] For that very reason, it's especially worth paying attention to the Creator's figurative maternity.[61] Reminders are everywhere—even, perhaps, in that first distant glimpse of the new world we get over the Tempter's shoulder:

> Far off th' Empyreal Heav'n, extended wide
> In circuit, undetermin'd square or round,
> With Opal Towers and Battlements adorn'd
> Of living Saphire, once his native Seat;
> And fast by hanging in a golden Chain
> This pendant world, in bigness as a Starr
> Of smallest Magnitude close by the Moon.
>
> (*PL* 2.1047–53)

A tiny (and poignantly de-"pendant") universe, more microcosm than cosmos, clinging to a great (and nurturant) universe by what resembles—in function as well as appearance—an umbilical cord.

The *process* of creation (*PL* 7) is a nested series of maternities, the oceanic womb of Waters taking over from that of Chaos and making way for the emergence of the Great Mother herself:[62]

> The Earth was form'd, but in the Womb as yet
> Of Waters, Embryon immature involv'd,
> Appear'd not: over all the face of Earth
> Main Ocean flow'd, not idle, but with warm
> Prolific humour soft'ning all her Globe,
> Fermented the great Mother to conceave,
> Satiate with genial moisture.
>
> (*PL* 7.276–82)

> The Earth obey'd, and strait
> Op'ning her fertile Woomb teem'd at a birth
> Innumerous living Creatures.
>
> (*PL* 7.453–55)

More centrally, the theological image from the proem to *PL* 1, of a masculine being in the act of giving birth, recurs benignly in Adam's (pro)creation of Eve:

> Mine eyes [Sleep] clos'd, but open left the Cell
> Of Fancie my internal sight, by which
> Abstract as in a transe methought I saw,
> Though sleeping, where I lay, and saw the shape
> Still glorious before whom awake I stood;
> Who stooping op'n'd my left side, and took
> From thence a Rib, with cordial spirits warm,
> And Life-blood streaming fresh; wide was the wound,
> But suddenly with flesh fill'd up and heal'd.
>
> (*PL* 8.460–68)

The Ground of Being—Great Mother *avant la lettre*—creates by sharing itself while losing nothing. Adam does the same, by a harmless Caesarean section; the "cordial spirits" and "Life-blood" he sacrifices are not only made up immediately, they're enhanced—and here the Advocate adopts the Hellenistic understanding[63] of the accompanying state of mind (Heb. *thardemah*, Gen. 2:21):[64] Adam has been lifted into *ecstasy*—mystic "transe" or "abstraction"; it seems he's never closer to the beatific vision than in the act of birth-giving.

By the same token, it seems that Satan is never further from the Creator than in the same act—but of course the whole point is that Satan's act is the same only if taken literally:

> All on a sudden miserable pain
> Surpris'd thee, dim thine eyes, and dizzie swum
> In darkness, while thy head flames thick and fast
> Threw forth, till on the left side op'ning wide,
> Likest to thee in shape and count'nance bright,
> Then shining heav'nly fair, a Goddess arm'd
> Out of thy head I sprung.
>
> (*PL* 2.752–58)

The rest of the episode rings changes on this grisly burlesque of love. Raped by the son she bears to her father, Sin anticipates the curse of Eve—with a vengeance. Dog-like things "kennel" in her womb (*PL* 2.658),

> hourly conceiv'd
> And hourly born, with sorrow infinite
> To me, for when they list into the womb
> That bred them they return, and howl and gnaw
> My Bowels, thir repast, then bursting forth
> Afresh with conscious terrors vex me round.
>
> (*PL* 2.797–801)

The Advocate is at a loss for parallels to their canine ugliness: Scylla's brood was no match for them; neither are the pets of the witch goddess, the dogs that Hecate's worshippers lure to their dances— *with the smell of infant blood* (*PL* 2.662–66). Exactly: Satan, Sin, Hecate, her child-murdering followers—a procession of Antimothers. For beings like ourselves, as we're told in *Areopagitica*, good is chiefly known by evil; the Advocate's leading metaphor for creation is being provided with a foil that illuminates by terror. As for the queen of infanticide, we might have seen her coming; the head of Satan's troops was the *king* of infanticide:

> First *Moloch*, horrid King besmear'd with blood
> Of human sacrifice, and parents tears,
> Though for the noyse of Drums and Timbrels loud
> Thir childrens cries unheard, that past through fire
> To his grim idol.
>
> (*PL* 2.392–96)

Eve and God

Much later on, the fallen Eve begins a better life by refusing to feed the cravings of another such king ("what seem'd his head / The likeness of a Kingly Crown had on" [*PL* 2.672–73]):

> miserable it is
> To be to others cause of misery,
> Our own begotten, and of our Loins to bring
> Into this cursed world a wofull Race,
> That after wretched Life must be at last
> Food for so foul a Monster.
>
> (*PL* 10.981–86)

For the Advocate's purposes, Death needs to be seen as the archetypal devourer of children—a foil both to Eve and to God: to the mother figure whose name is "Life"[65], and to the mother figure who created life. At the outset God enabled Adam to participate in the maternal act of creation by giving birth to Eve. Now, in the dialogue of reconciliation, he enables Eve to return the compliment. As I'm about to argue, the dialogue is a unique version of divine comedy: a shrewd celebration of a marriage reclaimed, and of the ingenious lovingkindness of God.

Male supremacist or not, the Advocate can hardly do justice to his assignment without beginning the story of renewal after the Fall with a reversal of roles; at this critical moment, moral authority shifts to Eve—by default; Adam is in no mood to exercise any:

> Out of my sight, thou Serpent, that name best
> Befits thee with him leagu'd, thy self as false
> And hateful.
>
> (*PL* 10.867–79)

Eve's "serpent" was the serpent—and Adam's "serpent" was Eve. (By inheritance from the Rabbinic [Aramaic] source, this is a bitter pun on the words for serpent and Eve.[66]) Adam's mistake was

> To trust thee from my side, imagin'd wise,
> Constant, mature, proof against all assaults,
> And understood not all was but a shew
> Rather than solid vertu, all but a Rib
> Crooked by nature, bent, as now appears,
> More to the part sinister from me drawn,
> Well if thrown out, as supernumerarie
> To my just number found.
>
> (*PL* 10.881–88)

Maybe there was no way of knowing, at the point of extraction, that the rib was "crooked by nature"; but Adam's suspicions, he now thinks, should have been aroused by the fact that the rib was "supernumerarie" to the "just" number of ribs. It was there waiting to be got rid of, like the suspect overgrowth in the garden. To repeat the question raised by the overgrowth, can there be good riddance to a *good* excess? The point of "just" (in "just number") transcends aesthetics: what distributive justice is to the moral arrangement of the world, proportion is to its architecture. Eve was *made* of something disproportionate—something perverse; no wonder she went bad.

Corruption seems to have turned Adam into a buffoon. But now he outdoes himself, rising to a kind of buffoonish sublime:

> O why did God,
> Creator wise, that peopl'd highest Heav'n
> With Spirits Masculine, create at last
> This noveltie on Earth, this fair defect
> Of Nature, and not fill the World at once
> With Men as Angels without Feminine,
> Or find some other way to generate
> Mankind? this mischief had not then befall'n.
>
> (*PL* 10.888–95)

This time Adam can't bottle up the real object of his resentment: the unwisdom (or worse) of this "creator wise." It won't do to reply on the creator's behalf that this afterthought—this "noveltie"—was the only way to fill a world; the populating of heaven shows otherwise. Even if the world wasn't to be filled with men "at once" but by successive generations, a *wise* creator would have known ways to generate mankind "without Feminine," and a *good* creator would have chosen one of them. (Never mind that a world without one sex is a world without the other; Adam is in no frame of mind to notice what he's pleading for.)

Silly and petulant as this stuff is, it gives the Adversary exactly what he needs, by dismissing the notion of free will. How could Eve have been created "wise, / Constant, mature, proof against *all* assaults" and still have collapsed under the *Tempter's* assault? The mere fact of the Fall (says Adam) exposes her "solid virtue" as mere "shew." So much for the Defense theory that the human mind before the Fall was "complete to have discover'd and repuls'd / Whatever wiles of Foe or seeming friend" (*PL* 10.10–11). On that theory—God's, Raphael's, even Adam's before the Fall—the moral armor promised by "proof," "solid," "complete," etc. isn't the *inability* to do wrong; on the contrary, absent the ability to do wrong, the act of doing right isn't an act at all, just the motion of a clockwork puppet. What's notable here is that free will doesn't get *formally* dismissed. It just drops out as if Adam had never heard of it, much less paid it the compliment of carefully explaining it to Eve (*PL* 9.350–63).

Eve is equally far gone—to start with, at least:

Forsake me not thus, *Adam*, witness Heav'n
What love sincere, and reverence in my heart
I bear thee, and unweeting have offended,
Unhappilie deceiv'd.

(PL 10.914–17)

This won't do, of course—not if we take the Creator as innocent until proved guilty (the ground rule of the forensic narrative): Eve was "complete" not only to have "repuls'd" Satan's wiles but to have "discover'd" them; whatever St. Paul means by her having been deceived, he can't mean to provide her with an *excuse* (she didn't know what she was doing). As for the protestation in "love sincere," it marks a faintly obscene lapse of memory: what Eve meant to share when she offered Adam the apple wasn't the power she would rather have kept to herself, but the death she would rather inflict on her beloved than face alone. Eve's conjugal love for Adam, as expressed by that act, was made of the same sick-sweet blend of sentimentality and malice as Satan's for the two of them:

> league with you I seek,
> And mutual amitie so streight, so close,
> That I with you must dwell, or you with me
> Henceforth.

(PL 4.375–78)

Misery "loves" company—"loves" it so much that it can't resist *making* the company it doesn't *find*.[67]

This is a terrible beginning—egoism redeemed only by what appear to be artlessness and confusion. It's not very clear what Eve wants of Adam beyond "peace" (*PL* 10.924)—or that she knows what she wants; maybe "thy gentle looks, thy aid / Thy counsel" (*PL* 10.919–20), maybe simply his protection: "forlorn of thee, / Whither shall I betake me, where subsist?" (*PL* 10.921–22). Yet after the *terrible* beginning comes something for which the Advocate has neglected to prepare us—a second and *real* beginning:

> on me exercise not
> Thy hatred for this miserie befall'n,
> On me already lost, mee then thy self
> More miserable; both have sinn'd, but thou
> Against God onely, I against God and thee,
> And to the place of judgment will return,

> There with my cries importune Heav'n, that all
> The sentence from thy head remov'd may light
> On me, sole cause to thee of all this woe,
> Mee mee onely just object of his ire.
>
> (*PL* 10.927–36)

No more talk of having offended "unweeting"; she not only offended *deliberately*, she outdid Adam by offending *twice*—first against God and then against Adam. And no more "importuning" of Adam; instead she will try to get him off by "importuning" God to divert all the punishment to her.

This last detail is remarkable; it deserves close attention: God will be asked to proceed on twin assumptions that Eve—by noting that "*both* have sinn'd"—has barely got through *ruling out*: that Eve is somehow (a) the "sole cause" of her accomplice's "woe," (b) the "onely just object" of God's anger. What's going on here? Does the speaker seriously expect to slip a brace of lies past this particular Judge?

These aren't lies. These are fictions that Eve is "importuning" God to adopt—fictions of a shape that ought to be familiar to the Advocate's Christian readers, especially if they manage to recall the Son's plea in *PL* 3.[68] God is being "importuned" to act *as if* something were the case—to let Eve not only undergo her own punishment but substitute for Adam in his; in this second capacity, Eve hopes to be allowed to *stand for*, and *suffer as*, Adam. (*Sub Adami persona*, as the theologians would say; playing Adam's part.) The moral principle her performance will serve, if any, is obviously not justice. As with the Son when he volunteers to pay "death for death" (*PL* 3.212), and (more to the point in the present context) as with the Creator who shares with the world an existence it has no particular right to, the moral principle Eve will be serving, if she gets her way, is love. Between the two principles, there's a deep, and maybe instructive, tension: in the context of justice, being a "respecter of persons" is a notorious vice; in the context of love, the case is otherwise.

Surely Adam can't help being deeply touched and replying in kind? It's a remarkable fact—as remarkable as Eve's unexpected access of moral authority—that he apparently *can* help it, with ease:

> Unwarie, and too desirous, as before,
> So now of what thou knowst not, who desir'st

> The punishment all on thy self; alas,
> Bear thine own first, ill able to sustain
> His full wrauth whose thou feelst as yet least part,
> And my displeasure bearst so ill.
>
> (*PL* 10.947–52)

There she goes again; her new resolve is just her old resolve to defy God, still driven by desire for the unknown; unknown fruit, unknown punishment—what's the difference? The new plan is beyond her puny strength anyhow—as her "unwariness" keeps her from realizing; if she finds Adam's mere *displeasure* ("out of my sight, thou Serpent") so hard to take, how can she hope to stand God's *wrath*? What we've just read (rightly or wrongly) as a gallant if quixotic reflex of love, Adam manages to read as a second fit of profane curiosity ("too desirous, *as before, so now*, of what thou knowst not")—a reckless lust for experience, in fact a presumptuous lust to *monopolize* the experience ("all on thy self"), and an arrogant refusal to accept one's own weakness ("bear thine own [assigned punishment] first").

A remarkable feat of interpretation, this. But Adam goes on to outdo himself in comic invention by smoking out something even more insidious in Eve's offer—a subversive attempt to upstage him:

> if Prayers
> Could alter high Decrees, I to that place
> Would speed before thee, and be louder heard,
> That on my head all might be visited,
> Thy frailtie and infirmer Sex forgiv'n,
> To me committed and by me expos'd.
>
> (*PL* 10.952–57)

He would have her know that the only reason he hasn't beaten her to this plan, and its execution, is that he isn't fool enough to think it would work. Anything she can do, he can do better. In a serious beau geste contest, he would outrun her ("speed before thee"), outpray her ("be louder heard"), and (in short) outshine her. In particular, he would turn his contempt for her autonomy into a plea on her behalf: she's a frail thing now, she was a frail thing then—too frail to resist the temptation he "expos'd" her to. (So much for the free will defense.)

This is reassuring; "out of my sight, thou Serpent" gave the vivid impression—happily put right here—that the furthest thing from his mind, before she spoke up, was magnanimity. Unfortunately, the Advocate has given us more to go on than an impression.

It's quite true that Adam has just now considered and rejected (as beyond his powers) the possibility of taking the punishment, as well as the blame, "on mee mee only" (*PL* 10.832). But his reason for taking the blame (echoed at *PL* 956–57) was a concern for justice, not for Eve. He genuinely believed that he alone was an autonomous agent, and hence "the source and spring / Of all corruption," on whom "all the blame lights due" (*PL* 10.832–33). He alone, that is, acted freely. Eve may be "that bad Woman" (*PL* 10.837), but she's a crooked rib by nature (*PL* 10.884–85) and not by choice. It's precisely her innate badness that exonerates her. The echo of Eve's "mee mee onlie" (*PL* 10.936) only serves to point up the difference between sacrificial love and moral contempt.

For Adam, it seems, the Fall gets two turns on the stage, the first as tragedy and the second as farce. The farce is a story of wilful misreading. In the dim light of a small mind, Eve's fumbling attempt at sacrifice becomes a plot to show Adam up, and the maudlin betrayal of God's trust that was Adam's part in the Fall gives way to his earlier decision to rely (as does God himself) on Eve's qualifications as a moral adult.

It's a measure of the smallness of the mind at work here that Eve's plea has partly succeeded—and partly (and ludicrously) failed: "As one disarm'd, his anger all he lost"; what we've been listening to is Adam's idea of "peaceful words" (*PL* 10.945–46), the last peaceful word being the suggestion that the two of them stop bickering—"no more contend, nor blame / Each other, blam'd enough elsewhere" (*PL* 10.958–59). Adam's generous response, as Eve lies there abjectly embracing his feet, is to act as if what's been going on were their quarrel and not his harangue. In short, for reasons we've already glanced at and will soon return to, Eve's début as a redeemer has been made to coincide with Adam's début as a prig.

Even a prig can get something right, of course: Eve's attempt to make amends *is* a sad affair; she's really no more than a would-be redeemer. Her next half-baked idea is an embarrassing case in point—crucial for our purposes because it focusses sharply on motherhood:

> miserable it is
> To be to others cause of misery,
> Our own begotten, and of our Loins to bring

> Into this cursed World a woful Race,
> That after wretched Life must be at last
> Food for so foul a Monster.
>
> (*PL* 10.981–86)

In Eve's horrific imagination, Death is the ultimate Moloch or Minotaur. The only way to save her children from the fate of sacrificial animals is not to bear them. No wonder "care of our descent" (*PL* 10.979) leaves her "perplexed": the objects of her mother love are nonexistent—and for their own good had better stay that way. For the salvation of these notional children, "Let us seek Death, or he not found, supply / With our own hands his office on ourselves" (*PL* 10.1001–2). Eve ends by converting despair into a homeopathic remedy: the least evil option is to destroy "destruction with destruction" (*PL* 10.1006).

Given the plea of weakness that accompanies Adam's fall, there's a mischievous irony in his staunchness at this point. Adam fell, not by rushing to his partner's assistance, but by electing to join her in self-destruction: "with thee / Certain my resolution is to die" (*PL* 9.906–7). This time—a bit belatedly—the counsel of despair leaves him "nothing sway'd"; his mind is "more attentive" than Eve's to hope (*PL* 10.1011). Unhappily it also seems to be a lot more attentive to hope than to Eve, for whose sake he's hard put to muster so much as a charitable interpretation.

Some tactical buttering-up leads to a frontal attack:

> *Eve*, thy contempt of life and pleasure seems
> To argue in thee something more sublime
> And excellent then what thy mind contemns;
> But self-destruction therefore sought refutes
> That excellence thought in thee, and implies,
> Not thy contempt, but anguish and regret
> For loss of life and pleasure overlov'd.
>
> (*PL* 10.1013–19)

He thought at first he was listening to a "sublime" contempt for life and pleasure. (He thought nothing of the sort; what would make him think this? And why are life and pleasure suddenly contemptible? Who made Eden?[69]) But the sublimity quickly disappears on closer inspection; people driven to "self-destruction" by the *loss* of something obviously love the something all too well. The voluntary barrenness scheme, in turn, has the unmistakable taste of

> Rancor and pride, impatience and despite,
> Reluctance against God and his just yoke
> Laid on our Necks.
>
> (*PL* 10.1043–47)

By plotting to avoid conception, Eve is committing the crime of "reluctance"; she's wrestling with her judge, whose justice includes the legitimacy of punishing sinners in their children.

Adam has already done the Advocate's work by settling this ticklish question in favor of God. He had asked himself, in his own fit of theological "reluctance":

> Ah, why should all mankind
> For one man's fault thus guiltless be condemn'd,
> If guiltless?
>
> (*PL* 10.822–24)

The weasel here was "if," as became clear in Adam's reply to his own question:

> from me what can proceed
> But all corrupt, both Mind and Will deprav'd,
> Not to do onely, but to will the same
> With me? how can they then acquitted stand
> In sight of God? Him after all Disputes
> Forc'd I absolve.
>
> (*PL* 10.824–29)

Adam now dismisses his question as a mere dodge: if the offspring really were guiltless, the question of why they should be condemned would answer itself. But of course they aren't guiltless (of eating the forbidden fruit): in fact, they not only *do* "the same / With me," they *will* it—where "same" defines a corporate act of will.

Adam has managed to persuade himself that getting corrupted by the Fall will somehow make accomplices of his offspring—not after but during the fact! "Same with me" is to be taken literally. We seem to be getting a reprise of God's Neoplatonic argument in the Heavenly Consult: all the members of a natural kind are (by "participation" or *methexis*) "in" the first, Adam is the "head" or "root" of his kind, so "in" him they live—and "perish"; Christ redeems human nature by replacing Adam as its embodiment (*PL*

3.286–87). The Hellenic ontology gets a boost from a Hebrew thought form: Jacob "is" Israel, Benjamin the patriarch "is" Benjamin the tribe, the king "is" his realm (for the Advocate this pill should be especially hard to get down). By the same token, Adam "is" Man—and (for guilt-assessment purposes) vice versa.

This old apologetic maneuver is the best Adam can do. All too clearly, it's also the best the Advocate can do; otherwise he wouldn't content himself with delegating a crucial part of his task to a weaker colleague. To the Advocate's credit, the old maneuver makes him uncomfortable, as it well might; it makes nonsense of the free will defense. On Adam's showing, the Judge of the World unjustly condemns people for things they couldn't help doing— things they "do" only in the sense that they share the nature of the actual doer. By the time the archangel Michael takes his turn, the *methexis* theory of doing has dropped away; the heirs of Adam's guilt

> never touch'd
> Th'excepted Tree, nor with the Snake conspir'd,
> Nor sinn'd thy sin.
>
> (*PL* 11.425–27)

Yet that sin has corrupted them—justly. Death is king, as St. Paul has it, "even over those that had not sinned after the similitude of Adam's transgression" (Rom. 5.13–14). This is the claim of divine justice that Eve is charged with rejecting.

Wrong thinking on this issue would simply add Eve to the list of people the Advocate has assumed the burden of putting right. But in fact she's innocent of wrong thinking—or any thinking—on the issue. Eve isn't aiming to defy God and his justice; only Death and his "glut" (*PL* 10.990). For all she says or implies to the contrary, Adam is right: children conceived by her and him are ipso facto guilty of a capital crime. The beings that inspire her "perplexity" and "care" (*PL* 10.979) are purely hypothetical—not children *conceived*, but children out of harm's way precisely because they're *unconceived*. Or does the stain of Adam's and Eve's parenthood reach beyond actual offspring to mere possibilities? Does God go after possible children, like a bounty hunter after convicts, to corral them into actuality? Again there's no sign in her speech that Eve (unlike Adam) is capable of having so refined an idea of divine justice, much less of rejecting it once she's had it. She reserves her refined ideas of the non-actual for the objects of her unconditional love, which is ample enough to encompass the children she can't allow herself to have. In short, "reluctance" against justice is well beyond her.

Adam, to repeat, is apparently too hard-pressed to waste time on the rule of charity; once again he moves to an ingeniously uncharitable reading of Eve's proposal. But the Advocate invites us to make allowances for him. After all, Adam's mind is "more attentive" than Eve's; by dint of "laboring" with that mind, he manages to catch sight of grounds for hope where his partner sees thin air (*PL* 10.1011–12). By itself, of course, the cognitive edge earns him no more credit than an edge in height and weight. He did nothing to deserve the gear he's born with. But the moral initiative of "laboring" with it is different. If the core of the episode is a dialogue between the affirmation and denial of hope—theological virtue and mortal sin—then maybe the balance of sympathy ends by shifting in Adam's favor. Maybe, but I think not. Adam's performance is too muddled for hope vindicated to be the central action—too muddled by half.

As it happens, the "hope" Adam speaks up for at first isn't the theological virtue anyhow: the reason Eve's proposal is hopeless in his view is, not (morally) that trying to dodge one's punishment is thumbing one's nose at the judge, but (prudentially) that this judge's sentences can't be dodged. The nose-thumbing ("contumacie") will just "provoke" him to "double" the punishment.

Evasion by *suicide* is especially self-defeating. The hoped-for result—"death in us"—isn't the refuge it seems to be; omnipotence includes the power to "make death in us live." It behooves us, at the very least, to look for a "safer resolution" than living death (*PL* 10.1020–29, 1040). The suicide plan also defeats itself on the positive side, by foreclosing on the promised "amends" of "crushing" our enemy's "head" (*PL* 10.1029–36). In short, the first hopes to vie for Adam's "attention," in all their banality, are revenge and "safety." We'll be taking a close look at the Hellish Consult in the next chapter; for now it's worth remarking that revenge and "safety" are what hope looks like to the damned. Adam's versions of these benefits, unlike Moloch's and Belial's, are not evil. But they are no reply to despair. In particular, what Adamic "safety" saves is, largely, one's skin.

Fortunately, Adam gets better as he goes along. The magnanimous interpretation he denies Eve, he reserves for his Judge, whose choice of punishments Adam reads as pure philanthropy—a study in correction rather than revenge. God's judicial "temper" (*PL* 10.1047)[70] comes out especially in the curse of labor he imposed, respectively, on women and men. The one kind of labor stops with childbirth and is "recompens'd with joy." The other (breadwinning) is a "curse aslope" that "glanc'd on the ground"; "idleness had been worse" (*PL* 10.1050–55). The curse on the ground—his contribution to it anyhow—also disappears at closer quarters: we never asked him to clothe us, as he just did, with his own hands; he won't refuse to teach us the arts of survival in a world whose "inclement Seasons" are all our own fault (*PL* 10.1056–81).

The problem the Advocate has set himself is to show Adam and Eve beginning to undo their divorce from God by undoing their divorce from each other—and from themselves. The riddle of these nested undoings is how the third and fundamental one—pulling oneself together once having gone to pieces—is remotely possible:

> For Understanding rul'd not, and the Will
> Heard not her lore, both in subjection now
> To sensual Appetite, who from beneath
> Usurping over sovran Reason claim'd
> Superior sway.
>
> (PL 9.1127–31)

The personification verges on mockery. The relevant self is nowhere in sight. The "persons" on view are the pathetic results of its disintegration: a bundle of impulses competing for "sway." A bundle—for the Advocate anyhow—no more constitutes a person than atoms in chaos a universe. To be halfway plausible, in short, the first stage in the process of undoing divorce needs to reenact the undoing of chaos—with one exception: the emerging cosmos was no moral agent.

The emerging Adam and Eve need to be shown *working*—"laboring"— with the "prevenient grace" that is recreating them, even before it has completely

> remov'd
> The stonie from thir hearts, and made new flesh
> Regenerat grow instead.
>
> (PL 11.3–5)

Above all, the heart's response to grace will need to be conspicuously short on grace. The inchoate heart is a clumsy thing. In the reconciliation sequence, the Advocate gives us (twice over) the likeness of such a heart. The best things we do, in Hooker's wry phrase, "have somewhat in them to be pardoned." Adam's rejection of Eve's despair, in particular, is the best thing he's done in a while; to do justice to his achievement, we need to grant the "somewhat to be pardoned" in it: the magnanimous interpretation Adam reserves for his Judge, he denies his wife.

Here the Advocate shows an unexpected flair for comic portraiture. Like all chronically poor listeners, Adam suffers from the auditory equivalent of a blind spot, or spots. The "somewhat to be pardoned" in Eve's speech—her despair—comes through with merciless clarity. Not so her clumsy attempt to sacrifice herself for her husband and spare her children; the best thing Eve has done in a while gets brutally garbled in transmission: sacrifice becomes self-promotion or self-indulgence, and compassion disappears altogether—readings natural enough, perhaps, to a listener whose objection to Eve's barrenness proposal is that it "cuts *us* [viz., Adam and Eve] off from hope" (*PL* 10.1043); and who thinks he's addressing the heart of her anguish by listing the prospects for the two of *them*.

One partner seems to specialize in compassion, the other in hope. Could the Advocate be suggesting a division of moral labor? Is compassion a woman's virtue rather than a man's? Consider Adam's first shattering insight into what he's letting his posterity in for:

> [Adam] wept,
> *Though not of woman born*; compassion *quell'd*
> *His best of Man*, and gave him up to tears
> A space, till firmer thoughts restrain'd *excess*.
>
> (*PL* 11.495–98)

Macduff grieves for his doomed children though he, too, is "not of woman born"—and apparently comes off with his manhood intact. It seems that the "excess" that momentarily "quells" Adam's best of man isn't too *much* compassion, but any at all.

This can't be right, of course. The Advocate knows better. His project, after all, has a second part: not only to trace "all our woe" to the disobedience of the first "Man," but to trace our eventual restoration to the *compassion* of a second, and "*greater* Man" (*PL* 1.1–5):

Beyond compare the Son of God was seen
Most glorious, in him all his Father shon
Substantially express'd, and in his face
Divine compassion visibly appear'd,
Love without end, and without measure Grace.

(PL 3.138–42)

In one pointed respect the God who is hidden has done his best to
come out of hiding, by seeing to it that his compassion is "substantially" expressed. Macduff, who scorns to "play the woman with
my eyes," was not born of woman. The "greater Man" of the Advocate's proem enjoys no such immunity. But then, his tears don't
seem to drive away "firmer thoughts." The unreservedly best of
Man, as we might expect, belongs to the Best of men. Apparently
Adam's intellectual collapse at the sight of history's "Lazar-house"
goes to show only that his "best of Man" isn't—yet—good enough.

As a scene of divorce undone, the dialogue of reconciliation is
less about hope and repentance than it is about love struggling to
repair itself. In this connection what Adam has to teach is less striking than what he has—barely—begun to be taught. To repeat, God
the Father in *PL*, in his essential roles as Creator and Redeemer, is
a mother figure, a figure of unconditional love. And so too, for all
the clumsiness of her performance, is the Eve who emerges partly
from the imagination of the Advocate and partly from the logic of
his Great Argument.[71]

Before the next step, a backward look.

On charges of criminal negligence, God the Creator joins God
the Judge in the dock. The core of the case for the Creator is Johannine: God is love (I John 4:16), a love expressed in creation by an
act of sharing that includes the creative power itself—in particular,
the power to give birth. Eve gets to exercise this very power in the
dialogue we've just been reading. She's finally being enabled—by
"prevenient Grace" (*PL* 11.3)—to live down her own fall, and her
role in Adam's, by living up to Raphael's prophetic "Hail," "the
holy salutation us'd / Long after to blest Marie, second *Eve*" (*PL*
5.385-87). In the jargon of *PL*'s official theory of history, the gift
of life to the first Adam "prefigures" the gift of life to the second.

Giving birth, in short, is one of the Advocate's two leading meta-

phors for the Creator's self-sharing. The other is giving food—as
Eve does perversely in abetting the Fall. The food metaphor, too,
deserves a closer look.

Soon after Raphael greets Eve, Adam apologizes for an earthly
meal that, for all he knows, may be "unsavourie" to "spiritual Natures"—though perhaps not, since "I know / That one celestial
Father gives to all" (*PL* 5.401–2). Adam's second thought turns out
to be on the right track, as Raphael confirms in his festive picture
of the nature of things:

> food alike those pure
> Intelligential substances require
> As doth your Rational; and both contain
> Within them every lower facultie
> Of sense, whereby they hear, see, smell, touch, taste,
> Tasting concoct, digest, assimilate,
> And corporeal to incorporeal turn.
> For know, whatever was created needs
> To be sustain'd and fed; of Elements
> The grosser feeds the purer, Earth the Sea,
> Earth and the Sea feed air, the Air those Fires
> Ethereal, and as lowest first the Moon;
> Whence in her visage round those spots, unpurg'd
> Vapours not yet into her substance turn'd.
> Nor doth the Moon no nourishment exhale
> From her moist Continent to higher Orbs.
> The Sun that light imparts to all receives
> From all his alimental recompense
> In humid exhalations, and at Ev'n
> Sups with the Ocean.
>
> (*PL* 5.407–26)

The world, it turns out, is a feasting as well as a coming to be born.
"Corporeal to incorporeal" (*PL* 5.413) is *pointed* here: the cosmic
feast easily betters the dreams of the "Empiric Alchimist"; it not
only "digests" dross into gold but, higher up the ladder of sublima-
tions, body into spirit. Spirit, too, partakes

> with keen dispatch
> Of real hunger, and concoctive heat
> To transubstantiate.
>
> (*PL* 5.436–38)

This last loaded word adds a refinement. The cosmic feast is not only a sublimation but a sacrament—and not just any sacrament, but the one especially favored by the Real Presence: the Feast of Love, writ large. It is the sacrament in which a being both human and divine somehow shares his body and blood.

"The images of food, nourishment, and concoction [i.e., digestion] are basic to Milton's [vision of] nature." "God is the 'Nourisher.' "[72] But why bring "concoction," etc., into this particular (forensic) narrative? For two reasons at least: (a) In *PL* 5 and 7 as elsewhere, the Advocate is plying his trade; establishing God's supreme nurturance, like establishing God's surrender of control over a part of creation (his creatures' choices), is equivalent to clearing him of a specific charge brought against him—the charge that love, like justice, is alien to him. (b) The humanistic moral of the "concoction" story (as we shall see) is that the thinking of a body in thought—the last refinement of matter—is not reducible to an interaction of its parts. If the Advocate's humanistic materialism fails, his theism can't succeed. The death of the concept of Man brings with it the death of the concept of God.

Ironically, the Advocate is exploring an epic theme—the feasting universe—on which Lucretius virtually holds a patent:

> The beings you see rejoicing in growth, climbing little by little the steps of their adulthood, take in more particles than they shed—so long as their veins give easy access to the food, and so long as they themselves aren't so spread out that many particles are released, and life is more squandered than stored.[73]

> Food is what is needed for the renewal and repair of all things, food for their support, food for the sustaining of all things.[74]

> [W]hether air flowing into the world from elsewhere steers the fires of heaven and drives them on, or else the flames themselves are capable of snaking along in the direction in which the food of each beckons and invites them as they go, feeding their flaming bodies in the pasture of the sky.[75]

The Lucretian touches in *PL* 5 are polemical, as they were in the Chaos episode. There, what doomed the Lucretian project wasn't atomism. It was false economy. For lack of making room in his theory for the craftily loving *designer* of atoms, the atheist gets to explain everything but the heart of the matter: atoms and their

"covenant." Deep facts are captured vividly, but without understanding, because the deepest have been blotted out of the text.

In *PL* 5 the polemic against atheist materialism takes a different
turn. Instead of disagreeing on whether a theory of everything can
get away with taking the laws of atoms for granted, the new issue
between the two materialisms is whether the atom "covenant" accounts for minds:

> O *Adam*, one Almightie is, from whom
> All things proceed, and up to him return,
> If not deprav'd from good, created all
> Such to perfection, one first matter all,
> Indu'd with various forms, various degrees
> Of substance, and in things that live, of life;
> But more refin'd, more spiritous, and pure,
> As neerer to him plac'd or neerer tending
> Each in thir several active Sphears assign'd,
> Till body up to spirit work, in bounds
> Proportion'd to each kind. So from the root
> Springs lighter the green stalk, from thence the leaves
> More aerie, last the bright consummate flowr
> Spirits odorous breathes: flowrs and thir fruit
> Mans nourishment, by gradual scale sublim'd
> To vital spirits aspire, to animal,
> To intellectual, give both life and sense,
> Fansie and understanding, whence the Soul
> Reason receives, and reason is her being,
> Discursive, or Intuitive; discourse
> Is oftest yours, the latter most is ours,
> Differing but in degree, in kind the same.
>
> (*PL* 5.469–90)

It seems that what brings "body up to spirit" (*PL* 5.478) is alchemi-
cal purification. The world is a crucible. Once body is "refin'd" (*PL*
5.475), it gets "indu'd" (*PL* 5.473) with life or sense. Life and
sense are "forms" (*PL* 5.473) of the whole "substance" (*PL* 5.473–
74). For fruit to "give" an angel "life and sense, / Fansie and understanding" (*PL* 5.482, 485–86) is for the matter of the fruit to be
"sublim'd" (*PL* 5.483) up to spirit—"converted" to the "proper
substance" (*PL* 5.492–93): given a similar "conversion," "from
these corporal nutriments perhaps / Your bodies may at last turn all
to spirit" (*PL* 5.496–97). If so, the human body will come to be
"all" spirit in the same holistic sense as it became (rather than

merely acquired) "a living soul" (*PL* 7.528). Sense, fancy, and understanding will be states of the whole rather than interactions among the parts.

Lucretius's holism about awareness is radically different. In the Advocate's perspective, the difference is all the more treacherous for occurring in the context of substantial agreement:

> Pain happens when a violent disturbance in the limbs or vital organs shakes up the atoms in their internal positions, and pleasure happens when the atoms resume those positions; so it's obvious that the atoms are incapable of being afflicted with pain or taking pleasure from their condition: atoms have no constituent atoms to give them pain or pleasure by a change in motion. In short, atoms are necessarily insentient.[76]

> Now this you have to admit: whatever proves to be sentient is made of insentient atoms. The commonplaces of daily experience cast no doubt on this, much less refute it. They lead us by the hand instead, compel us, to believe (as I say) that things *with* awareness arise from things *without*. Thus, when the earth rots after unseasonable rains, it's easy to see the worms quickening out of the grimness of dung. Everything else transforms itself in the same way—rivers into leaves, lush fodder into cattle, cattle into our bodies, and often, our bodies into the sinews of beasts and the wings of birds. The inference is inescapable: Nature transforms food of every sort into living bodies, and next into all the animal senses. By much the same principle, she unfolds dry wood into flame and reduces it to fire. Don't you begin to see the crucial dependence of the motions that elementary particles give and receive on the way those particles are arranged and combined?[77]

> It will be appropriate to bear this in mind: I'm emphatically not claiming that the senses arise automatically out of the ingredients of things that sense; the size and shape of the ingredients are critical—and above all their motion, order, position.[78]

For the Advocate, sense, fancy, and understanding are states of an individual. For Lucretius, they're movements in parts of the system of atoms—loosely divided into the subsystems of mind and soul—that extends (like a nervous system) throughout the body.[79] Thus a headache is a movement in the sector of the soul located in the head—and so on for other sensations.[80] Lucretius often speaks loosely of the movements of soul and mind atoms as "sense-conveying" (to whom?)[81], and of sense as being "kindled" (in whom?) by the movements of mind and body. But the hint of a receiver of something "conveyed" or "kindled" is a sop to folk psychology. Despite appearances, a phrase like "I sense" is for reporting an atom movement—"this movement for which our ordinary name is sense"[82]—not its effect on a mystifying Someone.

One's mind *is* a body (or at least an atom collection). Atheist materialism has the advantage of taking the mystery out of talk about minds and bodies moving each other; the talk is about garden-variety interaction between kinds of bodies,[83] not incommensurates touching magically across a category barrier. (Whole bodies turn no gears here—the parts or particles do all the real work.) Atheist materialism has the disadvantage—for the Advocate's humanist purposes—of turning personhood into a figment of grammar. On the atheist view, the singular subject-predicate structure of "I sense" had better not be taken literally; otherwise it's a gross misrepresentation (compare "the parade is passing" or "the trial is in recess" or "the war is still on"). Stare too hard at the woodwork and you end up seeing the little man who wasn't there. On Lucretius's showing at least, the interlocking notions of PERSON, FEELING, PERCEIVING, BELIEVING, THINKING, DESIRING, CHOOSING, etc., are so many language mirages.

Of course, this makes a mirage out of Lucretius's own project of getting the person he's addressing (his friend Memmius) to agree with the views of the person he venerates (the sage Epicurus).

From the Advocate's point of view, the figment is on the other foot; the attempt to think away the idea of PERSON is the second grand folly of atheism—the fool has said in his heart he doesn't exist. The alternative is a competing (Biblical) materialism. The bodies of men and women are living souls. Such bodies are as capable of "intellectual being" as the forms of angels. If all goes well— "if ye be found obedient"—such bodies begin as souls and in the end "turn all to Spirit."

Above all, Biblical materialism celebrates bodies ennobled by the power to choose. This, again, is a far cry from the story of choice told by atheist materialism, in which the event called volition starts with physical objects called sense images—films or membranes of atoms streaming from the surfaces of things seen;[84] on impact the images impress themselves on the atom system called mind. Take, for example, the mind event called "making up one's mind to take a walk":

I'm saying that, first, images of walking impinge on the mind and push it, as I've already described; the result is the willing. Nobody starts to do anything until the mind has had an advance look at what it wills to do. The advance look is the thing's image. Once the mind stirs itself up to the point of willing to walk, it abruptly strikes the soul [atoms] sewn broadcast throughout the limbs and joints.[85]

Note that the mind "stirs itself up" here only in the Pickwickian sense that it gets stirred up. It doesn't matter if the triggering event is random and causeless; willing is still something done *to* a collection of passive objects, not something done *by* an individual. As usual, the required notion of individuality dwindles, in the cold light of a Lucretian analysis, into a heap of empty words. The reply to all this, once again, is Raphael's divine alchemy.

The alchemy operates on a world of atoms. The coarser kinds or arrangements are sediment; what remains is automatically "more refin'd, more spiritous and pure" (*PL* 5.475). The atoms themselves come prefabricated, in structural "Clanns"—"light-arm'd or heavy, sharp, smooth, swift, or slow" (*PL* 2.902). Before creation, the "Clanns" form abortive "Factions" (*PL* 2.901) of "hot, cold, moist, and dry" (*PL* 2.898). Afterwards they combine in natural kinds at ever higher "degrees of substance" (*PL* 5.469–74). At the highest "degree" (spirit), matter purified to the point of consciousness gets released from the rigidities of body; organs turn out to be hindrances rather than instruments:[86]

> Spirits that live throughout
> Vital in every part, not as frail man
> In Entrails, Heart or Head, Liver or Reins,
> Cannot but by annihilating die;
> Nor in thir liquid texture mortal wound
> Receive, no more than can the fluid Air:
> All Heart they live, all Head, all Eye, all Ear,
> All Intellect, all Sense, and as they please,
> They Limb themselves, and colour, shape, and size
> Assume, as likes them best, condense or rare.
>
> (*PL* 6.344–53)

The God of the Proem to *PL* 1 has the powers of both sexes. He apparently owes this potency to the material "substance" in which divine alchemy begin and ends. Far from being purged of sexuality, disembodiment unleashes the sexual energy of matter, along with its powers of formal improvisation:

> Whatever pure thou in the body enjoyst
> (And pure thou wert created) we enjoy
> In eminence, and obstacle find none
> Of membrane, joynt, or limb, exclusive barrs:
> Easier than Air with Air, if Spirits embrace,
> Total they mix, Union of Pure with Pure
> Desiring.
>
> (*PL* 8.622–28)

>   Spirits when they please
> Can either Sex assume or both; so soft
> And uncompounded is thir Essence pure,
> Not ti'd or manacl'd with joynt or limb,
> Nor founded on the brittle strength of bones,
> Like cumbrous flesh; but in what shape they choose
> Dilated or condens'd, bright or obscure,
> Can execute thir aerie purposes,
> And works of love or enmity fulfill.
>
> (*PL* 1.423–430)

The organic hand is no more than a "manacle" to the spiritual hand—the irony being that the stuff the fallen angels are made of, even after they've surrendered their freedom, is the raw material of freedom ("as they *please* they limb themselves"; "in *what shape they choose* / Dilated or condens'd, bright or obscure"). The tragic ambiguity comes out in the uncanniness of the "condensation" we're shown just before the Hellish Consult:

> Behold a wonder! they but now who seemd
> In bigness to surpass Earths Giant Sons
> Now less than smallest Dwarfs, in narrow room
> Throng numberless, like that Pigmean Race
> Beyond the *Indian* Mount, or Faerie Elves,
> Whose midnight Revels, by a Forrest side
> Or Fountain some belated Peasant sees,
> Or dreams he sees, while overhead the Moon
> Sits Arbitress, and neerer to the Earth
> Wheels her pale course, they on thir mirth and dance

Intent, with jocund Music charm his ear;
At once with joy and fear his heart rebounds.

                                              (*PL* 1.777–88)

The "wonder" we're being invited to "behold" is just another
phase of what the Advocate has taken on as part of his second
brief—the glory of matter. As a corrective to the materialism of the
atheists we're getting the materialism of the Hermetics and late Pla-
tonics:

> We look up at clouds that give the appearance of men, of bears, of drag-
> ons and other things. So it is with the bodies of demonic beings, but
> with this difference, that the clouds that present a variety of shapes are
> driven from without, by the winds, whereas the demonic beings that
> vary bodily shape, now contracting themselves, now extending them-
> selves, do so by their own counsel and will.[87]

> The demonic body hasn't the solidity that would enable it to maintain a
> shape. Color infused into air and water, or shape impressed on them, is
> soon dissipated. Likewise with demonic beings; in them too, the shape,
> color, and look of anything, no matter what, quickly fall apart. This is
> why Marcus taught that the distinction between male and female in de-
> monic beings is not intrinsic but merely apparent, and that in them no
> such [sexual] form is stable and persistent.[88]

The Advocate pushes beyond these commonplaces of spirit lore
in the service of his brief. In *PL*, too, demonic substance is infinitely plastic, and demonic sexuality is infinitely volatile. But the
polymorphism of demons in *PL* isn't done with smoke and mirrors;
it's an awesome reality. Again, like the demonic fire or air of the
occult tradition, the "proper motion" of spirit is to rise (*PL* 1.75);
the rebel angels' escape into the deep took an effort of "compulsion
and laborious flight" (*PL* 1.80). But in *PL* demonic beings have
"proper shapes" as well as proper motions; Raphael comes back to
his in time to present his credentials to Adam and Eve (*PL* 5.276).
And at least at first, degrading one's proper shape, like descending
into Hell, takes a sustained effort; Satan's malicious compression
into a toad ends with an explosion:

                              As when a spark
          Lights on a heap of nitrous powder, laid
          Fit for the Tun some Magazine to store
          Against a rumor'd Warr, the Smuttie grain

> With sudden blaze diffus'd, inflames the Air:
> So started up in his own shape the Fiend.
>
> (*PL* 4.815–20)

In Raphael's account of divine alchemy, prime matter climbs endlessly up and down a Jacob's ladder of "degrees" of "substance" (*PL* 5.470, 473–90). The intervals in the traditional version of this "gradual scale" (*PL* 5.483) are vanishingly small, with "degrees" of rationality emerging well before the level of the human:

Porphyry says that he is presenting the real opinion of Pythagoras: every soul endowed with senses and memory is rational. Every such soul has not only reason but speech, both the inward kind and the outward kind by which animals communicate.[89]

Porphyry's other grounds for attributing rationality to animals, beyond their mutual signalling, are (i) the thoroughness and care of the plans they make to provide for future contingencies; (ii) the many things they learn from each other and from human beings, (iii) the fact that they teach each other. He adds that Aristotle, Empedocles, Democritus, and whoever else has made a close study of the facts about animals has discovered their share in reason and speech. But there's an observable variation in this sharing, as Aristotle also points out, like the supposed difference between gods and men—a difference in degree, not kind.[90]

Let's grant that animals are merely reasonable to a degree. But let's not deprive them of the faculty altogether. Let's not go from the premise that we're more intelligent than they are to the conclusion that they're devoid of intelligence. You might as well argue that, since partriches don't fly as fast as hawks, partriches don't fly![91]

In *PL*'s theist materialism too, the animal body is also a mind, and behaves accordingly. A circus of such thinking bodies "gambol'd" before Adam and Eve—"Bears, Tygers, Ounces, Pards," and an elephant who "us'd all his might" to "make them mirth" (*PL* 4.344–45). In the same vein, Eve's animal helpers (not yet corrupted into wildness) are "more duteous at her call, / Then at *Circean* call the herd disguis'd" (*PL* 9.521–22).

Eve doesn't need to be a Circe to elicit this attention to "duty." Even without a human nature "disguis'd" by black arts, matter at the right stage of "refinement" has risen to the level of intelligence. That's why the serpent can count on Eve's being less than shocked by his unexpected talents; she "demurs" on the issue of "human

sense" in animals, but it hasn't escaped her that "in thir looks /
Much reason, and in thir actions oft appeers" (*PL* 9.553–59).[92]

Long before he takes up his current brief, we can catch the Advocate playing with the idea that moral acts, including speech acts
("converse"), transfigure the body.[93] Now, at the end of Raphael's
description of the cycle of transformations, the idea reappears in the
form of a tantalizing hint: what if body that manages to stay unfallen naturally turns to spirit? The underlying materialism is not
only Jewish, Hellenic, and Alexandrian; more to the point, it's also
Pauline: "[The dead body] is sown a natural body, it is raised a
spiritual body. There is a natural body, and there is a spiritual body.
And so it is written, The first man Adam was made a living soul:
the last Adam was made a quickening spirit" (1 Cor. 14:44–45).
Resurrection takes up where divine alchemy left off after the great
interruption. In Paul's preferred agricultural metaphor, the dead
body is a buried seed (Lucretius's atoms are "the seeds of
things"[94]). Caring for the chosen is God's "husbandry" (1 Cor.
3:9).

But this is the Advocate's preferred metaphor too; the refinement
of body into spirit is of a piece with the gradual emergence of a
flower:

> So from the root
> Springs lighter the green stalk, from thence the leaves
> More aerie, last the bright consummate flowr
> Spirits odorous breathes.
>
> (*PL* 5.479–82)

The Advocate's client is the being "from whom / All things proceed, and up to him return" (*PL* 5.469–70); "all things" here include "one first matter" (*PL* 5.472). Matter, in all its pregnant
confusion, begins in Chaos as the stuff of God[95] and eventually (by
refinement or sublimation) as the stuff of heaven, of the world system, even of Hell and its inmates, whose intuitions tell them rightly
that their "substance" may be "indeed Divine, / And cannot cease
to be" (*PL* 2.98–99).

In atheist materialism, the notion of divine matter makes no
sense; divinity is a nonstarter as an atom property. In its other ancient version, materialism itself makes no sense *unless* matter is divine:

> God brought forth matter, having drawn the materiality out of his own
> essential nature. In the work of creation he took the matter, in its vital-

ity, to make the heavenly spheres, with their simplicity and freedom from passion. He used the last of the matter to make bodies—things that can be put together and taken apart.[96]

The material cause is something good, yet base and formless; something that participates in the One but not in the Beautiful.[97]

Matter and spirit—in other words, the cosmos and a certain divine force that spreads and flows through all things—didn't, while yet to be born, exist in a cosmic structure. But (says Asclepius) matter and spirit already existed in that from which they were born. What else did they exist in but the Divine Word by which all things were made, and in which everything that was made was Life, and from which issued forth at last, once made, whatever was made?[98]

There's a potentially embarrassing loose end here. Raphael's optimistic story of matter looks incoherent if matter begins and ends its career in God. Prime matter in the Chaos episode is "the womb of nature and perhaps her grave"; does the return of all things mean reabsorption? Do things return to God by getting "swallow'd up and lost / In the wide womb of uncreated night, / Devoid of sense and motion"(*PL* 2.149–51)? Is the destination of all things an "abortive gulf" (*PL* 2.441)? The return of matter to God isn't a return to its pristine condition. It's the last in a sequence of rebirths. (Satan is half right: "So ye shall die perhaps, by putting off human / To put on Gods" [*PL* 9.713-14].) Nothing comes home after a long journey the same thing it was on setting out.

There's another loose end that isn't so easily disposed of. Again it's an old speculation of the Advocate's: the world is due for a purge, when

> evil on itself shall back recoyl,
> And mix no more with goodness, when at last
> Gather'd like scum, and setl'd to it self
> It shall be in eternal restless change
> Self-fed and self-consum'd; if this fail,
> The pillar'd firmament is rottenness,
> And earths base built on stubble.[99]

The speaker is staking everything on the success of his de-scumming hypothesis; failure means the success of the criminal negligence charge. Just as the Judge of the World is innocent of the Fall of Man, the Creator of the World is innocent of sitting back and letting his temple become the Augean stable:

> See with what heat these Dogs of Hell advance
> To waste and havoc yonder World, which I
> So fair and good created, and had still
> Kept in that state, had not the folly of Man
> Let in these wasteful Furies, who impute
> Folly to mee, so doth the Prince of Hell
> And his Adherents, that with so much ease
> I suffer them to enter and possess
> A place so heav'nly, and conniving seem
> To gratifie my scornful enemies,
> That laugh, as if transported with some fit
> Of Passion, I to them had quitted all,
> At random yeilded up to their misrule;
> And know not that I call'd and drew them thither
> My Hell-hounds, to lick up the draff and filth
> Which mans polluting Sin with taint hath shed
> On what was pure, till cramm'd and gorg'd, nigh burst
> With suck'd and glutted offal, at one sling
> Of thy victorious Arm, well-pleasing Son,
> Both Sin and Death, and yawning Grave at last
> Through Chaos hurl'd, obstruct the mouth of Hell
> For ever and seal up his ravenous Jaws.
>
> (*PL* 10.616–37)

One trouble with this story is that "offal," too, is matter. Matter is the substance of God. How can sanitation call for "slinging" the substance of God into

> A Universe of death, which God by curse
> Created evil, for evil only good,
> Where all life dies, death lives, and nature breeds,
> Perverse, all monstrous, all prodigious shapes,
> Abominable, unutterable, and worse
> Then Fables yet have feign'd, or fear conceiv'd,
> Gorgons and Hydras, and Chimeras dire
>
> (*PL* 2.622–28)?

Raphael celebrates the sublime economy of a creation in which all things come home to their single common source, including a spiritualized prime matter. Now it turns out that not everything comes home. Some matter is hopeless "draff" (dregs, feces), and the best God can do with it is expel it into a travesty world—one of which it's true (as of the one we're in) that in the beginning is the word, but this time the word is a curse (*PL* 2.622). How can God condemn his substance to this fate? How can his substance degenerate into "draff," "offal," "scum," and "stubble"? How can it be "good" only in the ironic sense that it's "good" for evil?

The short traditional answer, of course, is that the ironic term here is "evil" (or "draff" or "offal," etc.), not "good." What matter is good for, in hell as elsewhere, is embodying things. Matter isn't to blame for the mischief done by, or with, the things it embodies. In this derivative sense (instrument of mischief), matter is "abominable, unutterable, and worse." This doesn't keep it from being at the very same time an instrument of good as well as good in itself, even in hell:

> Nigh on the Plain, in many cells prepar'd,
> That underneath had veins of liquid fire
> Sluic'd from the Lake, a second multitude
> With wondrous Art founded the massie Ore
> Severing each kind, and scumm'd the Bullion dross:
> A third as soon had form'd within the ground
> A various mould, and from the boyling cells
> By strange conveyance fill'd each hollow nook,
> As in an Organ from one blast of wind
> To many a row of Pipes the sound-board breathes.
> Anon out of the earth a Fabrick huge
> Rose like an exhalation, with the sound
> Of Dulcet Symphonies and voices sweet,
> Built like a Temple, where *Pilasters* round
> Were set and Doric pillars overlaid
> With Golden Architrave; nor did there want
> Cornice or Frieze, with bossy Sculptures graven,
> The Roof was fretted gold.

(*PL* 1.700–717)

Before he fell, the architect's hand "was known / In Heaven by many a structure high" (*PL* 1.732–33). Now one of his "structures high" graces hell. The defect of this one isn't the building material, much less the design, least of all the site. The defect is the (political) use Pandemonium is about to be put to.

The lesson is insistently driven home by the Advocate's comparisons between the worlds. In the fallen world, gold is simply a "bane" (*PL* 1.692); in heaven it's a "bane" only to somebody capable of mistaking a magnificent floor for the beatific vision (*PL* 1.681-84). By the same token, "Sulfurous and Nitrous Foam" (*PL* 6.512) is the stuff of gunpowder in both worlds—but also the stuff of fruits and flowers, gems and gold (*PL* 6.475); the "Deep" of both worlds is "pregnant" with the same "infernal" stuff (*PL* 6.483). For matter to be used as *everlasting* "draff"—to embody the damned—is for it to be singled out as an instrument of everlasting justice. That's not a debasement; it's a promotion.

Does this get rid of the difficulty? Only if changing the subject is a way of getting rid of difficulties. The defendant at this point is God the Creator, not God the Judge, and the charge this time isn't injustice, it's criminal negligence: absence of wisdom, absence of love. Exhibit A on this count (or close to it) is the sealing up of the "scum" of the universe—"scum" that thinks and suffers—in an eternal landfill. To reconcile this scheme with love, the Advocate can't hope to prevail by falling back on brute assertions like the sign over hellgate in the *Inferno*: that the Maker acted out of a desire for justice; that the gate was made by power, wisdom, and love. Made by power in the service of justice? Perhaps; one can see the outline of a case—the Free Will Defense. But made by love? By a love of which the love of a mother for her child is only a shadow?

The Advocate has no quarrel with the notion of an angry God. He's no sentimentalist, and no heretic in the tradition of Origen. One can be angry even though one loves, indeed angry *because* one loves. But a hating God is a different matter—a God who, as Adam complains, turns away infinitely from his finite creature. The notion that an infinite God is infinitely loving is no heresy. The whole point of the Advocate's survey of creation is to clinch the case for it. It doesn't help the case that the survey begins with a place (or state of mind) condemned eternally to God's hate. Characteristically, the Advocate knows this, thinks going there puts him in serious danger, and goes anyway. In the next chapter, we follow him.

4

God's Hatred

The current chapter, as I promised, will survey *PL*'s brave—or foolhardy—exploration of God's hatred; brave or foolhardy because God's hatred is one of the two counts against him: lack of justice, lack of love. I will argue that he cannot be acquitted of both. When the claims of justice and love conflict (on the Advocate's showing at least) there is no common measure (say, "utility") to decide which claim has priority. Even the Judge of the Universe is condemned to the ordeal of choosing blindly. Even he is in for a goring on one horn of the dilemma or the other—whether to sacrifice love to justice, or justice to love. To salvage God's defense, the Advocate will need to look for a way of transcending (or mitigating) the inevitable defeat of an essential part of his case. I will argue that the way he finds serves his poem (if not his case) supremely well. But all this comes much later—after we study God's hatred and (to start with) the anger his hatred extends to infinity.

The Advocate has no quarrel with the notion of an angry God. He understands that epic is tragedy writ large.[1] He also understands that a central terror and quandary of tragic *action*—both the crime and the punishment—is that somehow it coincides with tragic *passion*, especially a tragic passion for justice; coincides, in short, with anger:

> No more of talk where God or Angel Guest
> With Man, as with his Friend, familiar us'd
> To sit indulgent, and with him partake
> Rural repast, permitting him the while
> Venial discourse unblam'd: I now must change
> Those Notes to Tragic; foul distrust, and breach
> Disloyal on the part of Man, revolt,
> And disobedience: on the part of Heav'n
> Now alienated, distance and distaste,

172

> Anger and just rebuke, and judgement giv'n,
> That brought into this world a World of woe,
> Sin and her shadow Death, and Miserie
> Deaths Harbinger: Sad task, yet argument
> Not less but more Heroick then the wrauth
> Of stern *Achilles* on his Foe pursu'd
> Thrice Fugitive about *Troy* Wall; or rage
> Of *Turnus* for *Lavinia* disespous'd,
> Or *Neptune's* ire or *Juno's,* that so long
> Perplex'd the *Greek* and *Cytherea's* son.
>
> (*PL* 9.1–19)

Unlike his battle-haunted predecessors in epic, the Advocate is

> Not sedulous by Nature to indite
> Warrs, hitherto the onely Argument
> Heroic deem'd.
>
> (*PL* 9.27–29)

The trouble with a martial ideal of courage is that it leaves

> the better fortitude
> Of Patience and Heroic Martyrdom
> Unsung.
>
> (*PL* 9.31–33)

But as an introduction to the current book of *Paradise Lost,* all this is curiously misleading; in *PL* 9 too, the "better fortitude" will be going "unsung."

The "Notes" due to be struck here are no more celebratory than Homer's or Virgil's.[2] Their "argument" is the Advocate's as well: the bad fruits of "wrauth," "rage," "ire," and the alienated two-ness he begins by harping on to the point of obsession: "*dis*trust," "*dis*loyal," "*dis*obedience," "*dis*tance," "*dis*taste," "*dis*espous'd." (The prefix *dis* is the archaic Latin dual.) War is simply the most unmistakable evidence of this tragic duality—a fact again inscribed on the original form of its Latin name: *bellum* < *du-ellum.* Another archaic Latin echo hovers in the background: "Dis" is the name of the god of the underworld, the violator of Proserpina, goddess of regeneration—Dis the enemy of second chances (*PL* 4.269–71).

The epic "argument" (narrative aim) of accounting for God's anger is, to say the least, "not less but more heroic" than accounting for Achilles' or Turnus's or Neptune's or Juno's. "Anger" this

time is no adolescent or demonic tantrum; a "just rebuke and judgment" (*PL* 9.10) has cost us our partnership in the only benign
"dis" in the Advocate's list: "*dis*-course" between us and God or
his messengers (*PL* 9.5).

Adam thinks of this partnership as raising him above his mere
humanity:

> Thou in thy secresie although alone,
> Best with thy self accompani'd, seekst not
> Social communication, yet so pleas'd
> Canst raise thy Creature to what highth thou wilt
> Of Union or Communion, deifi'd.
>
> (*PL* 8.426–31)

But Adam is clearly wrong. These words come up precisely in a
discourse with God, and the speaker has *not* been promoted to
deity; his non-deity, in fact, is the core of his argument at the moment. The mistake, apparently, is to think that God needs to rede-
sign his creatures to make himself understood to them. In the "talk"
broken off by the Fall, God's partner is simply "Man" (*PL* 9.2),
not deified ex-"Man." By thou-ing his creature and letting himself
be thou-ed in return, God makes Adam in his image (*PL* 7.527) a
second time; he puts the finishing touches on Adam's humanity.
The taste of God's anger is the taste of a radical loneliness.

God is incapable of loneliness though transcendently alone. He
needs no "social communication." On the other hand, he's obviously "pleased" to engage in it. The supreme recluse manages to be
the supreme communicator. On the Protestant reading of the Fourth
Gospel (Junius-Tremellius version), the "Word" that was with God
in the beginning (John 1:1) isn't *Verbum* but *Sermo*: that is, precisely, "talk." The image-grounding likeness to God, in short, is
partnership in *sermo*. Not accidentally, the first glimmer of self-
knowledge comes to both Adam and Eve by way of an interior
sermo, in the form of a thou-ing by God:

> One came, methought, of shape Divine,
> And said, thy Mansion wants thee, Adam, rise,
> First Man, of Men innumerable ordain'd
> First Father, call'd by thee I come thy Guide
> To the Garden of bliss, thy seat prepar'd.
>
> (*PL* 8.295–99)

What thou seest,
What there thou seest fair Creature is thy self,
With thee it comes and goes: but follow me,
And I will bring thee where no shadow staies
Thy coming.

(*PL* 4.467–71)

"In the Beginning was the Word and the Word was with God and the Word [*Lógos*] was God" (John 1:1). "He who loveth not, knoweth not God. For God is love [*Agápe*]" (1 John 4:8). On the Protestant analysis, this comes out as "He who converseth not, knoweth not God. For God is Discourse." The Johannine nicknames of God—*Lógos* and *Agápe*—pick out the same creative action, or transaction. Martin Buber's "I-thou" is a late expression of the same analysis—of discourse, of love, and (not incidentally) of what it is to be a person. Even for the Creator—especially for the Creator—the game of personhood is not solitaire; it is hardly accidental that he chooses to take up membership in a cooperative "we" at the moment of his début:

And thou my Word, begotten Son, by thee
This I perform, speak thou and be it don.

(*PL* 7.163–64)

The Omnipotent
Eternal Father (for where is not hee
Present) thus to his Son audibly spake:
Let us make now Man in our image.

(*PL* 7.516–19)

"Audibly" in the second passage isn't as redundant as it looks. We've already had occasion to think about Adam's conversational reflex as he spots the "glow" of "distemper" (another ominous "dis") in his partner's cheek (*PL* 9.887): "First *to himself* he *inward* silence broke" (*PL* 9.895). This has an air of perverse novelty—not because the speech getting introduced is a soliloquy; soliloquy has already been invented. And not because it's an interior monologue; if we give mental "inwardness" the benefit of the doubt, why shouldn't a language-using creature experience thinking as a kind of inner speaking?

No, what's perverse here is that remarks *addressed to Eve* are somehow being uttered by Adam in silence—uttered "to himself" alone. So far the only silence he breaks is inward. This is why "audible" has a job to do in the description of the Creator-in-conference: unlike God making Adam, Adam unmaking himself is suddenly powerless to be open—"audible"—to the only interlocutor in sight. The result is a speech act in the subjunctive mood: Adam goes through the "inward" motions of telling Eve things he *would* tell her *if* he could bear to. As things stand, he is back to being his own partner; if it is "not good for the Man to be alone" (Gen. 2:18), it is particularly "not good" here: what's left after discourse is broken off is discourse mocked.

We've already been shown even more terrible mockeries. Later on we'll take a closer look at Satan's theory that "The mind is its own place, and in it self / Can make a Heav'n of Hell, a Hell of Heav'n" (*PL* 1.254–55). Satan is dressing up a banality ("nothing's good or bad but thinking makes it so") as a paradoxical insight. What's relevant here is that the rhetoric is pure bluff. Not all paradoxes make up for being logically absurd by being true. Absent a cue in the context, even metaphorical containers don't contain themselves. Satan himself is clearly well aware that his mind isn't a place he's in, but something he can't help *bringing along* to the places he's in (*PL* 1.252–53). Soon enough he'll also be aware, if he isn't already, that the same goes for hell: "My self am Hell" (*PL* 4.75); "within him hell he brings" (*PL* 4.20–21). "the hot Hell that always in him burns" (*PL* 9.467).

Just now I gave the benefit of the doubt to the metaphor of "inwardness." It may be elusive, but it had better not be nonsensical; it isn't easy to see how commonsense talk about the mind can stay afloat without it. The idea is that experience is radically private property, accessible to its owner directly. Everybody else's access is through natural or conventional signs (frowning, wincing, blushing, pulse rate, temperature, gestures, avowals, etc.). Knowledge of one's own states of mind is almost as direct, as "inward," as anything gets—excelled only by the sacred "inwardness" of the "talk" destroyed by the Fall, the "inwardness" of the Pauline "temple":

> And chiefly Thou, O Spirit, that dost prefer
> Before all Temples th' upright heart and pure,
> Instruct me.
>
> (*PL* 1.17–19)

What's left behind by the alienated "Friend," "Guest," "Familiar" (*PL* 9.1–2) is an abandoned temple, a crooked heart—in short, Satan's portable hell. This is the meaning of God's anger.

Anger in God—unlike anger in Turnus and Juno—can't literally be a passion, much less a passion out of control. By the usual logic of the Advocate's religious tradition, "anger" here names a deliberate action. *PL* 9 improves on the tragic "argument" of the *Iliad* and the *Aeneid* by showing us a just anger: God wouldn't be God if he didn't "alienate" himself from his betrayer by withdrawing all the way from intimacy to "distance" (*PL* 9.9).

But that can't be the whole story. In fact, it can't be the story at all. Angry or not, the Client of our (forensic) storyteller is not only loving; he is love itself. The Advocate's quarrel, to repeat, is not with the notion of an angry God. It's with the notion of a God who cherishes his anger forever. It's with the notion of a God who hates. The trouble is that this is a quarrel the Advocate seems bound to lose. Hell looks for all the world like the handiwork of such a God.[3]

The Hardened Heart

A warning is in order before I begin. In discussing the predicament of the fallen angels, I will court the danger of sounding a bit like the Advocate, having at God's enemies with a fierce irony that may seem almost personal. This is impossible to avoid. My business here is precisely with irony and fierceness. They are not mine. Ultimately, they aren't even the Advocate's. They are the characteristic idioms of God's hatred.

Satan is sentenced by order of law ("doomed" in the old courtroom jargon) to an eternity of "rowling in the fiery Gulf" (*PL* 1.52). The "wrath" of the physical punishment is as terrible as it is just. But there's worse:

> his doom
> Reserv'd him to more wrath; for now the thought
> Both of lost happiness and lasting pain
> Torments him; round he throws his baleful eyes
> That witness'd huge affliction and dismay
> Mix'd with obdurate pride and steadfast hate.
>
> (*PL* 1.53–58)

It seems that the pain of loss is nothing to the pain of never being able to stop thinking about it. The sharper the thought, the sharper the pain. What "lost *happiness*" mercifully blurs, "obdurate" and "steadfast" spell out implacably: the "happiness" forfeited here is agency—the ability to do, rather than to go through the motions of doing, like figures on a belltower. Satan's pride and hatred started out as acts. Now they've dwindled into clockwork.

Aquinas regularly defines freewill as will "indifferently [i.e., neutrally] disposed to well or ill choosing"[4]—will that could have chosen otherwise than it actually chooses (the jargon term for this indeterminacy is *libertas indifferentiae*). So newcomers to Scholastic theology will find it surprising that Aquinas endorses Gregory the Great's claim that the malicious will of fallen angels is both "free" and *incapable* of choosing anything but malice.[5]

Here is Gregory's usefully neat summary of this line of thought (the italics are mine): "Abandoned by grace, the devil has stayed *fixed* in malice, *so that* he wills nothing good, and wills nothing out of goodwill. Freewill he has, but freewill *depressed* and ceaselessly inclined to evil, *so that* he always shuns good and never stops choosing evil. For this reason what *happened to him* was a fall from the extreme of good to the extreme of evil."[6] Clearly the point of the italicized phrases is that incessant malice *results* from the "fixity" or "depression"—that is, the paralysis or restraining—of so-called free will. Without *eternal* freewill of some sort or other, *eternal* punishment would be hard to justify. The need is filled, at least rhetorically, by invoking a *Pickwickian* sense of "freewill" compatible with inability to choose otherwise than one actually chooses. The crucial point of Scholastic teaching to hold onto here is that, in the *ordinary* sense of the word, "freewill" is a casualty of the angels' fall.

Against this view, consider the following comment of Louis Martz: "Milton goes on [in *PL* 4] to create a more striking unorthodoxy as he reveals a Satan who still seems to possess the power of choice, a Satan who starts to curse God and then turns to curse himself, 'since against his thy will / Chose freely what it now so justly rues' (*PL* 4.71–72). It even seems to Satan that a way out might still remain in repentance: 'O then at last relent,' he cries, that is, repent, give up your obstinate course: 'is there no place / Left for Repentance, none for Pardon left?' (*PL* 4.79–80). Milton is boldly raising here another of his ultimate questions: would not a just God prefer to see Satan repent, and give him the chance to repent? Milton seems to leave the question open by showing that Satan's pride would never have accepted the chance, and that therefore God has not offered it [*PL* 4.103–4]."[7]

There are four difficulties with this reading; they are fundamental, and (as with all interesting mistakes) they shed an oblique light on the text. (1) If Satan's pride *would never* let him accept the offer of a chance to repent, then he seems, and is, powerless to choose acceptance, contrary to Martz's conclusion (that Satan "still seems to possess the power of choice"). (2) If God is prepared to give Satan a chance at repentance only on a condition that God knows full well Satan is powerless to meet, then clearly God has no intention of giving Satan a chance at repentance. But (3) if Satan has been denied the chance to repent—where "chance" has to include "wherewithal"—then, once again contrary to Martz's desired conclusion, Satan no longer has the power of choice. (4) Not only doesn't Satan "seem" on the available evidence to have the power of choice, he doesn't "seem" to have it even to himself. That's the point of "Disdain [of submission] *forbids me* [to repent]" (*PL* 4.82; italics mine). (A non-person "forbids" by *preventing*.) It's also the point of the condition-contrary-to-fact "say [for the sake of argument] I could repent" (*PL* 4.93).

To answer Martz's question directly ("would not a just God prefer to see Satan repent, and give him the chance to repent?"), the inability to repent is a kind of death—the death of the moral agent. In particular, it's allegorically apt for *Satan's* Sin to give "birth" to *Satan's* Death; the working assumption of *PL* is that, morally, the betrayal of God is both a capital offense and its own punishment. In short, it's a contradiction in terms—*PL*'s terms at least—to say that the God of *justice* would prefer to see Satan repent. The God of *justice* prefers to see justice done—retributive justice in this case; no more and certainly no less. Martz would be better advised to apply to the God of *mercy*. The crucial issue here is whether the two Gods could possibly be one and the same.

I beg readers' pardon for plaguing them with niceties. The point of being fastidious about (1)-(4) is that Milton is fastidious about them; the logical texture of *PL* doesn't blur under high magnification. If, as the old adage has it, God's dwelling is in the details, Milton is a frequent visitor.

"Obdurate" abbreviates the standard metaphor for moral death—hardening of the heart (*obduratio cordis*). The metaphor is Biblically inspired. It will mean nothing to Satan; his appointment with the awful truth comes later. (In this respect, among many others, the wrath reserved for the damned is a work in progress.) In the meantime, every brag of this braggart soldier chimes with the same mocking truth:

> Yet not for those [dire Arms],
> Nor what the Potent Victor in his rage
> Can else inflict, do I repent or change,
> Though chang'd in outward lustre, that fix'd mind
> And high disdain, with sense of injur'd merit,
> That with the mightiest rais'd me to contend.

$$(PL\ 1.94–99)$$

"That fix'd mind . . . that . . . rais'd me": Satan didn't *rise* against God; his "mind" *raised* him—once its motion got "fix'd."[8] That fixity *won't* be changed by its owner—precisely because it *can't*:

> What though the field be lost?
> All is not lost; the unconquerable Will,
> And study of revenge, immortal hate,
> And courage never to submit or yield:
> And what is else not to be overcome?

$$(PL\ 1.105–9)$$

Rebel *might* has been overcome—but not rebel *will*; an unconquerable will, in fact, is the one thing that's not to be overcome *by anything, even by its owner*. Here the speaker becomes his own heckler; if a so-called act of will merely *happens* to its owner, the "action" is really a passion. By the same token, "study" and "courage" are passions too. The hate getting "studied" is "immortal" because its agent is really a patient; the outside agency it would take to stop it will never oblige.

Satan needs more time than we do to catch on to the cruel joke in "unconqerable" and "not to be overcome"; he hasn't had the benefit of drill in the relevant commonplaces:

> But [you will object] he had a soul invincible. What praise [I reply] is that? The stomach [i.e., tantrum] of a child is ofttimes invincible to all correction. The unteachable man hath a soul to all reason and good advice invincible; and he who is intractable, he whom nothing can persuade, may boast himself invincible; whenas, in some things, to be overcome is more honest and laudable than to conquer.[9]

The demonic self is no longer an unmoved mover, a thing that *acts* (in the strict sense of acting). From now on (to repeat), "will," "study," and "courage" are passion in thin disguise.

The motor of passion, in turn, is "delight":

> But of this be sure,
> To do aught good will never be our task,
> But ever to do ill our sole delight,
> As being the contrary to his high will
> Whom we resist.

$$(PL \ 1.158\text{--}62)$$

It's a crucial symptom of obduracy that, in hell, "delight" and "task" are opposites. To be fallen is to be delighted (and moved) *exclusively* by the chance to refuse or frustrate a task. The sad apology for *action* remaining to the fallen is *reaction*. What the rebel angels do, and whether they do anything at all, will depend on what, if anything, they think God wants them *not* to do—a dependency that the grammar of "[such] courage [as] never to" neatly mimics. In the new construction, "courage" takes an infinitive of result: to be "courageous" is to be so *arranged* (or deranged) as never to submit or yield.

The case of "will," "study," "courage," "task," and "delight" is a warning never to take demonic Newspeak for its benign twin, the moral vocabulary we know and love.

Not that the deformation is total; overlap in fact is precisely the trouble. Take "courage" again. In the Advocate's lexicon as in Satan's, virtues are habits—inclinations arranged for triggering by particular challenges; and the virtue of courage in particular is the habit of responding to a present danger with no more (and no less) fear than honor allows. The catch is that Satanic virtue, unlike ours, is a habit that can't be kicked, and the Satanic virtue of courage is exercised by avoiding a feared enemy altogether, and launching a sneak attack on someone the enemy loves.

Before we resume, let me repeat the warning I began with. To a rapid reader, this and much of what follows is apt to sound like moralizing. But there can be no moral objections to the doings (or what pass as doings) in Hell. The result of taking the measure of God's anger won't be an indictment of Satan and his crew—far from it. From here on, they are to blame for nothing they do. The result will be a diagnosis. We are emphatically not itemizing demonic choices; the demons have no choices. We are surveying in detail the chart of the disease to which they have been abandoned forever. In short, a diagnosis isn't enough. For God to hate his betrayers is for him to leave them to a disease that is intricate as well as cruel. In fact, the intricacy is part of the cruelty. We need to look squarely at both to appreciate what it is for God to hate.

Consider the quip of the old Roman satirist: the hardest thing to take about being down and out is that it makes one ridiculous.[10] By that standard, being damned is being down and out with a vengeance. The feather in this boaster's cap is his curse. To hear the boasting, we might well think Satan magnificently deluded as well as obsessed, if we didn't know better: "So spake the Apostate Angel, though in pain, / Vaunting aloud, but wrack'd with deep despair" (*PL* 1.125–26).[11] This is a general of the army talking; a display of nerves would be bad for the troops. The mock-Stoic rant in *PL* 1–2 falls short of dramatic irony because the ranter falls short of total self-ignorance. But not far short. Hell is a place of darkness visible, where the typical use of eyes is to see the dark. In the standard account, obduracy goes with blindness.

We don't have to wait long for bizarre specimens of visual impairment:

> High on a throne of Royal State, which far
> Outshon the wealth of Ormus and of Ind,
> Or where the gorgeous East with richest hand
> Showrs on her Kings Barbaric Pearl and Gold,
> Satan exalted sat, by merit rais'd
> To that bad eminence, and from despair
> Thus high uplifted beyond hope, aspires
> Beyond thus high, insatiate to pursue
> Vain Warr with Heav'n, and by success untaught,
> His proud imaginations thus displaid.
>
> (*PL* 2.1–10)

The cautionary examples are a commonplace of Renaissance political theory. Pearl and gold aren't "barbaric" by nature. "Eastern" despotism[12] keeps up a bogus legitimacy by a parade of gorgeousness, and by a satrap culture that turns the basic metaphor of distributive justice ("high," "rais'd," "exalted," "uplifted") upside down. The result is slavery by consent. Richard II's sneer about throwing away "reverence" on "slaves" is barbaric enough to damn him: the "slaves" are freeborn Englishmen. The citizens of hell, too, were at least born free; despotisms that hope to survive, says Aristotle, had better make believe they're republics.[13]

So far the barbarian king hasn't asked himself if a bad "eminence" is any more of an eminence than a bad penny is of a penny. Self-examination isn't what he's about at the moment. The Advocate has a more pressing use for him: no portrait of the corrupted will is complete without a portrait of the corrupted wit. For a display of that wit in flight, consider Satan's appeal to the uniformity of nature: when despair has been pleasantly surprised by getting "thus high," what's to keep it from being even more pleasantly surprised by getting *"beyond* thus high" (*PL* 2.7–8)? If the past tells us anything about the future, despair is virtually a promissory note! Genuine induction is taught by "success" (results), fake induction by "proud imaginations" (*PL* 2.9–10)—imaginations that go to show that despair is more hopeful than hope.

Another symptom of the *blindness* of the hardened heart is its *politics*. This despotism, like others to follow—to repeat—is a fake republic. What we're looking at, on its face, is an elective monarchy, an ideal mixed constitution buttressed against overthrow by civil liberty. Under the constitution, one wields power only if one has a right to, and one has a right to only if one deserves to. In particular, Satan was "created" leader by "just right and the fixt Laws of Heaven" (*PL* 2.18–19). He "achiev'd" merit "in Counsel or in Fight"—a "highest worth" he's "conscious" of even as he volunteers to add to it (*PL* 2.429). And not the least of his merits is that this throne was "yielded"—that is, paid to him—"with full consent" (*PL* 2.24); he earned the vote—the "free choice"—of his fellow citizens (*PL* 2.19–21).[14] This is one Malvolio who belongs to all three classes of magistrate: born great, achieved greatness, had greatness thrust upon him.

Ironies proliferate here. (As usual, the speaker himself isn't quite listening yet—he's the last to appreciate them.) Thus it's true enough that Satan was "created" leader by "right" as well as law (law in heaven is "fixt" by right, rather than vice versa); he was *endowed with an archangel's nature* (theological sense of "create"), and not simply *promoted to an archangel's rank* (political sense of "create"). Like this initially good eminence, Satan's bad eminence—measured in "endless pain"—also came by "merit"; he busily worked his way up to the "greatest share" of this reward (*PL* 2.20, 29–30).

Another irony at the speaker's expense: this despot governs (if we believe him) with the guaranteed consent of the governed. His throne is as "safe" (*PL* 2.23)—that is, as "faction"-proof (*PL* 2.32)—as its unique wretchedness can make it; though in fact this is less "safe" than his fitful self-understanding lets him see. He thinks of faction as concerted envy, and takes it for granted that nothing disarms envy like the unenviable:

> none sure will claim in Hell
> Precedence, none, whose portion is so small
> Of present pain, that with ambitious mind
> Will covet more.
>
> (*PL* 2.32–35)

The trouble with this assumption, of course, is that the "ambitious mind" needn't covet pain to accept it as a price to be paid. Satan knows better; he's the prisoner of such a mind. The climax of this very debate will find him moving briskly to deprive the likeminded of the chance to outbid him.

Ambition owes its name, in fact, to the political art of outbidding one's competitors (for control of public "opinion" or "repute," *PL* 2.471–72). It's an art that Satan is just now busy inventing:

> Thus saying rose
> The Monarch, and prevented all reply,
> Prudent lest from his resolution rais'd
> Others among the chief might offer now
> (Certain to be refus'd) what erst they fear'd;
> And so refus'd might in opinion stand
> His rivals, winning cheap the high repute
> Which he through hazard huge must earn.
>
> (*PL* 1.466–73)

Ambitio is the art of the hustings, the political art of climbing— effective enough on its own terms. The master tyrant is a master illusionist, with a demagogic genius for getting himself "created" by "free choice" or "full consent" (*PL* 2.19, 24). But once again there's a catch; the *same* catch, in fact. No art of climbing will serve a climber who takes "down" for "up"—just as no code of "honor" can turn revenge into justice. Satan himself eventually sees this with a sickening vividness:

> what will not Ambition and Revenge
> Descend to? who aspires must down as low
> As high he soar'd, obnoxious first or last
> To basest things.
>
> (*PL* 9.168–71)

To complicate the theme of political blindness, the stage business tells an ironic story of its own:

Forthwith upright he rears from off the Pool
His mighty Stature, on each hand the flames
Drivn backward slope thir pointing spires, and rowl'd
In billows, leave i' th' midst a horrid Vale.

(PL 1.221–24)

The billows of this Red Sea part obediently for a deliverer who promises to "set free" his fellow captives "from out this dark and dismal house of pain" *(PL* 2.822–23); promises, in fact,

to lead ye forth
Triumphant out of this infernal Pit
Abominable, accurst, the house of woe,
And Dungeon of our Tyrant; now possess,
As Lords, a spacious World.

(PL 10.463–67)

If Satan is the Moses of this house of bondage,[15] then the fallen angels are the Israelites; their Egypt is Hell, and their Canaan, if Satan's mission succeeds, will be the newly created world. In terms of the inevitable parallels in the Gospel of Nicodemus, Satan is Christ harrowing hell, and the fallen angels are Adam, Eve, and the Patriarchs waiting to be released from Limbo. At one point, even more outrageously, the same parallels give us a Satanic Christ harrowing heaven:

I in one night freed
From servitude inglorious welnigh half
Th' Angelic Name.

(PL 9.140–42)

If the speaker enjoyed God's privileged access to the future, all of this would be a malicious play of wit at the expense of figural history rather than a dramatic irony at the speaker's expense. As it is, the Advocate is letting us peer at the world astigmatically again, through the eyes of the hardened heart. The view through those eyes gives us a measure, in empathy, of what it is to betray God's love and lose it beyond recall. It gives us another measure of the hatred of God.

The Exodus material is more than a comment on Satanic delusion; after all, the central confirming text for the theology of the hardened heart is the story of Pharaoh ("I will harden his heart, that he shall not let the people go" [Exod. 4:21]). In Satan's scenario, of course, *God* is the Pharaonic slavemaster. But the Advocate finds an elaborately telling way to tag the real Pharaoh in the scene:

> on the beach
> Of that enflamed Sea, he stood and call'd
> His Legions, Angel Forms who lay intranc'd
> Thick as Autumnal Leaves that strow the Brooks
> In Vallombrosa, where th' Etrurian shades
> High overarch'd embow'r, or scatter'd sedge
> Afloat, when with fierce Winds Orion arm'd
> Hath vex'd the Red-Sea Coast. . . .
>
> (*PL* 1.299–306)

"Thickness" is beside the point, of course; the real point in one of the Advocate's patented similes isn't so much *made*, as gradually *insinuated*.

What is it like for defeated angels to be sprawling around the "sea" of hell? First pass: like a thick layer of fall leaves in a Tuscan wood. Second pass: like seaweed on a wind-swept Red Sea Coast. Like something innocuously physical, in short. Or *is* it innocuous? We're teased by details that look far from innocuous. Is "Vallombrosa" mere gingerbread, or is the wood actually situated in the "Valley of the Shadow [of Death]"? Is "shades" (for "foliage") a pointless allusion to the placename "Vallombrosa," or a pointed Virgilian idiom for dead souls? Why an abrupt shift of scene to the Red Sea? Why Red Sea winds doing duty for weapons ("with fierce winds . . . arm'd")? Why a raid by a tutelary nature-god ("Orion arm'd")? Why a raid at all (Latin *vexare* = "harry")? These details are poised on the brink of relevance. Third and final pass:

> the Red-Sea Coast whose waves o'erthrew
> Busiris and his Memphian Chivalry,
> While with perfidious hatred they pursu'd
> The sojourners of Goshen, who beheld
> From the safe shore thir floating Carcases
> And broken Chariot Wheels, so thick bestrown
> Abject and lost lay these, covering the Flood,
> Under amazement of thir hideous change.
>
> (*PL* 1.299–313)

Satan in defeat is a Pharaoh left by God to his obduracy—to his death as a moral agent. So far in *PL* 1, the angels, unlike the "Mem-

phian Chivalry," are perfidious fugitives rather than perfidious pur-
suers, but in a little while Satan will be busy pursuing his own
"sojourners of Goshen" (candidates for enslavement).

In short, the central point of likeness turns out to be moral and
not physical after all. Both defeated armies, angelic and Egyptian,
are "thick bestrown"; both are physically "abject" (cast off). But
above all, both are morally "abject"—disowned by God. God can't
"lose" what he disowns; being "abject" means being "lost" to
oneself.[16]

Not surprisingly, the divided self gets to play antagonistic parts
in the Exodus drama:

> As when the potent rod
> Of Amrams son in Egypts evil day
> Wav'd round the Coast up call'd a pitchy cloud
> Of Locusts, warping on the Eastern Wind,
> That o'er the Realm of impious Pharaoh hung
> Like Night, and darken'd all the Land of Nile,
> So numberless were those bad Angels seen
> Hovering on wing under the cope of Hell
> Twixt upper, nether, and surrounding fires.
>
> (*PL* 1.338–46)

"Amrams son" is Moses, of course—the invoker of plagues on
God's behalf. Satan is playing Moses to his own Pharaoh. And one
of the self-inflicted plagues—the cognitive side of obduracy—is an
airborne invasion of darkness.

With his troops passing in review, Satan suffers another such invasion, in the form of a telltale whim; the general calls for a head
count:

> Thir number last he sums. And now his heart
> Distends with pride and, hardning, in his strength
> Glories.
>
> (*PL* 1.571–73)

The census is part of figural history; it carries the retroactive
"stamp" (*typos* in the jargon) of a future census: David too is
"moved" to order his head count by a God intent on punishing him
and his people (2 Sam. 24:1). And David too takes his movements
for acts, with a revulsion that is no longer possible to Satan: "David's heart smote him after that he had numbered the people. And

David said unto the Lord, I have sinned greatly in that [which] I have done: and now, I beseech thee, O Lord, take away the iniquity of thy servant; for I have done very foolishly" (2 Sam. 24:10).

We've already learned that the logic of obduracy is capable of transforming despair into a kind of hope (*PL* 2.7–8). The new census-generated hope is made of the same crazy material; this enemy can't be outnumbered, as Satan has very good reason to appreciate:

> So much the stronger prov'd
> He with his thunder: and till then who knew
> The force of those dire Arms?
>
> (*PL* 1.92–93).

"Till then" is still another manic touch. Who knew the force of those dire arms? Satan and his troops knew it; a new arrival in the field just before the last battle in heaven left them in no doubt. What to do in the face of Christ in arms, short of surrender? Enter the obdurate mind, with its delusional creativity:

> This saw [Christ's] hapless Foes but stood obdur'd,
> And to rebellious fight ralli'd thir Powers
> Insensate, hope conceiving from despair.
> In heav'nly Spirits could such perverseness dwell?
> But to convince the proud what signs avail,
> Or Wonders move th' obdurate to relent?
> They harden'd more by what might most reclaim,
> Grieving to see his Glorie, at the sight
> Took envy, and aspiring to his highth,
> Stood reimbattel'd fierce, by force or fraud
> Weening to prosper, and at length prevail
> Against God and Messiah, or to fall
> In universal ruin last.
>
> (*PL* 6.785–98)

The lover in Marvell's sardonic poem boasts of a love "begotten by despair / Upon impossibility." "Insensate" hope comes of the same parentage:

> Henceforth his might we know, and know our own
> So as not either to provoke or dread
> New war provok'd.
>
> (*PL* 1.643–45)

In the neat parallelism, "*his* might" goes with "not provoke" and "*our* might" goes with "not dread"—with bizarre illogic. His superiority in "might" to us and our inferiority in "might" to him are two versions of precisely the same state of affairs. Why the bogus distinction between knowing his (relative) "might" and knowing ours? Along with the quibble on "provoke" (the first occurrence denoting our act, the second occurrence God's), it's another piece of word magic in the service of another exercise in face-saving: somehow a "might" that is dreadfully inadequate for offense is dreadlessly adequate for defense.

Still (the speaker goes on to argue), why make a fetish of war? War isn't the only option. It isn't even the most eligible:

> Our better part remains
> To work in close design, by fraud or guile
> What force effected not: that he no less
> At length from us may find, who overcomes
> By force, hath overcome but half his foe.
>
> (*PL* 1.645–49)

Astigmatism again. The "better part" of valor that survives the defeat of force is—of all things—fraud. God doesn't know that his foe is only half defeated. He'll find out "at length"—that is, after the undefeated half defeats him. With the speaker's usual talent for selective inattention, he has neglected to tell us just how we manage to blindside an enemy with a notoriously unobstructed view:

> For what can force or guile
> With him, or who deceive his mind whose eye
> Views all things at one view? he from heav'n's highth
> All these our motions vain sees and derides,
> Not more Almighty to resist our might
> Than wise to frustrate all our plans and wiles.
>
> (*PL* 2.188–193)

The story *PL* 1 and 2 are designed to tell with relentless irony is the story of an imprisonment more radical than the hell Satan is about to break out of. Obduracy is the state of being locked up in one's malice, one's lies, and—strangest and bitterest imprisonment of all—in oneself. Here again, as with the boast of "unconquerable will," a terrible irony is lost on the braggart: "The mind is its own place, and in it self / Can make a Heav'n of Hell, a Hell of Heav'n"

(*PL* 1.254–55). Mind (Satan argues in effect) isn't literally "in" the thinker, much less "in" the thinker's surroundings. The only place the mind is "in" is "it self," its own processes. Actually, the morally *relevant* "in" for a mind isn't what it's *in*, but what's "in" *it*—what it "contains." This last will include a "hell"—or thought of hell—that the thinker can make a "heaven" at will, by replacing it with pleasanter thoughts.

The canard that "Descartes argues the irrelevance of body to mind" would qualify Satan's new boast as a "Cartesian error."[17] But in fact Descartes argues for the *relevance* of body to mind—a relevance intimate enough to fool the mind itself into identifying thoughts with "concurrences" of brain parts. True, Cartesian minds not only aren't bodies, but can't be; hence the absurdity of claiming that "it's impossible for mind to be given an existence apart from body, at least by God." But on Descartes' showing the absurdity can't help being seductive: creatures like us "never know existence without a body, and often have to work against the body—as if somebody chained at the ankles from infancy had drawn the conclusion that ankle chains are part of the body's equipment for walking."[18]

Satan's error isn't Cartesian. It isn't even Satanic; as usual, he has recent reason to know better than he speaks:

> Then *Satan* first knew pain,
> And writh'd him to and fro convolv'd; so sore
> The griding sword with discontinuous wound
> Pass'd through him, but th'Ethereal substance clos'd
> Not long divisible.
>
> (*PL* 6.327–31)

The sword of Michael passes through *Satan*, not through a "substance" he's somehow attached to. *He's* the only "substance." This intellectual being is a material object. For such an object, to be "incarnated" is not to be joined with flesh somehow, but "mix'd" with it: "obnoxious [i.e., vulnerable] first or last / To basest things" (*PL* 9.165, 171–72). Taken literally, the boast that the mind is its own place is simply false.

Again the ironic *truth* of Satan's boast is more terrible than its literal falsehood. Only the universe—the uncontained container par excellence—is *literally* its own place. But figuratively at least, Satan too is an uncontained container, a container with nothing inside it but "the hot Hell that always in him burns" (*PL* 9.467):

> within him Hell
> He brings, and round about him, nor from Hell
> One step no more then from him self can fly
> By change of place.
>
> (*PL* 4.20–23)

Satan eventually comes to see this:

> Which way I flie is Hell, my self am Hell,
> And in the lowest deep a lower deep
> Still threatening to devour me opens wide,
> To which the Hell I suffer seems a Heav'n.
>
> (*PL* 4.75–78)

If Satan is hell, the mouth waiting to devour him is his own. In a narrative stuffed with perverse examples of eating, a more perverse example would be hard to imagine; like the cursed Erysichthon ("earth-savior") in the myth, this cannibal is reduced to devouring himself, with no hope of satisfying his real hunger:

> thus these two
> Imparadis'd in one another's arms
> The happier Eden, shall enjoy thir fill
> Of bliss on bliss, while I to Hell am thrust,
> Where neither joy nor bliss, but fierce desire,
> Among our other torments not the least,
> Still unfulfill'd with pain of longing pines.
>
> (*PL* 4.505–11)

In boasting that his mind is its own place, Satan managed to overlook a crucial detail: the relevant place is a prison, and the relevant state of mind is a radical incapacity to love.

Love is the essential paradise in *PL*, and the incapacity to love is the essential paradise lost—to Satan at least, lost forever. The resulting hell, to repeat, is the state of being locked up in one's malice, one's lies, and (above all) oneself. This is the point of the allegory of Sin the Jailer:

> The key of this infernal Pit by due,
> And by command of Heav'ns all-powerful King,
> I keep, by him forbidden to unlock
> These Adamantine gates.
>
> (*PL* 2.850–53)

The key is Sin's by "due"—it's both her right and her duty to keep the sinner locked up in endless self-repetition; to abuse freedom is to forfeit freedom. This makes trenchant allegorical sense. So does Sin's eventual attempt to release the sinner:

> But what ow I to his commands above
> Who hates me, and hath hither thrust me down
> Into this gloom of *Tartarus* profound,
> To sit in hateful Office here confin'd?
>
> (*PL* 2.856–59)

"Due" implied a debt of justice. Here Sin tries to take "due" back ("what ow I?") and immediately bungles the attempt: her post may be "hateful," but it's admittedly an "office" (i.e., a duty). She also tries to desert her post by releasing Satan from malice in intent—to malice in action: in the lowest deep, a lower deep opens wide. And she justifies the (abortive) release attempt by appealing to gratitude, of all things—the principle whose betrayal she personifies. In the allegory as in the straight narrative, ironies proliferate.

What event in Satan's life does the whole allegory represent? His failure to understand his doom has been constant from long before this encounter—in fact from his first appearance. The encounter simply makes the self-ignorance explicit: Sin is his "dear Daughter," Death is "the dear pledge / Of dalliance" (2.817–18). The allegory is telling us that on the threshold of his expedition, Satan is having an unplanned moment of self-examination. He sees that he's done radical and complicated and repellent things to himself, things he's able to put the names "Sin" and "Death" to; but exactly what the names mean is still a mystery to him. Meanwhile, he speaks the language of family romance cheerfully enough. It has the effect of self-deception by euphemism.

We've already noticed that obduracy generates a politics. The politics in turn is a diagram of the mentality that generates it: compulsion masquerading as decision. The key episode here is the debate in Pandemonium, beginning with its fake agenda:

> With this advantage then
> To union, and firm Faith, and firm accord,
> More then can be in Heav'n, we now return
> To claim our just inheritance of old,
> Surer to prosper then prosperity
> Could have assur'd us; and by what best way,

> Whether of open Warr, or covert guile,
> We now debate; who can advise, may speak.
>
> (*PL* 2.35–42)

With the ensuing charade of parliamentary liberty, Satan adds a telling detail to the picture of an Asian "king *Barbaric*" that launches *PL* 2; Xerxes, another enemy of freedom, will convene a similar sham parliament on the eve of the invasion of Greece: "That I may not seem to you to be taking counsel in private, I put the matter in the midst, bidding him among you who so wishes to show his mind."[19] Like Xerxes, Satan has already settled on a policy of imperialist annexation (the isolationist version of "empire" is a nonstarter [*PL* 2.296, 378]), and his spokesman Beelzebub is waiting for the climactic moment to produce it (*PL* 2.378–80).

In the meantime, the point of having three debaters talk at each other fruitlessly is to show us that each embodies a different aspect of the emperor's despair—that is, abandonment of hope for a reconciliation with the ground of his being (and hence with himself). Each despairing angel exhibits the empty forms of prudence and republican virtue: of prudence, by giving priority to the greater good or (for lack of good) the lesser evil; of republican virtue, by subordinating individual to national interest. The madness has method in it, and a kind of nobility:

> O shame to men! Devil with Devil damn'd
> Firm concord holds; men onely disagree
> Of creatures rational, though under Hope
> Of heav'nly Grace.
>
> (*PL* 2.496–99)

The classification scheme is recognizably Scholastic (drives are assigned either to the *irascibile* or the *concupiscibile*). The first despair we hear from is a perversion of the drive to anger—"Moloch homicide" (*PL* 1.417). After the war in heaven, revenge at the price of suicide is cheap at the price (*PL* 2.126–29); better not be at all than be defeated (*PL* 2.47–48). If recklessness is courage and revenge is honor, Moloch has both.

Appropriately enough, the first of two rebuttals comes from a perversion of the drive to lust—Belial, "than whom a Spirit more lewd / Fell not from Heaven" (*PL* 1.490–91). Against Moloch's call to action, Belial speaks up for *in*action, or moral sloth, in a se-

ductively "humane" version (*PL* 2.109). The personified lust for
moral death, like perverted lust in general, is a sophist—that is, an
adept at making the worse appear the better reason (*PL* 2.113–14);
a gift of persuasion that reminds the Advocate of manna, that corruptible food from heaven (*PL* 2.12–13; Exodus 16:20). Belial's
signature virtue, not surprisingly, is a passion for the contemplative
life: "Who would lose, / Though full of pain, this intellectual
being?" (*PL* 2.146–48). Granted, pain can force one to give up
one's intellectual being whether one "would" or not; but Belial
supplies the antidote: hellfire stops being painful as soon as one
manages—intellect and all—to be "conform'd" to it (*PL* 2.217-
18). Apparently even an intellect made of darkness visible is a terrible thing to lose.

The third and most effective parliamentarian—"his Sentence
pleas'd" (*PL* 2.291)—is another member of the peace party. But
unlike Belial (whose advice is castor oil), Mammon's is the happy
face of despair. The only rational answer to the loss of hope is good
riddance. Mammon asks us to swallow a paradox worthy of Andrew Marvell: contrary to appearances, hope is the negative term,
not unhope; it's just dependency by another name. What's positive
is *un*hope or (to give it a less misleading name) *in*dependence (*PL*
2.252–54). Mammon's colleagues think they have to settle for
some lesser evil or other—nonexistence or anesthesia; for the third
speaker, despair isn't an evil at all. If not a good, it's at least the raw
material of one. Despair is the fertile nothing out of which virtue
"creates" a good of its own, a good that includes the fact of "creation" itself (*PL* 2.260). Mammon offers his audience a chance at
a "liberty" all the more splendid for being "hard" (*PL* 2.256).

At least Belial has held onto the knowledge that the being whose
love is not to be hoped for is all-good (*PL* 2.138) as well as all-
knowing (*PL* 2.189–90) and almighty (*PL* 2.144). All three versions of despair are incorrigible. But in Belial and Moloch, what's
been perverted is an animal appetite. In Mammon, the disease of
obduracy—the darkness of the blinded heart—has spread to reason
itself.

In the parliamentary annals of Hell, the debate comes to nothing;
it's a non-event, with no bearing on the legislation that will shortly
override it. The effect of introducing it is simply to isolate for allegorical inspection three phases of the emperor's despair. With Moloch and Belial, Satan says farewell (respectively) to fear and
remorse; with Mammon, he becomes one of "them that call evil

good and good evil, that put darkness for light and light for darkness; that put bitter for sweet and sweet for bitter" (Isaiah 5:20–21):

> So farewell Hope, and with Hope farewell Fear,
> Farewell remorse: all Good to me is lost;
> Evil be thou my Good, by thee at least
> Divided Empire with Heav'ns King I hold.
>
> (*PL* 4.108–11)

Actually, to give the devil his due, Satan hasn't stopped calling good and evil by their right names. "*My* good" here is idiomatic—and telling. Evil is the fallen angel's good in the same scare-quote sense that gruel is the beggar's caviar. Far from implying, in the manner of Hobbes, that to call something good is to express one's desire for it,[20] Satan's command ("be thou my good") assigns to moral evil the mere *role* of the moral good that's lost to him. It's precisely because good is lost to him that, from now on, he'll have to make do with a functional equivalent. If moral goodness is a source of power, so is moral evil—imperial power that God will soon be forced to share ("divided Empire"). If moral goodness is a source of delight, so is moral evil; to make it, as Satan has already done, "our sole delight" (*PL* 1.160) is still another way of casting evil in the role of good.

Unlike Aristotle's *akrates*, or victim of weak will, Satan has all his wits about him when he goes against his better judgment. The *akrates* is a city with good laws that occasionally go unheeded. By contrast, the *akolastos*, or incorrigible wrongdoer, is a city with perverse laws that get meticulously obeyed. Like the *akolastos*, the Satanic city obeys perverse laws—but only because the legislature has wilfully and consciously revised the originals.

Aristotle (the inventor of this particular city metaphor)[21] is surely not alone in excluding the possibility of such legislation. What is it to have a better judgment if not to prefer it? ("Better judgment," as usual, abbreviates "judgment of what it's better to do in the current circumstances.") What is it to prefer it if not to be ready to follow it? On the orthodox view of the will—as the rational appetite—Satan's evil deliberateness makes no sense. He's a disturbing twin of the classic *sophron*, or morally rational agent—with the exception of the rare bouts of misgiving or indecision, when he threatens to become an equally disturbing twin of the *akrates*.

Specimen One:

> cruel his eye, but cast
> Signs of remorse and passion to behold
> The fellows of his crime, the followers rather
> (Far other once beheld in bliss) condemn'd
> For ever now to have thir lot in pain,
> Millions of Spirits for his fault amerc'd
> Of Heav'n, and from Eternal Splendors
> For his revolt, yet faithfull how they stood,
> Thir Glory wither'd.
>
> (*PL* 1.604–12)

For a moment Satan is distracted from his resolve by "[com]passion" for the eternal pain of millions—millions who have resisted the temptation to blame him for the injustice of their sentence: they were just his "followers" (recruits), and thanks to him they're being punished as his "fellows" (co-conspirators). The sight of them ("faithfull how they stood") fills him with remorse; he knows very well that the only "fellow" of Satan was Satan. For a moment, in short, Satan succumbs to the sentimental illusion that his comrades' disproportionate suffering is his fault; it was his incitement (not their free choice) that made them revolt, and his incitement (not the Enemy's revenge) that got them "amerc'd / of Heav'n."

At least for the moment, the general has lost his nerve. Manly "scorn" would snap him out of his funk, yet "thrice he assay'd, and thrice in spight of scorn, / Tears such as Angels weep burst forth" (*PL* 1.619–20). In a moment he'll recall (for himself and his troops) that acts of glory are threatened with "withering" only if—absurdly—the glory is in the outcome and not the act: "That strife / Was *not* inglorious, though the event was dire" (*PL* 1.623–24). As for the revolt itself, the Enemy was to blame for that if anyone was; by mischievously concealing his real strength, he "tempted our attempt and wrought our fall" (*PL* 1.642). Next time we'll show him we're quick learners; what force "effected not," we'll "effect" by fraud (*PL* 1.647).

No misgivings here. The fit of "weak will"—shrinking from a malicious "better" judgment—is over; honorable malice is back in full strength.

Specimen Two:

> And should I at your harmless innocence
> Melt, as I doe, yet public reason just,
> Honour and Empire with revenge enlarg'd,

By conquering this new World, compels me now
To do what else though damn'd I should abhorr.

(PL 4.388–92)

Again sentimentality is threatening the speaker's "moral" clarity; a conscientious public servant always respects the fundamental maxim "be just before you're generous"—that is, always prefer your public (and impartial) to your private (and biassed) reason for acting. Satan is rescued from a morally self-indulgent "melting" by his "better" judgment—his judgment of what's better under the circumstances: there are duties of feeling as well as action; under the circumstances, it's Satan's duty to destroy these people, and to do it without abhorrence.

Specimen Three:

> Her graceful innocence, her every Air
> Of gesture or least action overaw'd
> His Malice, and with rapine sweet bereav'd
> His fierceness of the fierce intent it brought;
> That space the Evil one abstracted stood
> From his own evil, and for the time remain'd
> Stupidly good, of enmitie disarm'd,
> Of guile, of hate, of envie, of revenge.

(PL 9.459–66)

Again everything has been rotated 180 degrees. Again the role of Satan's "better" judgment is being played by malice and the role of tempter by a prospective temptee. Again the battle for "moral" integrity has been temporarily lost. The temptress has "disarm'd" the warrior of his weapons—in fact, of his identity. The result is the metaphysical equivalent of death; what's left of a paragon of fierceness "bereav'd" of fierce intent? of an Evil one par excellence "abstracted" from evil? Aristotle's *akrates*, like a drunkard, is stupidly bad. Intoxicated by Eve, the Advocate's looking-glass *akrates* lapses into a heartbeat's worth of stupid goodness.

A weak-willed Satan, as I remarked a few paragraphs ago, is the exception that proves the rule. The rule is a Satan of perfect self-possession. In a world in which the functional roles of good and evil have been systematically exchanged—"Evil be thou my Good"—being possessed by a demon does duty for a virtue.

In the usual jargon of theology, God "permits" Satan to do his worst:

> So stretch'd out huge in length the Archfiend lay
> Chain'd on the burning Lake, nor ever thence
> Had ris'n or heav'd his head, but that the will
> And high permission of all ruling Heav'n
> Left him at large to his own dark designs,
> That with reiterated crimes he might
> Heap on himself damnation, while he sought
> Evil to others, and enrag'd might see
> How all his malice serv'd but to bring forth
> Infinite goodness, grace and mercy shewn
> On Man by him seduc'd, but on himself
> Treble confusion, wrath and vengeance pour'd.
>
> (*PL* 1.209–20)

The Advocate muddies the waters a bit by informing us in passing that the aim of God's permission was nearly thwarted by Satan's nose dive in Chaos. He might have been falling "to this hour"— thereby sparing Adam and Eve a disastrous temptation, and sparing us the ordeal of history. What saved us, we're told, was the "ill chance" of a collective swerve of atoms in the opposite direction; by accident, they all somehow decided to be capricious in unison, saving God's plan into the bargain (*PL* 2.931–38). But (to repeat) the Advocate himself has taken care to prepare us for an irony. Even the fallen angels know better than to allow for the possibility that "everlasting Fate shall yeild / To fickle Chance, and *Chaos* judge the strife" (2.232–33). For God at least, permitting and facilitating are two sides of a coin.

It's just as well to avoid two possible misunderstandings growing out of the ambiguity of "permit." To take the more obvious first, there's no such thing, of course, as God's *granting* a creature *permission* to do wrong—that is, giving the creature to understand (absurdly and countereducationally) that God doesn't forbid wrongdoing. What's harder to see is this: though it makes sense to speak of "permitting" a guilty creature to "reiterate" a past crime it's strictly nonsense to speak of "permitting" an innocent creature to commit a pending crime—one the creature is *about to commit if not prevented*. The point to be reckoned with, in short, is that there's no such thing as a "permission" to fall.

There is, of course, such a thing as allowing the creature the *means* to fall; but in the usual sense of "means," giving agents the means to fall is not the same as refraining from preventing their fall.

"Preventing" is the key notion here: to permit act A in the relevant sense is to refrain from preventing A; to refrain, that is, from breaking the chain of causes that would otherwise lead straight to A. That's why nobody, not even God, "prevents" an act of free will from happening; the whole point of a free act (if there is a point) is precisely that nothing *makes* free will happen—it's not the last link in a causal chain. But if there's no such thing as preventing a free action, there's no such thing as *refraining* from preventing it; that is, no such thing as permitting it.

God's tragedy, as creator, is that he doesn't want his free creatures to act badly, yet knows that they will. What he doesn't know (because it's false) is that they are *about to, unless prevented.* And it makes as little sense for him to undo a future fall as to prevent it. Under his tragically penetrating gaze, the future is a domain of garden-variety facts, not possibilities or likelihoods or necessities. All-powerful as he is, he's as powerless to undo the future as to undo the past.

Unchaining the "Archfiend" from the burning lake is quite different. What God knows about the *fallen* Satan is precisely that *Satan is bound to do his worst unless prevented.* In short, God declines to prevent Satan's malice from *running its course.* In the relevant and precise meaning of "permit," God deliberately permits the malice; he wills the intactness of the causal chain between Satan's last free act and the processes of his hardened heart. Permitting in this sense goes with occasioning; that is, with giving Satan an opportunity—an opportunity he can't help taking.[22] In the Advocate's terms, Satan reiterates his crimes by God's "high permission" as well as God's "will" (*PL* 1.211–12).[23] No divine tragedy here. Instead we have justice: crime reiterated is punishment—the doom of the hardened heart.

Given that hardness, releasing Satan to his dark designs is clearly just launching the designs.

Tender consciences are apt to find this reality hard to take. The usual case history, of course, isn't Satan but his counterpart in Exodus. The Erasmus-Origen vindication of divine love for Pharaoh, a love that ends by hardening his heart, tips over into self-parody: God *does* try to cure what ails Pharaoh—with a prescription that aggravates the ailment! Medicine is medicine; the patient brought his allergy to it on himself. Granted, the allergy gets worse with each dose; but why should that encourage us to suspect the physician's motive? After all, by choosing a therapy that has the effect of hardening rather than softening Pharaoh's heart, God doesn't *cause* the resulting malice; he merely *occasions* it.[24] With enemies like Erasmus and Origen, the theology of anger doesn't need friends.

After a few more contortions, Erasmus supplies an analogy that is as revealing as it is evasive: A certain master knows that, for one of his servants, malice and opportunity are fire and tow; the servant's automatic response to favor is betrayal of trust. So the master entraps his servant by favoring him. Still (argues Erasmus), rest assured that the favoring doesn't cause its effect (the betrayal), it only activates the malice that is the real cause. In short, it only "occasions" the betrayal. Thanks to the subtle but crucial difference between occasioning and causing, the master contrives to will the servant's destruction, to gratify his will—and to avoid being even slightly to blame for the result.[25] Besides, the destruction is a "good" thing, worthy of a master who is "good" as well as just.[26]

Erasmus fails to suppress a flinch at the image of a love that serves vindictiveness like the strings of a puppeteer. Luther is less nervous. Still, even Luther doesn't avoid the anxious redundancy of a speaker protesting too much:

> Here you see that when God is at work *in* evil deeds and *through* evildoers, the evil deeds are done, but God is incapable of doing evil [directly], even though he does evil [indirectly] *through* evildoers. The reason is that he, being good, cannot do evil; but he avails himself of evil instruments that cannot help being seized and moved by his power. The vice is in the instruments, then. God doesn't let them be idle. Evils are done when God himself sets the evils in motion.[27]

Calvin, as usual, is beyond embarrassment:

> I have already shown rather clearly that Scripture calls God the *author* of all the things that these critics wish to happen by his mere idle *permission*. God bears witness that he creates the light and the darkness, and forms good and evil [Isaiah 45:7]; that no evil happens that he has not caused to happen [Amos 3:6].[28]

Calvin easily disposes of an equivocation on "obey"; for a sinful will to move in "obedience" to God's will is not for it to obey a sinful command, but merely to comply with the law of its nature—its sinful "disposition." In fact, obeying in this sense is perfectly compatible with an irresistible urge to *disobey* God's commands[29]—which, of course, is precisely the hole in this way of exonerating God: the second chance denied to the obdurate heart is the chance to perform any morally significant action at all, even an act of disobedience.

The Advocate argues that God's purpose in leaving Satan "to his own dark designs" was "That with reiterated crimes he might / Heap on himself damnation." This defense of "permission" is just a notational variant of the defense of occasion that Erasmus found in Origen, which "unties the knot" of God's apparent injustice by "attributing the *occasion* of hardening to God but throwing the *guilt* back on Pharaoh. In his malice, Pharaoh was hardened by what should have brought him to repentance." But of course this notion of compounded guilt can't be right; the heart once hardened is no longer capable of agency, only of automatic self-repetition. On the charge of a life of crime after his fall, Satan is not guilty by reason of depravity.

In short, the "permission" enjoyed by the hardened heart is God's joke, in a derisive style God indulges more than once in *PL*. Here he is, battling sudden doubts at the sight of a rebel force that apparently caught him napping:

> Neerly it now concerns us to be sure
> Of our Omnipotence, and with what Arms
> We mean to hold what anciently we claim
> Of Deitie or Empire.
>
> (*PL* 5.721–24)

The Speaker and his Son had better mobilize "what force is left, and all imploy / In our defence." Their opponent in imperial tennnis is threatening to drive an unreturnable ball into the crucial "hazard" (= "pocket in wall of tennis court"). If they don't block the maneuver, they may well "lose / This our high place, our Sanctuarie, our Hill" (*PL* 5.729–32). Later, an equally feckless God contemplates the "rage" of a mighty opposite

> whom no bounds
> Prescrib'd, no barrs of Hell, nor all the chains
> Heap'd on him there, nor yet the main Abyss
> Wide interrupt can hold
>
> (*PL* 3.81–84)

The supreme being has ransacked his wisdom and power and come up empty; his best "prescription" for restraining a captive is child's play to this wicked escape artist.

Still later the Jester turns the cold stream of his pleasantries on a second generation of fallen creatures:

> O Sons, like one of us Man is become
> To know both Good and Evil, since his taste
> Of that defended Fruit; but let him boast
> His knowledge of Good lost and Evil got,
> Happier had it suffic'd him to have known
> Good by it self, and Evil not at all.
>
> (*PL* 11.84–89)

The knowledge on offer is a "taste" of the thing known—or rather two things known: "I've lost Good"; "I've gained Evil." (So much for the ostensible promise of insight into the ground of the distinction.) God is impressed—and alarmed; Adam and Eve have somehow become peers to himself and his sons.

Never mind the strange implication that God belongs to a peerage. And never mind the curiously distorted echo of a recent outburst of one of the new peers:

> O *Eve*, in evil hour thou didst give ear
> To that false Worm, of whomsoever taught
> To counterfeit Mans voice, true in our Fall,
> False in our promis'd Rising; since our eyes
> Open'd we find indeed, and find we know
> Both Good and Evil, Good lost and Evil got,
> Bad Fruit of Knowledge, if this be to know,
> Which leaves us naked thus, of Honour void,
> Of Innocence, of Faith, of Puritie,
> Our wonted Ornaments now soil'd and stain'd,
> And in our Faces evident the signes
> Of foul concupiscence, whence evil store;
> Ev'n shame, the last of evils; of the first
> Be sure then. How shall I behold the face
> Henceforth of God or Angel, earst with joy
> And rapture so oft beheld? those heavn'nly shapes
> Will dazle now this earthly, with thir blaze
> Insufferably bright.
>
> (*PL* 9.1067–83)

The full horror of the fraud—"tree of the 'knowledge' of good and evil"—is just now dawning on Adam. The worm promised a "rising" to godlike knowledge. It lied—or rather equivocated on "know." An insight into the nature of good and evil is one thing. A taste of what it's like to *be* evil is another. If tasting is knowing, then Adam and Eve enjoy a knowledge that God and his Sons will never come close to matching. Tasting isn't knowing—not in the promised sense. Adam is aware of this. So, of course, is God; it's the cream of God's newest jest: by falling (not "rising"), those obdurate creatures have become "like one of us."

The Son appreciates a joke at Satan's expense if not at Adam's and Eve's:

> Mightie Father, thou thy Foes
> Justly hast in derision, and secure
> Laugh'st at thir vain designes and tumults vain.
>
> (*PL* 5.735–37)

In the Psalms, just this note of mockery accompanies the begetting of the Son: "He that sitteth in the heavens shall laugh; the Lord shall have them in derision. Then shall he speak unto them in his wrath, and vex them in his sore displeasure. Yet have I set my King upon my holy hill of Zion. I will declare the decree: the Lord hath said unto me, Thou art my Son; this day have I begotten thee" (Ps. 2:4–7). "The wicked plotteth against the just, and gnasheth upon him with his teeth. The Lord shall laugh at him: for he seeth that his day is coming" (Ps. 37:12–13). Part of God's joke on his enemies is that they plot and gnash by his "permission." The Homeric Olympus is filled with "the gods' unquenchable laughter"; so is God's holy hill.

Before leaving "permission," it will be instructive to glance back at a skeletal version of the standard defense. "Satan's evil will," says Luther, "is something God finds, not something he creates. God works by seizing a will already made evil by God's desertion and Satan's offense."[30] By God's desertion? *Deserente Deo et peccante Satana malam factam?* The verb describes something base, in fact a crime—*peccatum desertionis.* Surely Luther understands enough Latin to know that this is the worst word he could have chosen to gloss "permission." It is also the best—if candor has any claim on our admiration.

The inner Hell we've been surveying inch by inch is not of God's making. If we grant the Advocate the libertarian premise he needs to get his narrative off the ground (that the offenders had it in their power to act otherwise), God wasn't the hardener of Satan's heart. God only *abandoned* it to its (self-inflicted) hardness. In the jargon, he only "permitted" the hardness to proceed. The sublime of God's anger isn't fury but withdrawal. The anger is all the more terrible for being expressed by absence. Extended infinitely, it merges into hatred.

In *PL*, the measure of that hatred is the forgiveness it bans forever:

> I will clear thir senses dark,
> What may suffice, and soft'n stony hearts
> To pray, repent, and bring obedience due.
> To prayer, repentance, and obedience due,
> Though but endevor'd with sincere intent,
> Mine ear shall not be slow, mine eye not shut.
> And I will place within them as a Guide
> My Umpire Conscience, whom if they will hear,
> Light after light well us'd they shall attain,
> And to the end persisting, safe arrive.
> This my long sufferance and my day of grace
> They who neglect and scorn, shall never taste;
> But hard be harden'd, blind be blinded more,
> That they may stumble on, and deeper fall;
> And none but such from Mercy I exclude.
>
> (*PL* 3.188–202)

"Forgiveness" isn't quite right here, of course. Forgivenesss doesn't turn the obdurate heart from stone to flesh (Ezek. 11:19). It doesn't restore the power to decide whether to "hear" one's conscience or "neglect" it. What the favored child of God enjoys and the rejected one is denied, in short, is not mere forgiveness but the re-created power to make amends, to stand once more "on even ground against his mortal foe, / By me upheld" (*PL* 3.179–80).

This is God talking about resistible or sufficient grace—the kind that consists in the repair of free will. At least in the forgiven, God "creates" a heart that once again starts "clean" (Ps. 51:10–11).

Here it's worth noting a curious discrepancy. In the case of Adam and Eve, at least, the Advocate lets both himself and God talk as if the power to make amends could be restored without restoring the power to make a botch of things again—as if these powers weren't two sides of a coin. With the first generation of the Fallen, in other words, the Advocate endorses a grace that's irresistible and efficacious—the kind that (benignly) annuls free will. That's the point of "prevenient" or anticipatory grace in the Augustinian version of divine forgiveness: "Unto man's good purpose doth subsequent grace lend its aid; but the purpose itself would not *be*, had not grace gone before."[31] In the immediate aftermath of the Fall in *PL*, the clean heart has grace to thank not only for its ability to form good purposes, but for the good purposes themselves.

It's more than a little odd that free will should figure so crucially in the Advocate's treatment of Adam's and Eve's Fall and should be treated so cavalierly in his treatment of their Redemption:

> from the Mercie-seat above
> Prevenient Grace descending had remov'd
> The stonie from thir hearts, and made new flesh
> Regenerate grow instead, that sighs now breath'd
> Unutterable, which the Spirit of prayer
> Inspir'd, and wing'd for Heav'n with speedier flight
> Then loudest Oratorie.
>
> *(PL* 11.2–8)

> He sorrows now, repents, and prayes contrite,
> My motions in him, longer then they move,
> His heart I know, how variable and vain
> Self-left.
>
> *(PL* 11.90–93)

In the first passage, God simply makes repentance happen ("inspires" it); for flesh to be "regenerate" is precisely for it to breathe God's breath—that is, to pray sincerely (not merely to have the option of doing so). In the second passage God himself flouts his earlier libertarian ideal of grace: he cuts off the "variableness" of Adam's heart by refusing to leave the heart to itself; in short, he cuts off Adam's power to "vary" by choosing wrong. In this connection at least, the Advocate's God sheds his libertarian idiom and talks in the idiom of Luther.[32]

Actually, invoking the Augustinian Luther here is a bit misleading. The major historical precedent for a two-tiered redemption scheme—for some, absolute election; for others, election conditional on the right use of freewill—is the position of Augustine's heretical opponents. According to Julian, the fiercely libertarian Bishop of Campania, God predestines the Apostles outright, and the rest of the Elect only if he foresees that they will try to act rightly.[33] The Advocate's God, like Julian's, has chosen a few of the Fallen—notably Adam and Eve—"of peculiar grace / Above the rest" (*PL* 3.183-84), and promises to reward the rest for acts of faith "though but endeavor'd with sincere intent" (*PL* 3.192). Where Julian goes badly wrong, on the showing of *PL*, is his failure to see that for the power of sincere "endeavor" fallen creatures have only grace to thank—grace that some will act on and some "neglect." (Here the Advocate seems to side with the pre-Augustinian Greek Fathers.[34])

I just remarked that this discrepancy in the treatment of free will is more than a little odd. But of course it isn't really odd, given the overarching enterprise of vindicating (i) the fairness and (ii) the lovingkindness of God to man. This double enterprise encourages two competing versions of a second chance. Vindicating God's fairness requires (in his creature) a power to break faith with God as well as keep it. For vindicating God's infinite love and creativity, that ambivalent power is not so clearly an advantage, much less a requirement. We'll need to revisit this problem a bit later on.

For now, the point of this exploration of God's lovingkindness is that it gives us a measure of God's capacity to hate. To repeat, that hatred compounds the Advocate's difficulties manyfold. How can infinite hatred be justified in a being whose essence is perfect love? Here is a possibility: perhaps, under the circumstances, it's either bad or absurd to forgive this particular betrayer of God. Perhaps either the ethics or the logic of Satan's crime somehow rules out a second chance for him. Adam and Eve also betray God and yet retain his love. The Advocate's Great Argument is seriously at risk if he can't locate the difference.

Eventually the Advocate adds a footnote to his Great Argument by justifying God's rejection of Cain's gift in favor of his brother's: the difference is simply that Cain's was insincere (*PL* 11.432-43). It would have been helpful if the insincerity had been remotely hinted at in the canonical account. The ancient Rabbinic paraphrase of Genesis fills in a crucial gap (Cain's harangue to Abel just before the murder), but unfortunately what the killer resents—with no trace of insincerity—is precisely God's caprice; the first brother-murderer starts out as the first disillusioned free thinker, spewing negations: there's no universal justice, no universal judge, no last

judgment, and no original creation born of the compassion of a supreme being incapable of partiality ("respect of persons").[35] On the
Advocate's working assumptions, of course, Cain is simply misreading the evidence, including his own motives: not everyone
makes the best of a second chance, moral anarchy was inflicted on
the world not by God or Satan, but by human choice, and moral
anarchy is precisely what a last judgment (if there is one) is designed to sort out.[36]

Put the same speech in Satan's mouth, and it acquires a disturbing force. Here at least, it looks as if a double standard *is* at
work—or a double God: if not the doubleness of a Manichaean
standoff between good and evil, then a favoritism worthy of a despot out of the "gorgeous East." (Satan, of course, is such a despot
[*PL* 2.3]; but favoritism doesn't stain the republican virtue of the
Hellish Consult in *PL* 2.)

We had better be wary of tracing sources here. Calvin's God, too,
seems to use a coin toss to decide whom to favor. But divine favoritism, for Calvin, doesn't take "no" for an answer; to be favored is
to be saved, not merely given a chance to *qualify* for salvation. At
least on the point at issue, the Advocate isn't "readmitting" Calvin-
ism by a "back door";[37] even Calvin's opponents stipulate that the
fallen angels get no second chance.[38] On this issue as on others, one
central difference between Calvin and the Advocate is that Calvin
has not taken on the Great Argument; on the contrary, in his view
no human court has standing to bring this Defendant up on charges.
The Advocate, by contrast, is an officer in just such a court; it had
better make sense for the angels to be alone in having sinned the
unforgivable sin, the sin that even an infinitely loving God can't or
shouldn't forgive. If this is nonsense, the Advocate has crucially
failed his Client (to say nothing of the Jury).

The tradition offers two possible solutions. One is that Satan is
paying the penalty for the excellence of his nature, which is as in-
flexibly certain in its acts of will as in its acts of knowing;[39] but this
comes uncomfortably close to saying (in the cadences of Mickey
Mouse) that hardness of heart is beyond cure in angels because in
angels it's . . . beyond cure. The premise of the other solution is that
to sin is to yield to persuasion; to sin unforgivably is to persuade
oneself—to succumb (in Augustine's account of self-persuasion) to
a "spontaneous thought":[40]

> The first sort by their own suggestion fell,
> Self-tempted, self-deprav'd; Man falls deceiv'd
> By the other first: Man therefore shall find grace,

> The other none: in Mercie and Justice both,
> Through Heav'n and Earth, so shall my glorie excel,
> But Mercy first and last shall brightest shine.
>
> (*PL* 3.129–34)

In short, it *just occurred* to Satan to defect; if it had just occurred to Adam and Eve in turn, then they too might have been expelled from the love of God.

The difficulty with this theory is that one isn't to blame for entertaining a thought unless one has thought it over and *decided* to entertain it—that is, unless one *already* entertains it; but by the same token one isn't to blame for *already* entertaining it unless one has *already* thought it over and decided to entertain it—and so on (viciously) to infinity. Something that just occurs to us, in short—like whatever else just happens to us—is precisely *not* something we do. Hold us accountable for our spontaneous thoughts, and you might as well hold us responsible for our spontaneous itches and twitches. The unfallen Adam knows better:

> Evil into the mind of God or Man
> May come and go, so unapprov'd, and leave
> No spot or blame behind.
>
> (*PL* 5.117–19)

The evil thought that's prompting this reflection of Adam's, for all he knows, is entirely spontaneous—"wild work" of the sleeping Eve's imagination (*PL* 5.112). Notably, it doesn't worry him precisely because he has reason to hope that "what in sleep thou didst abhorr to dream, / Waking thou never wilt consent to do" (*PL* 5.120–21). Clearly, the same rule applies to internal as to external temptations: the only way a spontaneous thought could leave behind a spot, much less an indelible spot, is by winning the thinker's approval.

Besides being incoherent, the spontaneity explanation doesn't explain *enough*. For one thing, it doesn't explain the unforgivableness of Beelzebub's surrender to temptation. The temptation was no more spontaneous than Adam's or Eve's:

> So spake the false Arch-Angel, and infus'd
> Bad influence into th'unwarie brest
> Of his Associate.
>
> (*PL* 5.694–96)

What Beelzebub yields to is not only not a suggestion from within, it's not a suggestion at all; it's a poisonous *influence,* and (still worse) the poison is "infus'd" into him without his being aware of it. Why no mercy in *his* case? Why, for that matter, doesn't he earn clemency as a matter of simple justice? And what about the rest of the rebel army? They're as innocent of "self-temptation" as Adam and Eve, let alone Beelzebub. Why no grace for *them*?

For that matter, where is the grace or even the justice in the curse on the serpent? Perhaps (with apologies to the ASPCA) this misgiving would be a mere quibble—if the Advocate didn't work so hard, and with such pitiable results, to forestall it:

> without delay
> To Judgment he proceeded on th'accus'd
> Serpent though brute, unable to transferr
> The Guilt on him who made him instrument
> Of mischief, and polluted from the end
> Of his Creation; justly then accurst,
> As vitiated in Nature.
>
> (*PL* 10.163–71)

> God at last
> To Satan first in sin his [the Serpent's] doom apply'd,
> Though in mysterious terms, judg'd as then best.
>
> (*PL* 10.171–73)

Serious questions multiply here—questions at least as obvious and gnawing to the Advocate's educated contemporaries as to us. Where is the "justice" (*PL* 10.70) in cursing a helpless victim of demonic possession? Why is an omnipotent being, not to mention a transcendently just one, "unable" to transfer the guilt for an offense from an involuntary "instrument" to the real offender? Where is the "justice" in punishing in absentia an offender robbed of freewill by irreversible obduracy? Why should misusing a creature "vitiate" its nature, even if it "vitiates" a particular instance of the nature? Why, in other words, should one serpent's "pollution" be the pollution of serpenthood? Why, for that matter, should the vitiating of one pair of human beings vitiate humanity? The serpent didn't tempt itelf, much less consent to temptation; so how did it forfeit mercy? No doubt—if we accept Christian materialism—the pollution of a species can proceed *ex traduce,* by propagation; but then why is a hereditary disease incurable by this Physician of infinite resource? And if curable, where's the fairness in letting it spread?

Among these motes in the mind's eye, the spontaneity explanation is the grain of sand. Grant (for the sake of argument) that self-tempters are ipso facto not entitled to grace. Well, neither are *non*-self-tempters like Adam and Eve. Grace is a gift, not a reward. Besides being incoherent and explaining too little, the spontaneity explanation explains the wrong thing. What urgently calls for explaining here is not why a just God *needn't* cure what ails the fallen angels, but why a loving God *won't* and *shouldn't* cure it. If this latter proposition is nonsense (to repeat), then the Advocate has crucially failed his Client.

With this burden of proof, the prospects for an acquittal are bleak. Everyone in the Advocate's religious culture knows that the quality of mercy is not (con)strained; that's what makes it mercy. *PL* tries for a plausible constraint on the acts of forgiveness that shall count as mercy. The attempt is desperate. So is the self-congratulation assigned to the character called God the Father, who assures us that, in spite of powerful appearances to the contrary, mercy survives its retrenchments not only intact but magnified:

> in Mercie and Justice both,
> Through Heav'n and Earth, so shall my glorie excel,
> But Mercy first and last shall brightest shine.
>
> (*PL* 3.129–34)

As Adam's remarks on spontaneously evil thought show, the Advocate knows better, or rather has reason to know better (even the author can't be held to total recall of *PL*). In this context, the glory talk is not a note of triumph. It's a note of pathos.

Not that glory itself is an unseemly aim for God—not in the Advocate's tradition at any rate. The author of *Christian Doctrine*, for one, comes back to this theme, in strikingly similar terms, again and again: the point of God's exercising mercy is precisely "to lay open the glory of his mercy, grace, and wisdom."[41] God's "primary purpose" in foreordaining mercy is achieved when "the form and excellence of his grace, and of his wisdom and justice as well, shines the brighter."[42] The whole point of the creation, too, was "to lay open the glory of his power and goodness."[43] Open to whose inspection? Open for whose profit? Not God's, according to the same tradition: "Knowing God is in *our* interest, not his; each of knows him only if he, who has that knowledge, makes himself known to us."[44] "God seeks his own glory not for his sake but for ours."[45] In fact, God does nothing for his own sake: "Acting to fill a need argues an imperfect agent, an agent born to act and be acted on simultaneously. This imperfection is alien to God, which is why he is supremely liberal: he acts in accord with his goodness, not his utility."[46]

Yet—to play devil's advocate—doesn't this suggest a benign form of obduracy or unfreedom? It looks as if God can't help being good; it looks as if he has no alternative. In short, it looks as if God's will is no freer than Satan's.

The author of *Christian Doctrine* supplies half the standard reply: nothing is free to achieve logical absurdities; an essentially good being is no more free to be bad than to square circles.[47] The other half is this: God acts freely if there's nothing to keep him from acting otherwise; and in fact there isn't: he chooses every act of his from an infinity of equally good alternatives. Yes, the infinity lacks alternatives that are *less* good, much less ones that are bad. But obviously this doesn't keep the chooser from choosing otherwise than he does. God is precisely—and without paradox—a being barred from an infinity of actions who remains infinitely free.[48]

This is the kind of infinite freedom that the loyal angels end up with, and that Satan would have earned if he had chosen not to misuse the kind of freedom all the angels started out with, the freedom to do the wrong thing. Erasmus finds a hint of it in the Apocryphal Wisdom of Sirach: "The Lord made man from the beginning and left him in the power of his own counsel. If you are willing, you will keep his commandments and be faithful to your covenant. He has set down beside you fire and water; to whichever you wish, you will stretch out your hand. Over against man stand life and death; whichever it pleases him to have, that shall be given to him" (Sirach 15:14–17). "This passage," explains Erasmus,

> makes it clear that Adam, first of our kind, was created with an uncorrupted reason fit for telling apart what is to be sought and what avoided. To that reason, will was added, uncorrupted in its turn, but free none the less (if it so willed) to turn from good to evil. The angels were created in the same state, before Lucifer with his comrades defected from his

creator. In the fallen, will has been so utterly corrupted that they cannot turn back to the better course. In the persevering, good will has been so far confirmed as to be incapable of swerving toward impiety.[49]

We have two contrasting ideals of will: "free" and "confirmed"; piety that can swerve and piety that can't, the latter being what persevering spirits, human and angelic, wind up with. But this last detail is an embarrassment to Erasmus's case, which is the Advocate's case as well: if you can't have morally significant action without "free" choice, then how can a loving God let history culminate in an eternity of "firmness"—hence moral insignificance—for his favorite creatures? Even if he can, how does he rescue his *own* infallible (hence "firm") will from moral insignificance? On the other hand, if "confirming" a will leaves its significance intact, then how can a loving God endow his creature with a will that's *less* than "firm"?

Well, the "unconfirmed" will, the will that can go wrong, is the kind that lets God mete out rewards and punishments—that is, lets him exercise the virtue of justice; all other things being equal, the better worlds are the ones in which God has at least a chance to exercise his virtues. But all other things are *not* equal in such worlds. Love, too, is a virtue. Is it an exercise of love to create a world in which cruel justice has a chance for exercise? But lack of the chance to do justice is a blemish. Exactly where *is* the blemish in a scheme of things that dispenses God from exercising one of his virtues, especially a cruel one? For that matter, where's the blemish in leaving *all* of them idle? Does a God who forgoes the *exercise* of his virtues forgo the *virtues*? Is he tied, like an athlete, to the maxim of "use it or lose it"? But when it comes to virtues, practise makes perfect. What happened to God's celebrated freedom—without damage to his perfection—to refrain from creation *altogether*?

No more evasions. The Free Will defense vindicates God's justice by impugning his love. It clears the Judge by convicting the Creator.

It seems that the Advocate's case was doomed quite literally from the Beginning (of everything). No wonder images of that Beginning haunt his narrative. The horns of the Creator's dilemma, like the hero's quandary in a Restoration tragedy, are love and justice. As usually defined, they're at odds. Yet each has to be accommodated somehow if the maker of history is to review his handiwork and call it good.

The solution is to find a way of accommodating love *under the name* of justice—a Hebraic form of the virtue (*tzᵉdaqah*; "justness" or "righteousness" or "charity"). The Hellenic measure of justice (*dikaiosyne*) is the *receiver's* due; by contrast, *tzᵉdaqah* qualifies as "justice" by changing the measure from the receiver's due to the giver's: "When you spare evildoers, it is just—not as it is due to their merits but as it is due to your bounty."[50] "God exercises mercy not by acting *against* justice but by doing something *above* it. . . . Mercy doesn't undo justice; it fulfils it."[51] Rising above justice (and thereby fulfilling it) means giving up the policy of treating people "according to their desert"; after all, "use every man after his desert and who shall 'scape whipping?" The great thing (as Hamlet implies here) is to treat people "after your own honor and dignity. The less they deserve, the more merit is in your bounty." The paradox of a character in a revenge play showing an unexpected (if momentary) fluency in the language of mercy simply recapitulates the uncomfortable paradox we've been exploring, which comes to a crisis when God finds himself grasping both horns of his dilemma:

> He with his whole posteritie must die,
> *Die hee or Justice must*; unless for him
> Som other able, and as willing, *pay*
> The *rigid satisfaction*, death for death.
> Say Heav'nly Powers, where shall we find such *love*?
> Which of ye will be mortal to *redeem*
> Mans mortal *crime*, and *just th'unjust to save*?
> Dwels in all Heaven charitie so dear?
>
> (*PL* 3.209–16; italics mine)

When it comes to standards, "rigidity" is a virtue; a flexible standard is no standard at all. Thus the satisfaction a criminal is asked to pay should be no more and no less than his debt—in this case, death for death. But there's no lapse in this "rigidity" when a "just" benefactor "redeems" (pays for) the "crime" on the criminal's behalf, thereby "saving" the criminal the ordeal of paying his own debt. After all, what does it matter who pays a debt so long as it gets paid? Thanks to divine ingenuity, everybody comes out a winner. Two things were under threat, (a) the criminal, and (b) the justice of his getting his due: "Die hee or Justice must." The Redeemer manages to rescue both the person and the principle. In the old Roman law of contracts—the basis of the metaphor in play here—the guarantor of a debt is the *auctor*. God the Son is Adam's Author in more ways than one.

God the Father is being understandably meticulous here. We need to return the compliment.

Something strange has happened. We have two kinds of justice, one austere and the other magnanimous. The rule of magnanimity trumps the rule of austerity. Each is strict in its own way. Austere justice goes by what *the receiver deserves to receive*, magnanimous justice by what *the giver deserves to give*. Applied to the question of second chances for the fallen, austerity delivers an unequivocal "no," magnanimity an unequivocal "yes". The rules are irreconcilable, then; tragedy can't be avoided. But it turns out that at least this once, thank God, it's possible to eat one's cake and have it too. Better still, this feat of gastronomy isn't mere sleight of hand. The magic here is nothing more devious than a maxim of common sense: *it doesn't matter to the creditor if the debtor or somebody else does the paying, so long as the debt gets paid.*

In this case a subtle argument is also a subtle request. God the Father is asking us to take a familiar metaphor very seriously: *getting punished is paying what one owes—giving one's creditor "satisfaction."* God the Father is also relying on us to reject an equally familiar metaphor: *getting punished is getting paid what one is owed*. Unfortunately, the whole practice of punishment is bound up with the second metaphor: the whole point of making the punishment fit the crime is to pay the offender no more and no less than what his offense has earned him. Maybe a creditor needn't worry about who pays him back; but if the second metaphor is the right one for the current situation (as it seems to be), that's neither here nor there. The offender is not a debtor in the first place. Thanks to his guilt, he's a creditor. Justice—whoever ends up meting it out— owes him the wages of his offense. In short, being punished is precisely on a par with being rewarded: both are ways of being paid; the difference is the currency of payment. Both make sense to us precisely because they are intricately bound up with the second metaphor.

For God the Father, of course, the first metaphor is more conve-

nient, if less apt. Opportunistic metaphors cheat the eye by imposing on the usual conversational rule of charity: it's second nature
for us to give them the benefit of the doubt. The illusion is harder
to resist when second nature is reinforced by wishful thinking;
what's at stake in this particular conversation is the prospect of
being spared a distinctly less-than-agreeable fate.

In the meantime, to repeat, something strange has happened.
"Die hee or justice must," we were warned. Well, "hee" (Adam)
doesn't die; so by process of elimination—if the warning is to be
trusted—justice does. True to this warning, the Judge lets the culprit
off scot-free—on the astonishing grounds that it makes no difference if an innocent party pays the guilty party's "satisfaction." Justice is finessed, in short, by a pettifogging argument in the service
of love. In the language of Jesus' advice to his disciples, the wisdom of serpents has been enlisted in the service of the innocence of
doves. On the other hand, God has conspicuously *not* affirmed the
principle that "the less they deserve, the more merit is in your
bounty." All his ingenuity is bent on seeing to it that the convict
gets not one throe or pang less than he deserves; his concession to
mercy is to be merciless by proxy.[52]

We can wash our hands of the Advocate's failure by writing it
off as the inevitable result of taking on an impossible assignment:
defending the moral coherence of a hopelessly incoherent faith—a
faith safely obsolete, in which modernity is not invested. But that
would be a mistake. The faith the Advocate has failed to vindicate
is not mere Christianity. The conscience whose incoherence he has
run afoul of is ours.

Counsel or therapy or the scalpel (we will suppose) can somehow
reform Hitler into a fountain of good works—if we just agree to
forget about punishing him. The choice: (a) add to the sum of goodness by returning good for evil; or (b) right an incalculable wrong
by repaying in kind an incalculable evil. Afflicting this monster
won't bring back his victims, it won't undo their suffering; it
merely adds to the sum of evil in the world. Improving this monster
into a paragon is a desecration of those victims; it adds obscenely
to the sum of injustice in the world. On the face of it, these are
starkly contrary notions of what ought to be done to Hitler; no dis-
agreement could be more radical. But consider an unnerving possibility: what we're listening to isn't a radical difference of
opinion—unhappily for both parties. It's merely a radical difference between two meanings of "ought"—the "ought" of doing

good and the "ought" of doing right. Well, perhaps there's a third "ought" that might settle which of the other two to adopt. And perhaps there isn't.

Suppose there isn't. (*Admit* there isn't?) Then there just is no fact of the matter about which of the rival "oughts" we ought to embrace, any more than there's a fact of the matter about whether somebody is happier than he is tall. In the arguments we most urgently long to resolve, we're doomed to talking past each other, or past ourselves. Reason fails us, but reason is clearly not to blame; the space of values is a chaos of incommensurates. The Advocate is committed to denying this; so is the court of which he is an officer. He had better be right. If he's wrong, he's in deep trouble. And he's not alone.

GOD'S NOMADS

A few paragraphs back, I suggested that the Advocate's case is doomed by the Hobson's choice his Client faces at the Beginning. Short of logical absurdity, God cannot have both of two kinds of justice, or of two kinds of freedom, or of justice and mercy. In each case, he resolves the dilemma in favor of a grimmer virtue. It's hard to find a desire to give love, much less a need to give it, in his gift of a freedom to do the wrong thing. It's less hard to find in that gift a desire to *get* love, as well as the telltale mark of a divine risk-taker. The Advocate's Client is the ideal Muse for an "adventrous Song" (*PL* 1.13).

In *PL* the divine risk-taker is shown rolling the dice of his creatures' indeterminacy. Nothing in the toss determines the outcome. God *knows* the outcome, of course; he's the timeless witness of what *will* happen as well as of what *has* happened, as helpless to undo future facts as past ones. (If they could be undone, they wouldn't be facts, much less objects of knowledge.) He has no alternative to enabling his creatures to give him love at the heavy cost of enabling them to withhold it; these abilities are precisely equivalent ("Not free, what proof could they have giv'n sincere / Of true allegiance, constant Faith or Love?" [*PL* 3.103–4]). Worst of all, he knows he will end up with nothing to show for the gamble. No wonder the stress of total knowledge tells on him, at least for an instant ("ingrate!" [*PL* 3.97]).

But the point to focus on here is the indeterminacy assumption we're asked to give the Advocate for the sake of (the Great) Argument: nothing in Adam's composition or Eve's makes either of them any more likely to fall than to stand; they were "sufficient" for both (*PL* 3.99). The canonical story that the Advocate is stuck with makes this assumption hard to grant, for a reason that adds yet another cruel twist to the tragedy of *PL*: given indeterminacy, we have reason to hope that God will at least break even, yet as luck would have it, the Eden experiment is a total failure. Still worse, later trials of free will show the same bias in the dice: the timeless view from the Hill called Visions of God (*PL* 11.377) shows a grand total of one unequivocally just man per generation. God's reward for betting on creation is a run of bad luck that will last as long as history.[53]

I began this section by remarking that it's easier to make out a desire to get love than to give love in God's gift of the freedom to do the wrong thing. Actually, given the run of bad luck that freewill lets him in for, neither of these desires leaps to the eyes. By making us indeterminate beings, God ends by inflicting history on himself as well as on us. The eventual mess, it seems, will be fit only for cancellation, in favor of a new heaven and a new earth (not to mention the sacrifice of his only begotten Son). But how can a belated salvage operation help the Advocate's case? In due course I will be suggesting that this misses the point; the point of adding a history lesson to the forensic narrative is that a God who bets the world on love has ways of hedging his bet. But more of this later.

The Advocate's honor role of splendid nonconformists—"the only righteous in a world perverse" (*PL* 11.701)—owes its implications to the parallel list in the Letter to the Hebrews. Once again Enoch earns exemption from death by daring to shock his contemporaries into sobriety with an "odious truth," a truth as ironic as it is odious: the last judgment will be inaugurated by Enoch himself (*PL* 11.702-9), reserved by God to join Elijah in challenging Antichrist on the last day.[54] Thanks to his faith, Enoch is "translated that he should not see death" (Heb. 11:5)—"translated into Paradise that he might give repentance to the nations" (Ecclus. 44:16). As a second "heir of the righteousness which is by faith" (Heb. 11:7), Noah also anticipates the life of Christ; in a time of "wrath," Noah becomes "reconcilement" (Ecclus. 44:17); he becomes, that is, "the one just Man alive" from whom God, having drowned one world, will "raise another" (*PL* 11.818, 890, 877).

Jewish history resumes the pattern. Abraham trusts God enough to leave "his Gods, his Friends, and native Soil" (*PL* 12.129, Heb. 11:8) without being told where he's being sent; his historic mission—and reward—is that "in his seed / All Nations shall be bless'd" (*PL* 12.125–26). The same brave transience and exile marks the careers of Isaac and Jacob (*PL* 11.153; Heb. 11:20–21), Joseph (*PL* 11.16; Heb. 11:22), and especially Moses, who bears Christ's "figure" (*PL* 11.240-41). "By faith Moses . . . refused to be called the son of Pharaoh; choosing rather to suffer affliction with the people of God than to enjoy the pleasures of sin for a season; esteeming the reproach of Christ greater riches than the treasures in Egypt" (Heb. 11:24–26).

The common denominator of the Hebrews list is that "these all died in faith, not having received the promises, but having seen them afar off." Thanks to this distant sight, they "confessed that they were strangers and pilgrims on the earth" (Heb. 11:13). Faith and pilgrimage go together: in each generation after the first (in which "the one just man" is the reunited Adam and Eve), somebody undertakes a moral as well as physical journey of unknown destination. He is God's nomad, "like one that had bin led astray" (with the moon in "Il Penseroso") "through the Heav'ns wide pathless way." He is lost, but well lost, being astray in heaven.

The Pauline "strangers and pilgrims on the earth" begin their historical career with the beginning of history itself, at the very end of the Advocate's narrative—though how this début is supposed to clinch the Great Argument remains to be seen. "In either hand the hastning Angel caught / Our lingring Parents" (*PL* 12.637–38). Adam and Eve obviously aren't yet quite grown up; in maturity at least, "parents" is a little misleading. We've surprised them in the last "lingering"—ambivalent—moments of a kind of adolescence. Holding each by the hand, the guardian angel hurries them toward the exit. So much for the project of sheltering moral innocence from moral experience, a project whose mythology the sly Advocate has already evoked:

> not that fair field
> Of *Enna*, where *Proserpin* gathring flowrs
> Her self a fairer Flowr by gloomie *Dis*
> Was gather'd, which cost *Ceres* all that pain
> To seek her through the world; nor that sweet Grove
> Of *Daphne* by *Orontes*, and th' inspir'd
> *Castalian* Spring might with this Paradise

Of *Eden* strive; nor that *Nyseian* Ile
Girt with the River *Triton*, where old *Cham*,
Whom Gentiles *Ammon* call and *Lybian Jove*,
Hid *Amalthea* and her Florid Son
Young *Bacchus* from his stepdame *Rhea's* eye;
Nor where *Abassin* Kings thir issue Guard,
Mount Amora.

(PL 4.268–281)

The parental ideal of sheltered (and suspended) childhood that Lybian Jove shares with the Abyssinian kings is clearly not the Advocate's—or his Client's, for that matter; Eden is a sheepfold
expressly designed for access to wolves, a garden of experience
rather than innocence.

In fact, the fallen Eve speaks less rebelliously than she knows
when she invokes experience as the "best guide" to "wisdom" (*PL*
9.808-10). Unfortunately "wisdom" means natural fact to her. The
opportunity to put her experience to work in a moral engagement
with life awaits her somewhere east of Eden. In that territory—
which is also a place of trial and hence (morally) part of Eden
("Through Eden took thir solitarie way," *PL* 12.649)—good is
known chiefly by evil, and doing the right thing is as taxing to the
wit as to the will:

> Good and evil we know in the field of this world grow up together al-
> most inseparably; and the knowledge of good is so involved and inter-
> woven with the knowledge of evil, and in so many cunning
> resemblances hardly to be discerned, that those confused seeds which
> were imposed on Psyche as an incessant labor to cull out and sort asun-
> der were not more intermixed.

> It was from out the rind of one apple tasted that the knowledge of good
> and evil, as two twins cleaving together, leaped forth into the world.
> And perhaps this is that doom which Adam fell into of knowing good
> and evil, that is to say, of knowing good by evil.[55]

In his speech to a notional Parliament against licensing of printing,
the Advocate supplies three senses in which good and evil are crops
that grow up together and not apart. (a) Some goods and evils are
conceptually "interwoven"; the given good just consists in sur-
mounting the given evil (no gallantry without danger, no fortitude
without suffering. (b) Often a given good and evil are identical

twins; it takes cunning (shrewdness? practical reason?) to tell them apart. (c) Good and evil were twins born "cleaving together"— joined by an overlapping (hence neutral or ambiguous) part; the short way with ambiguities kills the good along with the evil. Whenever you wind up with evil no matter how you choose, right choice calls for a trade-off.

Given (c), the innocence of doves won't see us through "the field of this world" without a touch of the virtues that smack of vice— virtues like courtesy playing the hypocrite, or shame holding back for fear of disgrace, or the cunning of serpents prescribed by the Son and occasionally practised by the Father. In this third sense at least, getting through the "field" takes somebody who has given up speaking or understanding or thinking as a child—somebody who has put childish things away (I Cor. 13:11). It takes an adult:

> Assuredly we bring not innocence into the world, we bring impurity much rather: that which purifies us is trial, and trial is by what is contrary. That virtue therefore which is but a youngling in the contemplation of evil, and knows not the utmost that vice promises to her followers and rejects it, is but a blank virtue, not a pure; her whiteness is but an excremental whiteness.[56]

Not the whiteness of the dove, that is, but the whiteness of the whited sepulchre. The adult's blackened hands, by contrast—where dirtying one's hands is the price of moral engagement—are a badge of honor. Ripeness is all.

The way back is barred by cherubim

> on the ground
> Gliding meteorous, as Ev'ning Mist
> Ris'n from a River o're the marish glides,
> And gathers ground fast at the Labourers heel
> Homeward returning. High in front advanc'd,
> The brandish'd Sword of God before them blaz'd
> Fierce as a Comet which with torrid heat,
> And vapour as the *Libyan* air adust,
> Began to parch that temperate Clime.
>
> (*PL* 12.628–36)

In the ancient rabbinical allegory, the menacingly energetic sword becomes Gehenna, "the type of hell" (*PL* 1.405), and the work of the garden that the sword cuts off forever becomes the work to fol-

4: GOD'S HATRED 221

low: after all, the law too, the moral part of it at least, is a thing to be cultivated—"a tree of life to them that lay hold upon her" (Prov.3:18).[57] The Advocate's narrative at this crucial stage is no allegory. But it carries the flavor of these traditions. The sword again plays the role of hell, scorching Paradise into a desert. But the educational effect of showing this is to wean the mind from a sentimental attachment to place:

> With thee to goe,
> Is to stay here; without thee here to stay,
> Is to go hence unwilling; thou to mee
> Art all things under Heav'n, all places thou.
> (*PL* 12.615–18)

Eve has already learned the lesson of the sword: partners in marriage stay in the true Paradise—the "Paradise within" (*PL* 12.587)—by leaving the outward Paradise *together*; either partner is driven from the true Paradise by staying in the outward one *alone*. In marriage at least, the mind is (or can be) its own place— one little room an everywhere, as Donne says. It turns out that the title of *PL* is a festive paradox: sometimes a paradise lost is a paradise regained.

Once Adam and Eve reach the plain below Eden, their guardian disappears, perhaps to rejoin the "dreadful faces" they see at the Gate as they look back for a moment. They are almost ready:

> Som natural tears they dropp'd, but wip'd them soon;
> *The World was all before them*, where to choose
> Thir place of rest, and Providence thir guide:
> They hand in hand with wandring steps and slow,
> Through *Eden* took thir solitary way.
> (*PL* 12.645–49; italics mine)

"The World was all before them" chimes with two later scenes in the history of God's nomads. In one, the righteous king Abimelech restores Sarah to her husband Abraham, whose status as a prophet of God has been revealed to Abimilech (Gen. 20:7): "Behold *my land is before thee*: dwell where it pleaseth thee" (Gen. 20:15). In the other, the captain of the Babylonian guard is moved, in spite of himself, to give Jeremiah his freedom: "Behold, I loose thee this day from the chains which were upon thine hand. If it seem good unto thee to come with me to Babylon, come, and I will look well

unto thee: but if it seem ill unto thee to come with me unto Babylon, forbear: behold *all the land is before thee*: whither it seemeth
good and convenient for thee to go, thither go" (Jer. 40:4).

In both scenes, God's nomad is finally on his own; his lines and
life, in Herbert's phrase, are "free, free as the road, / Loose as the
wind"—with no guide in sight. In the first scene, the work to be
addressed en route is domestic, the fashioning of a marriage; the
parallel with Adam and Eve is obvious. In the second, God's nomad
is outward bound on the work of prophecy (though in fact Abraham
too is identified as a prophet); left free to choose his resting place—
"behold, all the land is before thee"—Jeremiah elects to stay in
Judea, in a town named Watchtower (Mizpah)—like the "hill of
speculation" (*PL* 12.588) from which Adam surveys the future of
his race (*specula* = "watchtower"). A prophet like Jeremiah or
Abraham is God's sentinel as well as his spokesman.

Adam too is a nomadic partner in conversation with God. Michael's visit has the effect, among other things, of blocking a seductive misreading of the Advocate's preface to the temptation story:

> No more of talk where God or Angel Guest
> With Man, as with his Friend, familiar us'd
> To sit indulgent, and with him partake
> Rural repast, permitting him the while
> Venial discourse unblam'd. I now must change
> Those notes to Tragic.
>
> (*PL* 9.1–6)

The narrator is shifting key from idyllic "notes" to "tragic"—for
good; he will have no more to say about familiar talk between God
and Man. What he isn't doing is announcing that, thanks to the Fall,
familiar talk between God and man is about to end. When Adam
flirts with precisely this despair, Michael quickly puts him right:

> Yet doubt not but in Vallie and in Plain
> God is as here, and will be found alike
> Present, and of his presence many a sign
> Still following thee, still compassing thee round
> With goodness and paternal Love, his Face
> Express, and of his steps the track Divine.
>
> (*PL* 11.349–54)

In spite of the "dreadful Faces" that seem to have replaced it, the
Face of God hasn't been withdrawn after all. The interrupted dia-

logue with God has already been resumed, along with the interrupted dialogue between Adam and Eve. One episode in that
dialogue is the couple's free but "guided" choice of resting place
(*PL* 12.646–47). Another—with comic irony—is Adam's prophetic
history lesson on the hill of speculation.

Why should the Advocate interest himself in all this? How does
this final vision of ripening and pilgrimage help the precarious case
for his Client's lovingkindness? The obvious answer—maybe too
obvious—is that all the nomads of God are Christians *avant la lettre*. The "promises" they see afar off will be sealed by the ordeal
of the One Just Man par excellence:

> The Law of God exact he shall fulfil
> Both by obedience and by love, though love
> Alone fulfil the Law; thy punishment
> He shall endure by coming in the Flesh
> To a reproachful life and cursed death,
> Proclaiming Life to all who shall believe
> In his redemption, and that his obedience
> Imputed becomes theirs by Faith, his merits
> To save them, not thir own though legal works.
> For this, he shall live hated, be blasphem'd,
> Seis'd on by force, judg'd, and to death condemn'd
> A shameful and accurst, nail'd to the Cross
> By his own Nation.
>
> (*PL* 12.402–14)

This revelation of future history is enough to convert Adam to
Christianity (*PL* 12.572–73). He has learned that suffering for truth
ends in victory, and he acknowledges Christ as his redeemer (*PL*
12.569–70). But Christian triumphalism doesn't mend the gaping
holes in the Great Argument we've spent this chapter inspecting.
Triumphalism just energetically changes the subject. On the Advocate's own showing, the incapacity to sin doesn't rule out freewill,
and a plausible scapegoat jurisprudence is conspicuous by its absence. Except for some declamatory gestures, the end of *PL* isn't
about victory. It's about coming of age, and setting out on a journey
whose destination cannot be fixed before it is reached.

To make a connection to the Great Argument, we have to look in
another direction: remember that the Creator too embarks on such
a journey—the act of creation itself. The crux of God's defense[58] in
PL is the claim that there are feats not even an omnipotent being

can bring off, on pain of logical absurdity. God, as we've seen, is the supreme adult called on to make his peace with an ambiguous reality.

The capacity to give the kind of love God wants from his creatures doesn't come pure; it's born a Siamese twin, "cleaving together" with the capacity to withhold love. A world history in which that two-in-one ability is exercised doesn't unfold with lawful inevitability from its initial conditions; freewill breaks the chain of causes and thereby brings luck into the world—*bad* luck, as it happens. By the exasperating logic of foreknowledge, God can't call off the freewill experiment and thereby make prudent use of his *knowledge* that Adam and Eve will fall; what makes it knowledge is precisely that they *will* fall—that is, that he *doesn't* call it off.

The best God can do with the unspeakably bad luck that disfigures human history is to crown that history with a happy ending—an ending so abundantly happy that it puts Adam into a terrible quandary:

> O goodness infinite, goodness immense!
> That all this good of evil shall produce,
> And evil turn to good; more wonderful
> Then that which by creation first brought forth
> Light out of darkness! full of doubt I stand
> Whether I should repent me now of sin
> By mee done and occasion'd, or rejoyce
> Much more, that much more good thereof shall spring,
> To God more glory, more good will to Men
> From God, and over wrauth grace shall abound.
>
> (*PL* 12.469–78)

The Easter Proclamation in the ancient liturgy "echoes" Adam, but without his becoming hesitation ("full of doubt I stand . . ."):

(a) O surely needful was Adam's sin that by the death of Christ has been destroyed!

(b) O happy blame that has deserved to have such and so great a Redeemer![59]

For a sin to be needful is for it to bring about a good that would have been impossible otherwise. For a blameworthy act to be happy is for it to bring about (unintentionally) a happy result.

The danger of the first claim is the appearance of suggesting that this bonus of happiness depends on the failure of the freewill experiment. But the Advocate, at least, has already staked out the opposite position; success of the experiment would have meant happiness to the superlative degree, admission to the company of angels:

> And from these corporal nutriments perhaps
> Your bodies may at last turn all to Spirit,
> Improv'd by tract of time, and wing'd ascend
> Ethereal as wee, or may at choice
> Here or in Heav'nly Paradises dwell;
> If ye be found obedient, and retain
> Unalterably firm his love entire
> Whose progenie you are.
>
> (*PL* 5.496–503)

The danger of the second claim—with its central notions of happy blame and evil "turned to" good—is that at first glance it seems to represent the past (absurdly) as revisable; what happened is caused to be other than it was. But this would be to read the claim literally—that is, to *mis*read it. The Advocate is a metaphorist, not a weak logician. For past evil to *turn into* present good is for it to be *followed by* present good—by a consolation.

In the middle of the story, people go wrong and suffer badly and die worse, no matter what happens to them later. The horror isn't mitigated, much less turned into a non-horror, by coming in the middle, or by being misremembered from the vantage point of present good; the good isn't enhanced by coming at the end, or by showing the horror only through the wrong end of a telescope. It isn't after all quite true, on the showing of *PL* 12, that the best God can do with the unspeakably bad luck that disfigures human history is to compensate its victims at history's end. He can't do anything with it directly at all; facts can't be changed into non-facts.

The real point of the Easter Proclamation is that the best God can do with the fact of unspeakable suffering is to share it, by entering the natural order in the person of the Son:

> Thy punishment
> He shall endure by coming in the Flesh
> To a reproachful life and cursed death.
>
> (*PL* 12.404–6)

Once again, "thy punishment / He shall endure" clearly can't mean that he spares others the punishment of a reproachful life, etc., by enduring it himself; he isn't the only one who has been, or will be, "to death condemn'd / A shameful and accurs'd, nail'd to the Cross" (*PL* 12.412–13). That, in fact, is the point: he is very far from the only one. The punishment is "reproachful," "shameful," "accurs'd," because the Roman Empire reserves it as the last humiliation of the wretched of the earth, the obscene basis of the slavemaster's favorite sneer: that to be a slave is to be fit for nothing else.[60]

The currency of the Son's ransom—the Passion that buys the fallen a second chance—is *Com*passion (in the root sense of the word); only by "coming in the flesh," can he manage to *share* suffering. The value of this gift, in short, is only partly utilitarian; acts of radical compassion justify themselves even if they come to nothing. The Advocate has already tried to make sense of this difficult and perhaps implausible Christian idea in a much earlier reflection on the God of history:

> That glorious Form, that Light unsufferable,
> And that far-beaming blaze of Majesty,
> Wherewith he wont at Heav'ns high Council-Table,
> To sit the midst of Trinal Unity,
> He laid aside; and *here with us to be*,
> Forsook the Courts of everlasting Day,
> And chose with us a darksom House of mortal Clay.
> (*On the Morning of Christ's Nativity* 8–14)

By "emptying out" his divinity (Paul's term, Phil. 2:7), the Son contrives not only to redeem us, but quite simply to be *with* us.

The Gospel analogue (and perhaps prototype) of the Happy Blame Paradox is Christ's hard saying that "ioy shall be in heauen for one sinner that conuerteth, more then for ninetie and nine iust men, which need none amendment of life" (Luke 15:7). Does this really mean (as it seems to) that it pays to fail the first time around provided one manages to make the best of one's second chance? If so, the Prodigal's elder brother has reason to be bitter: "Loe, these many yeeres haue I done thee seruice, neither brake I at any time thy commandement, and yet thou neuer gauest me a Kidde that I might make merrie with my friends. But when this thy [Prodigal] sonne was come, which hath devoured thy goods with harlots, thou hast for his sake killed the fat Calfe" (Luke 15:19 [Geneva]).

But in fact it turns out that the elder son hasn't been slighted; true, there has been no kid to offset the Prodigal's fatted calf, but there has been something vastly better: "Sonne, thou art euer with me, and all that I haue, is thine" (Luke 15:31 [Geneva]). The question remains: why is it more joyful for God to find what he lost than simply to keep what he never lost in the first place (Luke 15:31, 15:6)? In both associated parables (Lost Sheep, Prodigal Son), suffering gets shared; both are rites of compassion: God has to "*goe after* that which is lost, till he find it*" (Luke 15:4 [Geneva]); the Prodigal "was *yet a great way off* [when] *his father saw him and had compassion* and ranne and fell on his necke, and kissed him" (Luke 15:20 [Geneva]). God ends by saving his fallen creatures. Better still, he begins by quite simply *being* (that is, suffering) *with* them.

By the last book of *PL* the idyllic "notes" have long since been transposed to "tragic" (*PL* 9.1–6); now the tragedy expands beyond the human sufferers to God himself, in the person of his Son—creator, redeemer, and judge—who joins his creatures as a human victim of the indeterminacy without which there can be no love. How does this parting vision of pilgrimage help the precarious case for his Client's lovingkindness? It *is* the case.

On the showing of *PL* 11–12, a profound sadness lies at the heart of life, in fact at the heart of being, in fact at the heart of God. By way of complement if not corrective to the notion of a God of just but terrible anger, the Advocate invites us to contemplate the notion (in Eliot's reticent phrase) "of some infinitely gentle / Infinitely · suffering thing."[61] At the end of *PL*, we watch Adam and Eve newly ripened to adulthood and to a tragic vision that they share with God. They are now ready to enter the world of adults, with all its ambiguity and complexity.

Taken together with everything that prepares the way for it, this vision has, I think, a magnificence unavailable to comedy, however divine. Maybe it has some claim to being an imaginative vindication of the humanistic idea that persons and their value are at least as much a part of the basic structure of reality as elementary particles and their powers.

Does it clinch the Advocate's case as he explicitly defines it? Have the ways of God been vindicated? I think not, for the reasons I've been exploring in this chapter. But I respect the Advocate's clear intention. At the end of the day, this question is not for me to decide. At least it is not for me to decide alone. Only the jury can decide it, acting in concert. The jury is still out.

Notes

INTRODUCTION

1. The intended figure of speech is metonymy. Compare ascribing blondness, loudness, blushing, etc., to the whole person rather than to the relevant part.

2. Stephen M. Fallon, *Milton and the Philosophers* (Ithaca: Cornell University Press, 1991); Harinder Singh Marjara *Contemplation of Created Things* (Toronto: University of Toronto Press, 1992).

3. Joan S. Bennett, *Reviving Liberty: Radical Christian Humanism in Milton's Great Poems* (Cambridge: Harvard University Press, 1989); J. M. Evans, *"Paradise Lost" and the Genesis Tradition* (Oxford: The Clarendon Press, 1968); Dennis H. Burden, *The Logical Epic: A Study of the Argument of "Paradise Lost"* (London: Routledge and Kegan Paul, 1967); C. A. Patrides, *Milton and the Christian Tradition* (Oxford: The Clarendon Press, 1966); Hugh MacCallum, *Milton and the Sons of God* (Toronto: University of Toronto Press, 1986); Dennis Richard Danielson, *Milton's Good God: A Study in Literary Theodicy* (Cambridge: Cambridge University Press, 1982), Helen Gardner, *A Reading of "Paradise Lost"* (Oxford: The Clarendon Press, 1965)

4. Barbara Kiefer Lewalski, *"Paradise Lost" and the Rhetoric of Literary Forms* (Princeton: Princeton University Press, 1985)

CHAPTER 1. GOD'S ATTORNEY: NARRATIVE AS ARGUMENT

1. Ludwig Rademacher, ed., *Quintiliani Institutionis oratoriae libri duodecim* (Leipzig: Ludwig Rademacher and Vincent Buchheit, 1959), 1:205, 201. Also: "Quid inter probationem et narrationem interest, nisi quod narratio est probationis continua propositio, rursus probatio narrationi congruens confirmatio?" (1:213).

2. "Nec quisquam reprensione dignum putet, quod proposuerim eam [scil. narrationem] quae sit tota pro nobis debere esse veri similem, cum vera sit. sunt enim plurima vera quidem, sed parum credibilia, sicut falsa quoque frequenter veri similia. quare non minus laborandum est, ut iudex quae vere dicimus quam quae fingimus credat" (Quintilian, *Institutio*, 1:205).

3. *Reason of Church Government*, 2.3; in F. A. Patterson, ed., *The Student's Milton*, (New York: Appleton Century Crofts, 1957), 529b.

4. Quintilian, *Institutio*, 1:219–20.

5. Ibid., 1:208–09.

6. Ibid., 211.

7. Ibid., 11–13, 18–20.

8. Ibid., 222.

9. "Demons" is the ancient Jewish rendering in Greek of Heb. *'elil*, "idol"; see *LXX* and the Vulgate ad loc.

10. Homer, *Odyssey* 1.34; quoted with approval in *De doctrina christiana*, *The Works of John Milton*, ed. F. A. Patterson et al. (New York: Columbia University Press, 1937), 14:174.

11. "Theodicy" is Leibniz's pseudo-Greek, of course, not mine. But in the venerable tradition Milton and Leibniz both inherit, the coinage is inescapable.

12. Richard Swinburne, "Does Theism Need a Theodicy?" *Canadian Journal of Philosophy* 18 (1988), 287–311. *"[The theist] does not need a theodicy in the sense of God's actual reasons for allowing some evil to occur.*. . . Barring very strong evidence of the existence of God, an inquirer does at any rate need a theodicy with respect to some of the evils in the world which seem to him to count against the existence of God, which would lead him to suppose that a theodicy is to be had with respect to other evils" (298; italics mine).

13. See Swinburne, 303–4. For e = evidence of evil, h = the hypothesis that e is due to providence, h_j = alternative explanations of e, and k = background knowledge, Bayes's theorem equates the posterior probability of h given e—i.e., $P(h|e.k)$—with $P(e|h.k)$ x $P(h|k)$ divided by $P(e|h.k)P(h|k)$ + $P(e|h_1.k)P(h_1|k)$ + $P(e|h_2.k)P(h_2|k)$ etc., where (i) $P(e|h.k)$ is the predictive power of h—i.e., how probable h makes e; (ii) the denominator sums up to the prior probability of e—i.e., $P(e|k)$; (iii) the explanatory power of h is measured by how many times more likely e is given h than e is in itself—i.e., $P(e|h.k)$ / $P(e|k)$. Note that the less likely the alternatives are in themselves and the less likely they make e, the more powerful h becomes as an explanation of e. Note also that $P(h|e.k) > P(h|k)$ if and only if $P(e|h.k) > P(e|k)$—i.e., e confirms h just in case (and to the same degree as) h confirms e (303–4). But then, if h entails f and f doesn't entail e, $P(h.f|e.k) > P(h.f|k)$ if and only if $P(e|h.f.k) > P(e|k)$; e.g., the existence of evil confirms (rather than disconfirms) the existence of a libertarian God if and only if the existence of a libertarian God confirms the existence of evil.

14. See Swinburne, 308: "This will depend on [the explanatory power of the theodicy $P(e|h.f.k) > P(e|k)$—i.e.,] how probable it is that, whether or not there is a God, evil will occur; how probable it is that if there is a God, he will bring about freedom; and how probable it is that freedom will lead to evil. Loosely, one may say that evil will confirm the existence of God only if it is very probable that God will bring about freedom and very probable that freedom will lead to evil, and not very probable that evil will occur if there is no God. Otherwise evil will be irrelevant or disconfirmatory."

15. Ibid.

16. J. M. Evans, *"Paradise Lost" and the Genesis Tradition*, 61.

17. The Greek formula is *so'dzein ta phainomena*; cf., e.g., Proclus, *Hypotyposis astronomicarum positionum* 5.10, ed. C. Manitius (Leipzig: Teubner, 1909). For the equivalent English phrase see, e.g., Bishop Edward Stillingfleet, *Origines sacrae* (London: Henry Mortlock, 1662) 3.1.9. The explanatory theories of the Ptolemaics and Copernicans invite Raphael's ridicule because (a) the only way they can "contrive / To save appearances" (*PL* 8.82) is by grotesquely multiplying entities in violation of the principle of parsimony (Ockham's razor) and (b) they do the job equally well—appearances decline to choose between them.

18. Targum ad loc. gives Aramaic *ya'aqem dina'*, "curve judgment," for Hebrew *ya'awweth mishp/at*, "make judgment crooked," and Aramaic *yqalqel tzidqa'*, "devalue righteousness," for *ya'awweth tzedeq*, "make righteousness crooked." *LXX* gives *adikései krínon*, "do wrong as a judge," and (*NB*) *taráxei to díkaion*, "disturb the [property of being] just."

19. Actually, on the showing of the text, God *is* somebody's debtor. His current argument is a rehash of Elihu ben Barach'el's at 35:7.

20. The Aramaic version has *bar nash* ("son of man").

21. *Mesítes* (*LXX*).

22. *Elénchein*(*LXX*).

23. Targum: *shechinah*.

24. Compare Heb. *'Iyyob*, "enemy," and *'Oy/eb*, "Job."

25. Aramaic *ba'al debaba'* has all these nuances.

26. Targum: *phitqa'*.

27. Note that at 36:22–23 *LXX* sees power where Targum and Masora see providence: we get *"tis estin kat' auton dynast/es"* for *"mi cam/ohu m/oreh"*.

28. Targum *shiqra'* for Biblical *'awel*, "iniquity".

29. Targum *melaph theritzutha'* for Masoretic *moreh*.

30. Targum *'ilitha'* for Biblical *'awla'*.

31. Significantly, the Targum uses the relevant technical terms borrowed by Aramaic from juridical Greek—*parakletos* and *kategor* respectively.

32. The Targum's *milcca'*, "counsel," is derived from the word for king. *LXX* supplies *boulé*.

33. Neil Forsyth, *The Old Enemy: Satan and the Combat Myth* (Princeton: Princeton University Press, 1987), 121, 123.

34. Martin Luther, *De servo arbitrio*, ed. A. Freitag, in *Luthers Werke* (Weimar: Boehlau, 1908), 18:633: "Fides est rerum non apparentium. Ut ergo fidei locus sit, opus est ut omnia quae creduntur abscondantur. Non autem remotius absconduntur quam sub contrario obiecto, sensu, experientia. Sic Deus dum vivificat, facit illud occidendo; dum iustificat, facit illud reos faciendo; dum in caelum vehit, facit id ad infernum ducendo, ut dicit scriptura [1 Sam. 2:6 Vulg.]: Dominus mortificat et vivificat, deducit ad inferos et reducit, 1 Regum 2. . . . Sic aeternam suam clementiam et misericordiam abscondit sub aeterna ira, iustitiam sub iniquitate. Hic est fidei summus gradus, credere illum esse clementem, qui tam paucos salvat, tam multos damnat, credere iustum, qui sua voluntate nos necessario damnabiles facit, ut videatur referente Erasmo delectari cruciatibus miserorum et odio potius quam amore dignus. Si igitur possem ulla ratione comprehendere quomodo is Deus sit misericors et iustus, qui tantam iram et iniquitatem ostendit, non esset opus fide. Nunc cum id comprehendi non potest, fit locus exercendae fidei, dum talia praedicantur et invulgantur, non aliter quam dum Deus occidit, fides vitae in morte exercetur."

35. Isa. 1:18, 43:26; cf. Micah 6:2, 5, Jer. 2:9.

36. Erasmus, *Hyperaspistes* I, quoted by Freitag, 633 n. 2.

37. See, e.g., Origen, *perì archôn* 3.1.21, Migne, *Patrologia Graeca* 11:297C ff.; Erasmus, *De libero arbitrio diatribe sive collatio*, ed. Hans von Walter (Leipzig: Deichert, 1935), 50 (3a6). Milton paraphrases "gratiam faciam cui faciam" (Ex. 33:19) as "ne nunc latius causas ⌐narrem." On Rom. 9:20–21: "hoc enim iuris vindicat sibi Deus ut quivis alius in res suas, ut statuat de iis pro arbitrio

suo nec rationem reddere cogatur quamvis iustissimam reddere si velit possit." See Milton, *De doctrina christiana*, *Works*, 146.

38. The aim of divine mercy is "ad gloriam misericordiae gratiae sapientiaeque suae *patefaciendam*" (Milton, *Works*, 14:102). Compare the aim of creation, "ad *patefaciendam* potentiae et bonitatis suae gloriam" (15:40), and the aim of predestination, "ratio interim adeoque laus divinae non solum gratiae verum etiam sapientiae ac iustititae aliquanto clarius elucet. Quem *finem* praedestinationi Deus proposuit sibi *primarium*" (14:140). Italics mine.

39. Lewalski, *"Paradise Lost" and the Rhetoric of Literary Forms* 120. Compare Louis L. Martz, *Poet of Exile: A Study of Milton's Poetry* (New Haven: Yale University Press, 1980): "Milton's God is pleading with mankind, *perhaps a little too anxiously*, to understand the gift of freedom" (98; italics mine). Just so—even though Martz fudges his point by deferring momentarily to a perverse but fashionable critic: "*Perhaps the speech is designed to have a neutral quality*, but it seems impossible to read this passage aloud without creating either a harsh defensive tone or a tone of grieved lament." (Italics mine.) What keeps the speech from accommodating a neutral delivery if not its "design"?

Actually the tone *isn't* neutral—precisely for reasons of rhetorical "design." It is—without the petulance implied by modern usage—defensive, even harsh. Unlike some of his modern readers, the Advocate thinks there are theological views that amount to inadvertent blasphemy; the false authority that gives them currency does harm to consciences. A God they didn't anger might be agreeably free of "harshness," but he would also be less than just. In defending himself—or rather rehearsing a defense—God is defending his creatures from the dangers of getting him wrong. He is not only "pleading *with*" mankind, he is pleading *for* it. Whether he does so "too anxiously" depends on one's assessment of those dangers.

40. Dennis Richard Danielson, *Milton's Good God*, 129: "The paradigms of theodicy we have considered—the Son's and Adam's requests for justification of God's ways . . .—have been characterized by a lack of any adversarial 'arguing with God.' " Maybe the critic would have better luck finding adversarial dialogue in *PL* 3 if he weren't averse to finding it—if (e.g.) he shared the Advocate's Socratic view that part of intellectual love is to call the beloved to account.

41. Both suggestions are due to Lewalski, *"Paradise Lost" and the Rhetoric of Literary Forms*, 94–95.

42. MacCallum, *Milton and the Sons of God*, 142.

43. Lewalski, *"Paradise Lost" and the Rhetoric of Literary Forms*, 210.

44. John Calvin, *Ioannis Calvini Institutio christianae religionis*, ed. A. Tholuck (Berlin: Gustav Eichler, 1834), 2:148 (3.23.2). Compare Aquinas: "Only God's will is the measure [*regula*] of [the rightness of] its act, because that will is not ordered to a higher end" (*Sancti Thomae Aquinatis Summa Theologica* [Turin: Marietti, 1922], 1:407a [1.63.1]). Actually Aquinas's language in the surrounding passage is decidedly more voluntaristic than Calvin's, though I think equally misleading.

45. Actually, *neo*platonist theme; see Plotinus, *Enneades*, ed. Émile Bréhier (Paris: Les Belles Lettres, 1963), 6 (2):145–46 (6.8.10): the Good isn't subject to law or necessity because it *is* law and necessity for what is subsequent.

46. Luther, *De servo arbitrio*, 18:712.

47. Ibid., 785.

48. Hobbes, *The English Works of Thomas Hobbes*, ed. William Molesworth (1840; reprint Aalen [Germany]: Scientia, 1962), 4:260.

49. Ibid., 3:257.

50. For Augustine and Plotinus, among many others, it isn't so obvious that animals don't enjoy at least a *prima facie* right not to be tortured—a presumption that needs to be defeated by argument. See (St.) Augustine, *De libero arbitrio* 3.23.69 (edition consulted William Green's, reprinted Berlin: Tempsky, 1956), *Enneades* 3.2.15.

51. Thomas Hobbes, *Thomae Hobbes Malmesburiensis Opera Philosophica quae latine scripta sunt omnia*, ed. William Molesworth (London: Longman, Brown, Green, and Longman, 1845), 3:256.

52. Milton, *Works,* 15:116.

53. Ibid., 114.

54. Just as the second "e" in "receptus" is an umlauted "a," (< "re-captus"), so the "oe" in "oboedire" is an umlauted "au."

55. Milton, *Works,* 15:114. Cf. *PL* 3.94–95.

56. Lewalski, *"Paradise Lost" and the Rhetoric of Literary Forms* 96, 95.

57. See, e.g., Augustine, *De libero arbitrio* 1.6.14–15. Compare 2.9.27.

58. Principle and circumstance supply the major and minor premises of what Aristotle calls the practical syllogism.

59. See, e.g., Michael Lieb, *Poetics of the Holy: A Reading of "Paradise Lost"* (Chapel Hill: University of North Carolina Press, 1981), 95, 99, 102, 104–6; John Stachniewski, *The Persecutory Imagination* (Oxford: Clarendon Press, 1991), 362.

60. Hobbes, *Opera latine scripta*, 3:42. Translation mine.

61. Hobbes, *The English Works*, 4:255–56.

62. Hobbes, *Opera latine scripta*, 2:96.

63. Ibid., 3:157–58.

64. Ibid., 100.

65. Ibid., 122.

66. Ibid., 3:102, 2:169–70.

67. Ibid., 3:198, 200.

68. Ibid., 2:195–96.

69. Hobbes, *English Works*, 3:117.

70. Ibid., 3:127.

71. Ibid.

72. Ibid., 115.

73. Ibid., 130–31.

74. Calvin, *Institutio christianae religionis* 4.14.6: "Dominus promissiones suas 'foedera' nuncupat." This metaphor becomes a term of art in the covenant theology of the Westminster Confession (1647). Actually, for the covenant theologians, the human obligation to obey God's command is grounded in subordination and the duty of thanksgiving, not in binding agreement. David A. Weir seems to slight the figurativeness of the passages he usefully reproduces in *The Origins of Federal Theology in Sixteenth-Century Reformation Thought* (Oxford: Clarendon Press, 1990).

According to the Confession, the binding force of the moral law derives from (i) its contents, and (ii) God's "author_ty" as its creator (chapter 19.5). The so-called covenant is no more and no less than God's "voluntary condescension"—

his unilateral promise to reward an obedience to which Adam and Eve were already bound (chapter 7.1). Strictly, "reward" is also metaphorical when it denotes a response to the act of meeting one's obligation: as Adam finally concedes, "thy [i.e., my—he's talking to himself] reward was of his grace [as opposed to his justice or fairness]" (*PL* 10.767).

Vossius (1618) says that the Fall entailed a total rejection of the "covenant between God and man"—but only by being fundamentally a sin of ingratitude toward God, and of *astorgia* (failure of fatherly and motherly love) toward posterity. As defined by Ursinus, the "covenant of nature" is not bilateral, and so not a contract; the divine promise isn't met with a counter-promise: "Lex requirit a nobis perfectam oboedientiam erga Deum et praestantibus eam [scilicet oboedientiam] promittit vitam aeternam, non praestantibus minatur aeternas poenas" (quoted by Weir, 113). This despite Ursinus's definition of covenant as "mutua pactio *duarum partium*" (Weir, 113; italics mine).

Dudley Fenner's version of the covenant: "Deus stipulatur se fore hominibus in Deum ad benedictionem vitae, prout condicionem annexam impletam habuerint; sin minus, contra" (quoted by Weir, 151 n. 23). "Homo recipit se fore Deo in populum ad benedictionem, prout condicionem annexam impletam habuerit" (ibid.). In other words, man's role is simply to receive a promise, not to make a counter-promise. Without the latter ("consideration"), Adam is no party to a literal contract. This is exactly the situation in *PL* 10. Milton's only quarrel with covenant theology, in short, is rejection of a misleading figure of speech.

75. "Status et Respublicas sine foederibus, non autem sine iustitia subsistere posse." See *John Milton's Writings in the Anglo-Dutch Negotiations 1651–1654*, ed. Leo Miller (Pittsburgh: Duquesne University Press, 1992), 192.

76. *Doctrine and Discipline of Divorce* 2.4; see *The Student's Milton*, 602a.

77. In *Torah and Law in "Paradise Lost"* (Princeton: Princeton University Press, 1994), Jason Rosenblatt, by dint of resolutely selective reading, succeeds in convincing himself of the virtual equation of sin and the Mosaic law in Romans 6 and the first verses of Romans 7. For a reliable commentary on these chapters see (besides Calvin, Bullinger, Wolleb, Cartwright, and Owen) the annotations in the Geneva Bible.

78. Calvin, *Institutio*, 1:233 (2.7.7). Rosenblatt, 172, quotes John Cotton's remark that "the obedience of [the Law], and comfort in that obedience, doth harden the hearts of others from Christ" because these "others" "come to find more comfort in their obedience than in the grace of God." According to Rosenblatt, Cotton is asserting here that "those who obey [the Law] avoid Christ out of hardheartedness." But Cotton is warning against the hardhearted—that is, obstinate—pride of taking "comfort" in one's obedience, rather than in the grace that makes obedience possible. The antinomianism, as usual, is an artifact of selective reading.

79. Calvin, *Institutio*, 237 (2.7.14).

80. See Aristotle, *Ethica Nicomachea* 1137b11–27 (consulted in Ingram Bywater's edition [Oxford: Clarendon Press, 1920]); also Guido Kisch, *Erasmus und die Jurisprudenz seiner Zeit* (Basel: Helbing & Lichtenhahn, 1960).

81. Milton, *Works*, 16:140, 141; 17:8.

82. Jacob Arminius *Iacobi Arminii veteraquinatis batavi sanctae theologiae Doctoris eximii OPERA THEOLOGICA* (Frankfurt: William Fitzer, 1631), 507. Translation mine.

83. Cf. Helen Gardner, *A Reading of "Paradise Lost"* (Oxford: The Clarendon Press, 1965), 25: "If, as I have said, I am unable to believe that when Milton declared that his purpose was 'to assert Eternal Providence' he thought of himself as providing a solution to the difficulties inherent in the Biblical doctrine of God that would satisfy the unaided reason, I am also unable to believe that he was happily unaware of the dilemma that the rendering of this conception in epic form inevitably posed. Indeed, *far from trying to disguise the problem, he again and again obtrudes it on the reader.*" (Italics mine.) *Pace* Gardner, the Advocate is entitled to be taken at his word; the "men" to whom the ways of God will be "justified" are men *tout court*, not men specially equipped. But she is clearly and crucially right about "the generosity and intellectual candour that reign in *Paradise Lost*" (ibid.).

84. But see Millicent Bell, 'The Fallacy of the Fall,' *PMLA* 68 (1953), 870; and Dennis Burden, *The Logical Epic: A Study of the Argument of "Paradise Lost"* (London: Routledge and Kegan Paul, 1967), 94.

85. Burden, *The Logical Epic:* 96.

86. Evans, *"Paradise Lost" and the Genesis Tradition* 252.

87. Pliny, *Naturalis historia* 8.78.

88. Cf. Italian "*a suo parere.*"

89. Cf. Augustine, *De civitate Dei* 13.21: "Nemo itaque prohibet intellegere . . . lignum scientiae boni et mali [figurata significatione] transgressi mandati experimentum."

90. Thomas à Kempis, *De imitatione Christi libri quattuor*, 1.13.6: "Vigilandum tamen est, praecipue circa initium tentationis: quia tunc hostis facilius vincitur, si ostium mentis nullatenus intrare sinitur; sed extra limen, statim ut pulsaverit, illi obviatur." "Primo occurrit mentis simplex cogitatio: postea delectatio, et motus pravus, et assensio." Quotation is from the Parma edition (*ex imperiali typographia*) of 1807.

91. Cf. John M. Steadman, *Milton and the Paradoxes of Renaissance Heroism* (Baton Rouge: Louisiana State University Press, 1987), 39: "[Adam's decision] to risk death rather than separation from his lady would be heroic in the context of chivalric romance." It's clear that risking death to rescue one's lady earns admiration in romance; less clear that incurring death to spare oneself the pain of missing her earns more than pity.

92. Cf. Dennis Richard Danielson, *Milton's Good God*, ix: "If Milton presents a God who is wicked, or untruthful, or manipulative, or feeble, or unwise, then his epic poem must suffer *accordingly*. But if that poem recognizes the case that is brought against the Christian God and counters it (even if not conclusively) with a high degree of philosophical and literary credibility, then the poem and the poet must be praised *accordingly*."

CHAPTER 2. FREE WILL IN *PARADISE LOST* AND ITS HISTORICAL ROOTS

1. Calvini, *Institutio christinae religionis*, 2:151 (3.23.7).
2. Ibid., 1.18.3.
3. Ibid., 3.23.8.

4. Aquinas, *Summa theologiae* 1.83.1 ad 3. Translation mine.

5. *De correptione et gratia* cap. 14, Migne, *Patrologia Latina* 44.

6. René Descartes, *Oeuvres de Descartes*, ed. Charles Adam and Paul Tannery (Paris: Léopold Cerf, 1897–1910), 8:20. Cf. Descartes, 5:269–70.

7. Luther, *De servo arbitrio*, 18:636.

8. Ibid., 615–16.

9. Erasmus, *De libero arbitrio*, 50 (IIIa6).

10. Cf. "Nobis ut quid impingitis crimen ob hoc, quod dicimus praedestinasse deum homines sive ad iustititam sive ad peccatum?" (Augustine, Migne PATROLOGIA LATINA 53:623a). "Ut autem peccando hoc vel hoc illa malitia faciant, non est in eorum potestate, sed dei dividentis tenebras et ordinantis eas" (44:984). "His testimoniis manifestatur, operari deum in cordibus hominum ad inclinandas eorum voluntates quodcumque voluerit, sive ad bona pro sua misericordia, sive ad mala pro meritis eorum" (44:909).

11. Erasmus, *De libero arbitrio*, 10.

12. Ibid., 33; IIa14. Cf. 34, 41.

13. Luther, *De servo arbitrio*, 18:719.

14. Ibid., 685–86.

15. "Illudit autem sese Diatribe ignorantia sua, dum nihil distinguit inter Deum praedicatum et absconditum, hoc est inter verbum Dei et Deum ipsum" (Ibid.).

16. Namely, *praeter fatum*. Milton, *Works*, 14:174. See *Odyssey* 1.34.

17. Milton, *Works*, 14:88: "quos refellere si coner idem agam ac si prolixe disputem Deum non esse Diabolum."

18. Cf. Augustine, *De libero arbitrio* 1.16.35.

19. Cf. the cognitive uses of Latin *concipio*, classical Greek *kyeo*, Biblical. Hebrew. *harah*.

20. For *fornicatio spiritualis*, see Aquinas, *Summa theologica* 2–2.151.2.

21. Thinking up the sin and sharing the thought aggravate the guilt of consenting. Thus Satan is guiltier than Adam (*De libero arbitrio* 3.10.29).

22. Arminius, *Opera*, 511.

23. Aristotle, *Politica* 1259a38-b4, 1260b15–20 (edition consulted, Franz Susemihl [Leipzig: Teubner, 1882]).

24. MacCallum, *Milton and the Sons of God* 155–56.

25. Cf. ibid., 154: "[Eve] is, in fact, simply echoing Raphael's final words to Adam, words that she confesses to having overheard." This useful remark is perfectly at odds with the rest of the critic's discussion.

26. Bennett, *Reviving Liberty*, 111, argues that Eve "feels an urge toward independent action and a greater personal efficiency than is possible, or necessary, or desirable in the prelapsarian balance." In particular, by claiming that she doesn't need Adam's help to keep faith, Eve is "declining" his help; she fails to understand that prelapsarian obedience is a "collaborative exercise" (115). In failing, Eve doesn't sin, but she does (along with compliant Adam) lose her "balance" and become "more vulnerable than usual to a push from the enemy" (111).

But Eve isn't declining Adam's help—that is, she isn't refusing to accept help. Whether or not she eventually accepts help, at this point she's saying that she doesn't need help to avoid sinning—and (by implication) that "sinning" for lack of needed help isn't sinning anyhow, because it isn't free. In short, she's rejecting an assertion, not an offer—the assertion that, as Bennett puts it, "perfect freedom is, in a way that Eve fails to realize, 'frail' " (116). The Advocate had better join Eve in her rejection if he means to win his case on God's behalf. If freedom unaided is "frail" ("vulnerable" to the Tempter's "push"), then it *isn't* perfect; in one fell swoop, "frailty" supplies the unaided Eve with an excuse for falling and deprives the Advocate's Client of a defense against the *prima facie* injustice of making the fall a hanging offense.

Bennett thinks that "Eve does not sin when she decides to leave, because the decision facing her is not a moral one; to go or to stay is itself a morally neutral decision" (116). But if Eve is (however unwittingly) indulging a "frailty" that puts her faith and her children in mortal danger, then it's hard to see how her decision comes out as morally neutral. If it does, then it's equally hard to see how it answers the question that, according to Bennett, the separation scene is designed to answer: "How do genuinely righteous persons fall?" (111). In any case, the "how" in Bennett's question seems to be requesting a causal explanation of the Fall. If the scene is designed to grant the request, then the Advocate aims to defeat the Free Will Defense and jettison his Client.

Cf. the Bennett-like argument in Danielson, *Milton's Good God*, 145.

In *The Muse's Method* (Cambridge: Harvard University Press, 1962), 171, 173, Joseph Summers argues that Eve thinks she is "Adam's intellectual equal" and immune from error. But this isn't implied by Eve's insistence that her faith can't be "shaken" by fraud; if fraud rather than Eve's free and knowing choice eventually shakes Eve's faith, then the whole case for God's justice collapses. Modern critics find it almost impossible to play by *PL*'s rules by allowing the Advocate his basic premises and waiting patiently to see if they generate contradictions (as I will later argue they do).

For reasons best known to himself, J. M. Evans, *"Paradise Lost" and the Genesis Tradition*, 274, like Summers, thinks that Eve "proceeds to assume an equality which the whole account of the state of innocence has insisted she does not have."

27. Cf. MacCallum, *Milton and the Sons of God*, p155: "[Eve] is [free] in Adam's presence as well as in his absence" (155). If so, Adam's main argument against her going collapses. Freedom entails the possibility of sinning. But Adam thinks this possibility shrinks if they stay together. MacCallum refers ibid. to Eve's perverse "wish to prove her inner freedom." But Eve's wish—not obviously perverse—is to prove her loyalty; or rather to be allowed to exercise it; she takes her freedom for granted.

28. Cf. Dennis Richard Danielson, *Milton's Good God*, 127: "[By forbidding her to go Adam] would not . . . violate Eve's freedom to go if she so chose, any more than God's commanding them not to eat of the forbidden fruit prevents their freely doing so."

The analogy is misleading. By forbidding her to go, Adam would be replacing a choice between going and staying, based on Eve's judgment of their comparative prudence, with a choice between obeying and disobeying her lord. By replacing the former choice, Adam would be depriving Eve of the freedom to make it—if she obeyed. And in commanding (hence expecting) her to stay, he would be compromising the Free Will Defense by putting less trust in her obedience to God than in her obedience to Adam.

To buttress his case for a uxorious Adam, Danielson quotes Eve's hindsight reproach: "Hadst thou been firm and fix'd in thy dissent, / Neither had I transgress'd, nor thou with me" (9.1160–61). But if the self-serving Eve is right, then it isn't only Adam's wisdom that's being indicted. The whole basis of the Free Will Defense is under challenge. Statements of the form "If P happened then Q would happen" make sense as factual claims because they're implicitly about the laws and likelihoods of the actual world. You evaluate the statements by holding those laws and likelihoods constant. In a world ordered mainly like this one, and differing as little as it is allowed to by the nonactual circumstance that A forbids E to go, transgression is ruled out. By what? *By just those laws or likelihoods.* So in any such world Adam's and Eve's choice between obedience and disobedience is constrained. By making such a world actual, Adam would make God's experiment impossible.

29. Cf. MacCallum, *Milton and the Sons of God*, 156: "[Adam] does not believe in the relevance of the argument that he provides for [Eve] (that it is easier to be alert if you actively seek trial)." If he doesn't think it's relevant, he has no reason to bring it up. In fact, the relative safety of the options is relevant to choosing the better option, and the test of safety he relies on is which option would keep them more alert. Earlier Adam claimed that staying together would. Here he admits that Eve, "thus warn'd," and seeking trial, seems alert enough; if she thinks she would be less alert if she weren't seeking trial, she should go. This is coherent only if Adam knows of nothing that would invalidate Eve's opinion about alertness and trial-seeking.

30. Joan S. Bennett, *Reviving Liberty*, 116, thinks that "Adam should not say, 'Go, if you think you should,' when he knows Eve's thought is mistaken." But for his belief to be a piece of *knowledge* it has to be (a) justified, and (b) true. Adam's justification for distrusting free will is conspicuous by its absence, and Bennett produces no textual evidence that Eve is not fully armed against temptation— "Complete to have discover'd and repuls'd / Whatever wiles of Foe or seeming Friend" (*PL* 10.10–11).

Bennett immediately adds (ibid.) a different version of Adam's alleged mistake in letting Eve go: truth (as *Areopagitica* assures us) always wins out in a free and open encounter; Adam "must not close the encounter before both participants have been freed of *the passions clouding their reasons* [my italics]." But *Areopagitica* guarantees victory to truth, not to something believed true by a believer whose reason is clouded by passion. Adam has yet to come up with a reason for distrusting Eve's or his own unaided freewill, much less a reason for thinking that he will come up with such a reason later if only he waits long enough. He doesn't close the encounter foolishly on the point of winning; he closes it magnanimously at the point of losing.

31. For another opinion, see MacCallum, *Milton and the Sons of God*, 150.

32. *Thomae a Kempis C. R. Ordinis S. Augustini de imitatione Christi libri quattuor*, 1.12.3, 4.

33. If an elementary fallacy (*post hoc ergo propter*) deserves to be called a "ground." For proof-of-the-pudding arguments to show that Adam was right all along, see Maccallum, *Milton and the Sons of God*, 151 and Louis L. Martz, *Poet of Exile: A Study of Milton's Poetry* (New Haven: Yale University Press, 1980), 135.

34. See Dennis H. Burden, *The Logical Epic*, 91–92. Burden tries to have his

cake and eat it too by claiming that Adam and Eve are blameable but unfallen, since what they're to blame for isn't "directly" connected with apple-eating even though it's "the first necessary stage in the process of their Fall." If this is really what Milton has in mind, then the title of Burden's book is a glaring misnomer.

35. Aristotle, *Ethica Nicomachea*, 1111a23–24.

36. *Ethica Eudemia*, 1224a10–12, 20–22. Cf. *Physica*, 192b8ff., 13–19; *Met.* 1023a17ff.

37. Aristotle, *De motu animalium*, 703b4–11.

38. *Ethica Eudemia*, 1225b25–26.

39. Ibid., 1220a22–23.

40. Ibid., 1223b26–27. For "better judgment," read "judgment of comparative (obligation? utility?)."

41. An immoral person may have both a desire and a rational preference for something unworthy, yielding a perverse analogue of the virtue of temperance; see *Ethica Eudemia* 124123–27.

42. Ibid., 1224b15–29.

43. Ibid., 1246a18–19. For moral sentiments (as supplements to moral virtues) see ibid., 1233b18.

44. Ibid., 1225a9–19.

45. *Ethica Nicomachea*, 1146b31–47b18; *Ethica Eudemia*, 1225b11–16.

46. *Ethica Eudemia*, 1240b11–37.

47. Ibid., 1223a9–20.

48. *Ethica Nicomachea*, 1114a32-b10.

49. Ibid., 1114b12–16.

50. Ibid., 1114b12–21.

51. Ibid., 1114a7–10.

52. Ibid., 1113b6–8.

53. *Ethica Eudemia*, 1223a5–9, 1225a9–10, 1225b8–9. Just as health is the natural and ill health the unnatural object of knowledge, so good is the natural and evil the unnatural (aberrant) object of will (*Ethica Eudemia*, 1227a25–31). Cf. *Ethica Nicomachea*, 1139a21–26.

54. *Parà tòn logismón; par' hò oíetai béltiston eînai.*

55. *Ethica Eudemia* 1223a29-b10.

56. Cf. Peter van Inwagen, *An Essay on Free Will* (Oxford: The Clarendon Press, 1983), 162–64.

57. *Mishneh Torah*, ed. Philip Birnbaum (Hebrew Publishing Co., 1944), 41.

58. *Politica* 1253a1–25.

59. Plotinus, *Enneades* 6.8.4. The text I'm using is Emile Bréhier's (Paris: Association Guillaume Budé, 1936).

60. Ibid., 6.8.5.

61. Ibid., 6.8.6.

62. Ibid., 6.8.7.

63. Ibid., 6.8.15.

64. Andrew Marvell, "A Dialogue between the Soul and Body," 7–10 *The Poems and Letters of Andrew Marvell*, ed. H. M. Margoliouth (Oxford: Clarendon Press, 1952).

65. Aquinas, *Summa theologica*, 1.29.1.

66. Ibid., 1.29.1 ad 5.

67. *De Anima* 434a12–15, in *Aristotelis De anima*, ed W. D. Ross (Oxford: Clarendon Press, 1956).

68. Aquinas, *Summa Theologica* 1.83.1 ad 5.

69. Ibid., 1.83.3 ad 2.

70. Ibid., 1.83.3.

71. Ibid., 1.83.1.

72. Ibid., 1.22.2.

73. Ibid., 1.23.5.

74. Ibid., 1.23.5.

75. Erasmus, *De libero arbitrio*, 29–30 (2a11).

76. Ibid., p. 64 (3b5).

77. Ibid., 20 (2a2; italics mine). Cf. Ecclus. 15:14–18.

78. Ibid., 52–53 (3a9).

79. Arminius, *Opera* 523–24.

80. "[Gratia efficax] sine qua actu non credet [homo] neque conuertetur" (Ibid., 523–24).

81. Luis de Molina, in "Epitome de Praedestinatione," *Geschichte des Molinismus*, ed. Friedrich Stegmüller, vol. 32, *Beiträge zur Geschichte der Philosophie und Theologie des Mittelalters* (Münster Aschendorff, 1935), I:339.23–30. Translation and italics mine.

82. Ibid., 352.22–353.1.

83. Ibid., 353.34–38. Cf. 343.9–22.

84. Compare Alvin Plantinga's argument in *God, Freedom, and Evil* (New York: Harper and Row, 1974), 39: "God did not bring into existence any states of affairs at all. What He did was to perform actions of a certain sort—creating the heavens and the earth, for example—which resulted [!] in the *actuality* of certain states of affairs. God *actualizes* states of affairs. He actualizes the possible world that does in fact obtain; He does not create it. God could not have created a world in which he does not even exist." Note that Plantinga's claim depends, among other things, on our managing to see a distinction between something's *resulting* from an act of God and something's being *caused* by an act of God. The word magic here is highly Molinesque.

85. Calvin, *Institutio*, 1.15.7.

86. 1 Cor. 9:7, 24, 25; 1 Tim. 6:12; 2 Tim. 2:3, 5, 6.

87. Erasmus, *De libero arbitrio*, 43 (2b4). Cf. *conatur*, 76 (3c13).

88. Descartes, *Oeuvres*, 3:249.

89. Ibid., 4:173 (Latin version), 3:379 (French). Italics mine.

90. Ibid., 4:174–75 (Latin version), 3:382 (French). For *impellor*, the French has *j'y estois poussé*.

91. Ibid., 4:433. Italics mine.

92. Erasmus, *De libero arbitrio*, 2.13.37.

93. Descartes, *Oeuvres*, 4:114.

94. Ibid., 4:116.

95. Ibid., 4:355.

96. Ibid., 8:20.

97. Ibid., 8:18–19.

98. Hobbes, *Opera latine scripta*, 1:333. Translation mine.

99. Hobbes, *The English Works*, 4:244.

100. Descartes, *Oeuvres*, 4:116.

101. Hobbes, *The English Works*, 4:252.

102. Hobbes, *Opera latine scripta*, 5:269.

103. Descartes' reply, printed in Hobbes, *Opera latine scripta*, 5:269–70.

104. Milton, *Works*, 14:70, 72.

105. Ibid., 14:126, 128. The "as it were" is asking forgiveness for the dubious grammar and logic of allowing degrees of "disposedness."

106. Ibid., 14:128, 130. Italics mine.

107. Ibid., 14:396.

108. Ibid., 14:166. Compare the appeal to *naturalis indoles* at 14:132, 134.

109. Plantinga, *God, Freedom, and Evil*, 29–30.

110. Milton, *Works*, 14:132, 134.

111. Ibid., *Works*, 15:212.

112. Ibid., *Works*, 14:130.

113. Ibid., *Works*, 15:214.

114. Ibid., *Works*, 14:140.

115. Ibid.

116. *Othello* 1.3.319–332 (1248b in the *Riverside Shakespeare* ed. Blakemore Evans Second Edition [Boston: Houghton Mifflin, 1997]).

117. Prudentius, *Hamartigeneia*, in *Prudenti opera omnia in usum Delphini recensita* (London: A. J. Malpy, 1824), 1:544–45. Translation mine.

118. *Othello* 1.1.61–65.

119. Boethius, *Boethii consolationis philosophiae* (Consolation of philosophy) (Hack: Leyden, 1671), p. 249 (5, prosa 4). My translation.

120. The situation with "was going to happen" and "will have happened" is more complicated: the former locates the event at a time *t2* later than a time *t1* earlier than the time of utterance; the latter locates the event at a time *t2* earlier than a time *t1* later than the time of utterance. In both cases, comparing the event time *t2* with a reference time *t1* other than the time of utterance allows a shift in point of view without resorting to make-believe—e.g., an anticipatory stance toward a past or present event in the case of "was going to happen."

121. Boethius, p. 249 (5, prosa 4).

122. Ibid.

123. Aquinas, *Compendium summae totius theologiae* (Rome: sacra congregatio, 1765) 133–34; Pietro Pomponazzi, *Petri Pomponati Mantuani libri quinque de fato, de libero arbitrio, et de Praedestinatione*, ed. Richard Lemay (Lucania: Thesaurus Mundi 1957), 7. 24–25.

124. Cf. the Theologian, in *Doctrina Christiana*, in Milton, *Works*, 14:78–80.

125. Cf. the use of "certain" to mean *distinct* in "Richard Roe was looking for a certain John Doe."

126. This is the core of Aquinas's argument in the first part of *Summa contra gentiles*. Natural causes operate only contingently—only if not headed off. Seen in their contingent causes, as creatures see them, future facts are uncertain. Seen in themselves, as God sees all facts, future facts are as determinate—as certain—as any others.

127. Milton, *Works*, 15:266, 268. Cf. Boethius, *De persona et natura* 3.

128. [*Ru'akh*] *memallela*'; see the *Targum Jonathan* ad loc.

129. For the Theologian's respectful reference to the targums as "antiquissimi paraphrastae," see Milton, *Works*, 15:282.

130. Ibid., 15:40.

131. Ibid., 15:48.

132. Ibid., 15:48.

133. Not even an ordered collection, if that's what Locke means by a "system of matter, fitly disposed"—the kind of material "system" Locke's God has it in his power to give a "faculty of thinking" (*An Essay concerning Human Understanding*, 4.3.6). See John W. Yolton, *Thinking Matter: Materialism in Eighteenth-Century Britain* (Minneapolis: University of Minnesota Press, 1983), 14.

134. *In toto [corpore] categorematice sumpto*, i.e., "in the whole [body] taken as subject to the [relevant] predicate [*categorema*]."

135. Pietro Pomponazzi, *Tractatus de immortalitate animae*, ed. Gianfrancesco Morra (Bologna: Nanni & Fiammenghi, 1954), 144. The Theologian seems to be making the same point, rather than simply contradicting himself, when he turns around and insists that thoughts are in the mind and not the body (Milton, *Works*, 15:228)—not the body, that is, taken as an organ collection.

136. The two alternatives to individualism would be: (a) that for me to walk is simply for my body parts to interact in a particular way; and (b) that for me to walk is for my body parts to interact in one or another of a loosely defined family of similar ways. In either (a) or (b), my walking is exhaustively described by reference to my parts; reference to me (as a whole) adds no information. (It's often falsely claimed that by invoking a family of part interactions rather than a single one, alternative (b) avoids "reductionism.")

137. Hobbes, *Opera latine scripta*, 1:331–32.

138. *Opera latine scripta*, 5:253.

139. Ibid., 5:263.

140. Ibid., 5:258. Italics and translation mine.

141. Descartes' thesis in the *Meditations* as challenged by Gassendi (Descartes, *Oeuvres*, 7:337).

142. Calvin, *Institutio Christianae Religionis*, 2.14.1. Translation mine.

143. Reprinted in Hobbes, *Opera latine scripta*, 5:259–60.

144. Descartes, *Oeuvres*, 7:133.

145. Ibid., 7:160–61.

146. Hobbes, *Opera Latine scripta* (1.333). Translation (and italics) mine.

147. Daniel Goleman, "Scientists Trace 'Voices' in Schizophrenia." *The New York Times*, 22 September 1993, C12.

148. Sandra Blakeslee, "Seeing and Imagining: Clues to the Workings of the Mind's Eye." *The New York Times*, 31 August 1993, C7.

149. Daniel Dennett, *Consciousness Explained* (Boston: Little, Brown & Co., 1991), 439. Italics mine.

150. "The Progress of the Soul," 246, "The Extasie" 51.

151. Milton, *Works*, 14:220.

152. Ibid., 14:194.

153. Ibid., 11:58, 60.

154. Spinoza's basic material individual ("substance") has no parts (*Ethics*, Part I, Corollary to Proposition 13; Proposition 15 [toward the end]).

So-called bodies turn out to be finite "expressions" of the attributes of the basic individual—its motion or rest at a given time and place (I. corollarium ad prop. XXV; II. lemma I).

The text of the *Ethics* I'm using is in *Benedicti de Spinoza opera quotquot reperta sunt*, ed. J. van Vloten and J. P. N. Land (The Hague: Martin Nijhoff, 1913), I:34–273.

155. A human thought is a finite thought of God's (*Ethica*, II. cor. ad prop. XI).

156. *Ethics*, Part II, Scholium to Proposition 7; ibid., Part III, Proposition 2. Decision and (effective) desire are one and the same thing under the aspect of mind and body respectively (ibid., IIIae scholium ad prop. II).

157. *Ethics*, Part I, Proposition 5; Definition 4; Proposition 4.

CHAPTER 3. THE CREATOR DEFENDED

1. See Chapter 1 [iv].

2. *Summum ius summa iniuria est.*

3. In the Scholastic jargon, *natura naturans*, not just *natura naturata*.

4. "Frugality" suggests that divine architecture has to meet a test of parsimony or mathematical elegance.

5. *Merachépheth.*

6. *Chagigah* (Talmud) 15ª. As a Judeo-French equivalent for *merachépheth*, Rash'i ad loc. supplies a term that means both "cover" and "hover." See *Trésor de la Langue des Juifs Français au Moyen Age*, ed. Raphael Levy (Austin: University of Texas Press, 1964) s. v. *acoveter*.

7. For the bisexual demiurge, see fragment 6.11 of the Orphic *Theogony* in *Orphica*, ed. Gottfried Hermann (Leipzig: Caspar Fritsch, 1805), 457, preserved in *Procli Commentarium in Timaeum* 2:95.34. Cf. the serpent Heracles hatching and impregnating the chaos egg in the Orphic theogony preserved by Athenagoras in *Pro Christianis* 18.20 Schwartz, Diehls 1B13.

Marjara, in *Contemplation of Created Things*, 216, finds a possible Orphic reference at *PL* 7.417–20, where we have a literal egg disclosing a literal bird and no hint of figurative overtones in the context—or at least no hint specified by the critic, who is following D. C. Allen, "Milton and the Creation of Birds," *Modern Language Notes* 63 (1948), 263–64.

8. *Ethica Nicomachea* 1113b18–19; compare ibid., 1120b13–14.

9. Cf. James 1:17, I John 1:5.

10. *Imitatio Christi*, 3.21.3: "O lux perpetua! cuncta creata transcendens lumina! fulgura coruscationem de sublimi, penetrantem omnia intima cordis mei: purifica, laetifica, clarifica et vivifica spiritum meum cum suis potentiis ad inhaerendum tibi iubilosis excessibus."

11. William Kerrigan, *The Sacred Complex: On the Psychogenesis of "Paradise Lost"* (Cambridge: Harvard University Press, 1983), p. 150, recommends that we "take the holy light [invoked in the proem to *PL* 3] to symbolize what becomes of orthodoxy's Holy Spirit after Milton has disassembled the triune Godhead and erected in its place his own dyad of uncreated Father and created Son." "Milton addresses the will of God 'put forth' in a form, light, symbolizing creative intent. In escaping the disjunction of created/uncreated, this light eludes the categories that necessarily define other creatures" (ibid., 153–54). But the speaker of the proem takes it for granted that

God is light,
And never but in unapproached Light
Dwelt from eternity, dwelt then in thee.

From "in unapproached Light / Dwelt from eternity," the speaker infers "dwelt
then in thee." So the speaker is answering his own initial question about created-
ness: the light being addressed is coeternal with God and hence uncreated—unlike
the Holy Spirit of *De doctrina christiana*. This light is the uncreated heaven of *De
doctrina*. It's also the light of the material world, since the Miltonic God is material
and created the world out of his own substance. The referent of "thou" is constant
throughout, so the light being addressed here gives not only vision but also the
intellectual illumination the speaker asks of it toward the end of his invocation . (If
God dwells in light, by the way, light is in effect his tabernacle; see *PL* 3.375–82,
7.248.)

12. *Targum Jonathan* at Gen. 2:7: *Ruach memalela' le'anharuth 'ayenayin
'ulemitzetuth 'udenin.*

13. Cf. John Rumrich, "Milton's God and the Matter of Chaos," *PMLA* 110
(1995), 1035–46, esp. 1035: "If the [monist and materialist] poet conceived of this
matrix as intrinsically hostile to God and creation, any attempt at theodicy would
seem pointless." Rumrich argues that *PL* presents chaos as a "complex disorder"
that "persists dynamically in any order" (ibid., 1041a); but structural principles of
contrast and dissonance, which is what the *Areopagitica* text he cites is about
(ibid., 1041b), don't imply disorder. With this exception, Rumrich's discussion
strikes me as brilliantly on the mark, and quite the best treatment of the Chaos
episode that I have seen.

14. Cf. Lucretius, *De rerum natura* 1.628–634, 2.335–37, 479–80, 514. The
text I am using is *T. Lucreti Cari De rerum natura libri sex*, ed. William Ellery
Leonard and Stanley Barney Smith (Madison: Univ. of Wisconsin Press, 1942.

15. For Lucretius's argument to the contrary, see *De rerum natura* 1.1021–37.

Lewalski, *Paradise Lost and the Rhetoric of Literary Forms*: "[In the Lucretian
echoes of *PL* 7.313–24 and 453–70] we are intended to see that the marvelous
processes of creation in Lucretius are begun and continued by the random motion
of atoms, whereas the yet more marvelous processes the Miltonic Bard describes
emanate from the prodigious vitality of a divine Father who makes his creatures
vigorous, active, and potent, and sustains them in continuous processes of growth
and generation" (135). But on the Advocate's showing "vitality" isn't the only
"marvelous process of creation" that Lucretius fails to account for; he fails to account for *any*. Atheist materialism (as opposed to the Christian kind) can't get creation off the ground.

16. According to Harinder Singh Marjara, in *Contemplation of Created
Things*, 93, the Chaos episode criticizes atomism by implicitly denying chance a
role in *created* nature. But on the showing of the Chaos episode, chance has no
role in *creating* nature; for all the episode shows to the contrary, the lawfulness of
nature once created could be a Swiss cheese of discontinuities.

17. *De rerum natura* 5.187–94.

18. Of course, infinitely many such runs *do* see the monkeys through to success; the improbability of the universe we know and love is an objection to atheism
only if we dismiss the notion that many possible universes coexist, some of them
playing out versions of Chaos and some of Cosmos. Roughly this seems to be the

winning card played by the inflationary cosmogony that is enjoying a vogue at the moment: many Big Bangs launching alternative evolutions governed by alternative laws of nature. In the end, the Advocate's thought experiment isn't the knockdown argument he sums up at *PL* 2.914–16.

19. Lucretius, *De rerum naturae* 1.586, 5.924, 6.906–7.

20. Ibid., 1.75–76, 1.586–87, 5.526, 5.545, 6.907.

21. For the notion of alternative worlds each obeying reason in its own way, see ibid. 5.527.

22. Ibid., 1.587.

23. Ibid., 1.77, 1.596.

24. Ibid., 1.77, 1.593, 5.160, 5.527, 5.1183, 5.1439, 6.41.

25. Cf. Rumrich, "Milton's God and the Matter of Chaos," 1042b.

26. For the cave of the Demiurge see Fragment 6.1 of the Orphic *Theogony* (Hermann 456), preserved in *Procli Commentarium in Timaeum* 2:95.34. For night as midwife of creation, see Fragment 10 of the Orphic *Theogony* (Hermann 471). For night as mother of creation, see Orphic Hymn 3.1 (Hermann 257). For original Chaos as a "necessity," see the Orphic *Argonautica* 12 (Hermann 4). For the body of the demiurge as the container of everything, see Fragment 6.12–20 of the Orphic *Theogony* (Hermann 457).

27. Cf. Lucretius, *De rerum natura* 2.253–55:

> declinando faciunt primordia motus
> principium quoddam quod fati foedera rumpat,
> ex infinito ne causam causa sequatur.

28. "Exiguum clinamen principiorum / nec regione loci certa nec tempore certo" (Lucretius, *De rerum natura* 2.292–93), where a fact is "certain" when it's covered by a law of nature, not when it's knowable beyond a reasonable doubt.

29. Lucretius claims that atom-swerve protects the mind from "necessum intestinum" (*De rerum natura* 2.289–90).

30. "Ut videas initum motus a corde creari / ex animique voluntate id procedere primum" (Lucretius, *De rerum natura* 2.269–70).

31. *The Winter's Tale*, 4.4.95–97.

32. John Milton, *Complete Poems and Major Prose* (New York: The Odyssey Press, 1957), 733a. Italics added.

33. Evans, *"Paradise Lost" and the Genesis Tradition*, 248. Elsewhere Evans shows a far sharper sense of what's at stake here: "The tendencies Eve exhibits at the sight of her own reflection or in her demonic dream, the forces inside him which Adam reveals in his questions about cosmology and his passion for his wife, these are no more wicked than the upsurging vitality of the plants around them. Hunger, thirst, curiosity, and sexual desire become evil only when they are not properly disciplined, when hunger, whether intellectual or physical, becomes gluttony, and desire lust" (ibid., p. 271).

34. Aristotle, *Ethica Nicomachea* 1146a10–12, 1151b34–52a6. Hellenistic philosophy is, notoriously, even more positive that real virtue ("wisdom") always goes with "apathy" or "ataraxy"; somebody virtuous can't conceivably be disturbed.

The Rabbinic tradition gives *encrateia* the status of a virtue; see Maimonides on overcoming impulse (*yetzer*), *Mishnéh Toráh*, ed. Paltiel Birenboim (New York: Hebrew Publishing Co., 1989), p. 43.

35. Greek for pruning (*kólasis*) also means castigation. Latin for pruning (*putatio*) also means ordering, e.g., one's accounts or thoughts.

36. Apparently influenced by Dutch *glans*, "luster."

37. Evans, *"Paradise Lost" and the Genesis Tradition*, 266.

38. Cf. Joseph Summers to the contrary, *The Muse's Method* (Cambridge, Mass.: HUP, 1962), p. 165.

39. Summers, *The Muse's Method*, 163–4, on *PL* 8.478–80 (Adam waking after Eve's creation—ready to "abjure" all other pleasures if he can't find her): "This is excess: anxiety so intense and desire so vehement that they seem to exclude all else." The fact remains that *Adam hasn't fallen yet.* On pain of incriminating Adam's creator, the "excess" has to be counted natural and innocent: the "abjuring" of other satisfactions simply registers the fact—built into Adam's nature by God—that it isn't good for Man to be alone (Gen. 2:18, *PL* 8.445).

It isn't open to the Advocate (pace Summers, 149 and *passim*) to allow Adam a moral failing so long as it's short of disobeying the ban on the apple. On the standard Christian view, any moral failing comes down to a failure of love for God.

40. As Evans himself says later: "[Adam] must not permit himself to be debased by his passion for his wife" (*"Paradise Lost" and the Genesis Tradition*, 268).

41. Lewalski, *"Paradise Lost" and the Rhetoric of Literary Forms*, 187.

42. Evans, *"Paradise Lost" and the Genesis Tradition*, 253.

43. Coming and going *with* Eve (line 469) strongly suggests, if not implies, being *other* than Eve. God's definition of "self" ("with thee it comes and goes") is mystifyingly unhelpful—not least because it works better as a definition of her "shadow" (see line 470). Not the least of the oddities of this definition is that it qualifies Eve to be Adam's "self"; she's *his* "image," after all (*PL* 4.472), and as his helpmeet "with [him] comes and goes." If it's wrong in principle to dally with one's image, why isn't it wrong for him?

44. *Thomae a Kempis C.R. Ordinis Beati Augustini de imitatione Christi* 3.6.1: "Certare autem adversus malos animi motus, suggestionemque spernere diaboli, insigne est virtutis et magni meriti. Non ergo te conturbent alienae phantasiae, de quacunque materia ingestae." "Nec est illusio, quod aliquando in excessum subito raperis, et statim ad ineptias solitas cordis reverteris. Illas enim invite magis pateris quam agis; et quamdiu tibi displicent, et iis reniteris, meritum est, non perditio." Cf. Augustine, *De libero arbitrio* 3.25.75.

45. Golda Werman, *Milton and Midrash* (Washington, D.C.: The Catholic University of America Press, 1995), 116, identifies these prelapsarian emotions with the Rabbinic *yetzer harah* (= "inclination to evil"). But the whole point of *PL* is that, in creating no less than in judging, God is the source of nothing but good. Werman goes on, 143, to read the discussion of original sin in *Christian Doctrine* 1.11 as an endorsement of the Rabbinic view that *yetzer harah* was inflicted on Adam and Eve by their creator. The culprit seems to be a misreading of *in generatione hominis* as "in man's creation."

46. Marjara, *Contemplation of Created Things*, 273: "The demonic influence [of the dream] does leave its spot behind, and Eve's animal spirits do take the taint." "Eve's susceptibility to temptation must be a part of her nature, since her

behavior, in order to be convincing, must give the sense of being caused, and it must be caused by Eve's own nature rather than by an external force."

But if something in her nature *caused* her to fall, how can she be to blame for falling? She's the victim of congenital sabotage by none other than the Advocate's Client, the kangaroo Judge who will soon be unjustly condemning her to death. Given compelling evidence that the Advocate has been willing to destroy his case in the interest of making Eve's behavior "convincing," he stands convicted of gross incompetence. Marjara produces no such evidence. The burden of proof that Milton and his surrogate are grossly incompetent, as usual, is on the accuser.

Curiously enough, the critic doesn't think of himself as an accuser; he sees no incompetence, gross or otherwise, in trying to show (a) that the Tempter's victims "stood little chance, and the battle was lost before it began" (276), while insisting (b) that Eve "cannot blame either her nature or her circumstances for the fall" (279).

Louis L. Martz, *Poet of Exile*, 122, claims that the "wild work" is "part of man's created perfection" and then goes on to argue that the Advocate uses it to motivate the Fall.

47. Plotinus attacks the foolhardy or self-defeating argument (*tolmëròs lógos*) that God operates either by necessity or by chance, and hence enjoys neither freedom (*eleuthería*) nor power over self (*autexousía*) (*Enneádes* 6.8.7). God's will (*thélësis*) is independent of both necessity and chance (*Enneádes* 6.8.16).

48. Compare *PL* 1.650–54.

49. Heb. *tzᵉdaqah* ("justice" = "righteousness" or "liberality") vs. Greek *dikaiosyne* ("justice" = "[the virtue of] rendering to each its due").

50. *Hamlet* 2.2.531–33.

51. Lucretius, *De rerum natura* 5.156–65: "quidve novi potuit tanto post ante quietos / inlicere ut cuperent vitam mutare priorem?" (5.168–69)

52. *Ethica Nicomachea* 1113b18–1.

53. *Ethica Eudemia* 1241a35–124b9.

54. Cf. Rumrich, "Milton's God and the Matter of Chaos," 1043a: "Chaos is boundless and infinite because God fills it . . . although God refrains from being there as a governing agent. How can God both fill the space and not be there?" Rumrich has already answered his own question; not being there *as Creator* does not imply not being there at all. There is no paradox in the quoted lines.

Pace Marjara (*Contemplation of Created Things*, 97), space coeternal with God doesn't saddle God with a "dualistic" partner so long as "filling space" names a family of properties—call them ways of being extended—rather than a relation to a second thing. Filling a given subspace will come out as exhibiting one of the family of extension properties. The family will need to be infinite, of course, like the being that exhibits them all; the reason the deep is boundless is that "I am who fill / Infinitude."

It's worth adding that "I am who fill" isn't just a long-winded way of saying "I fill": God isn't reporting a pastime here; he's defining himself as the extended being par excellence (compare God's paradigm act of self-definition at Ex. 3:13; literally translated, the original Hebrew means "I am who am").

55. God doesn't put forth his goodness in a place merely by being in it. For example, there are gulfs of "vast vacuitie" in Chaos; Satan falls into one (2.932). (a) The gulf is "vacuous" in the sense that, unlike the "smoke" leading up to it

and the "bog" leading away from it, there's nothing in it but God. (b) The gulf is *non*-"vacuous" in the sense that God is everywhere. *Pace* Marjara, *Contemplation of Created Things*, 96, 97, (a) and (b) are not in conflict; we just have different senses of "vacuity" in different contexts.

56. Compare Plotinus, *Enneádes* 6.8.16: the Good isn't everywhere; everywhere (every point in space) is the Good. Things exist—occupy points in space—by lying beside Him (*parakeîsthai*). Compare the Rabbinic use of *hammakóm* "the Place [par excellence]" as a nickname for God. For God and place, see also *Enneádes* 6.8.11.

57. Compare *De doctrina Christiana* 1.7: "Certe motum et tempus, quae mensura motus est, secundum prius et posterius, ante mundum hunc conditum esse non potuisse, quod vulgo creditur, nihil cogit assentiri; cum Aristoteles in hoc mundo, quem aeternum esse statuit, dari nihilominus motum atque tempus docuerit" (Milton, *Works*, 15:34). The author of the treatise is arguing that Aristotle, no mean logician, finds no contradiction in the notion of time-in-eternity; after all, eternity, in his view, is a property of the world we're in.

58. His mystical Hebrew name is *hammakóm*, the Place (par excellence).

59. Milton, *Works*, 15:20, 22.

60. We've already had occasion to notice the limits of the "supremacy" involved here; see section (e) above, on the innate awesomeness of Eve, and Adam's innate susceptibility to it; and on the unexpected republicanism of the Advocate's family politics.

61. Cf. Rumrich, "Milton's God and the Matter of Chaos," 1043a: "I suggest that chaos is God's womb, essential to his deity."

62. Invoking Berecyntia or *Magna Mater* invites us to imagine the associated visual image: titanic female figure crowned with allegorical towers.

63. *Ecstasis*, "withdrawal from self," *LXX* ad loc.; a neoplatonic usage?

64. Compare the prophetic level of *thardemah* distinguished in the *Midrash Rabbah* on Genesis, section 17.

65. Eve < Heb. *Khawwa*, "life."

66. *Khawwah*, "Eve," and *khiwei*, "serpent"; see *Genesis Rabbah* 20.

67. See Christopher Marlowe, *Doctor Faustus* 2.1.39–42, in John D. Jump's edition (Cambridge: Harvard Univ. Press, 1962).

68. Cf. Summers, *The Muse's Method*, 178: "Eve's attempt [*PL* 10.914–36] mirrors the redemptive actions of the Son, both in His first moment of undertaking and throughout the poem."

69. In *The Dialectics of Creation* (Amherst: the University of Massachusetts Press, 1970), 210, Michael Lieb endorses Adam's egoism reading of Eve's proposal for reasons unfortunately not specified.

70. Coming from a materialist, this particular anthropomorphism is especially telling; God is being provided with a *temperamentum humorum*, or emotional biochemistry.

71. Cf. Summers, *The Muse's Method*, 178. (This is a book of enduring value; it isn't likely to be superseded.)

72. Marjara, *Contemplation of Created Things*, 230.

73. Lucretius, *De rerum natura* (2.1122–27).

74. Ibid., 2.1146–47.

75. Ibid., 5.519–25.

76. Ibid., 2.963–72
77. Ibid., 2.865–85.
78. Ibid., 2.891–96.
79. Ibid., 3.124–27, 136–40, 5.126–43.
80. E.g., ibid., 3.147–151.
81. Ibid., 3.240, 245, 272, 570.
82. "Hunc motum quem sensum nominitamus," ibid., 3.352.
83. Ibid., 3.152–67.
84. Ibid., 4.161–65, 183–90, 234–36, 4.244–55, 4.524–25.
85. Ibid., 4.882–88.

86. Marjara, *Contemplation of Created Things*, 226: "Milton's angels are not totally incorporeal, nor are they made of a distinct ethereal or empyrean substance." But angels assimilate food precisely by turning "corporeal to incorporeal" (*PL* 5.413). Satan apparently relies on this fact to make it plausible that angels are "Ethereal Sons" that is, products of spontaneous generation from the ether (*PL* 5.863). Continued innocence would eventually have turned Adam's and Eve's bodies into spirit, enabling them to "ascend / Ethereal as wee" (*PL* 5.499). See also the passages discussed in the text.

87. *Iamblichus de mysteriis, Proclus de anima atque daemone, Idem de sacrificio et magia, Porphyrius de divinis atque daemonibus, Michael Psellus de daemonibus, Mercurii Trismegisti Pimander, eiusdem Asclepius, interprete Marsilio Ficino* (Leyden: Ioannes Tornaesius typographus regius, 1570), 348 (Psellus): "Sicut enim nubes suspicimus nunc hominum, nunc ursorum, nunc draconum, aliorumque praeferre figuras, sic et corpora daemonum; sed hoc interest, quod nubes externis agitatae ventis figuras varias agunt, daemones autem proprio consilio prout ipsi volunt, corporum formas in se variant, et modo in breviorem contrahuntur, modo rursus in longiorem se extendunt."

88. Ibid., 350 (Psellus): "Non enim solidum corpus daemonum, quo possint acceptas retinere figuras. Sed sicut in aere et in aqua contingere consuevit, videlicet sive colorem infundas sive figuram imprimas, mox diffunditur atque dissolvitur, simile quiddam daemonibus accidit. nam et in his figura colorque et species rerum quarumlibet cito dilabitur. Docuit itaque Marcus maris et feminae differentias non inesse daemonibus, sed apparere, nullamque eiusmodi formam in eis stabilem permanere."

89. Ibid., 323 (Ficino's paraphrase of Porphyry, *De abstinentia animalium*): "In libro tertio dicit [Porphyrius] se afferre opinionem veram et Pythagoricam omnem scilicet animam sensibus et memoria praeditam esse rationalem, habereque rationem, orationemque habere tum interiorem tum exteriorem, qua inter se loquantur animalia."

90. Ibid., 323 (Ficino's paraphrase of Porphyry's *De abstinentia*): "Contendit deinde animalia rationem habere, cum quia inter se sua significent tum quia diligenti sibi sollertia consulant, usuiqe futuro provideant, tum quia discant et ab se invicem et et ab hominibus multa, se ipsaque in vicem doceant. Subiungit Aristotelem Empedoclem Democritum aliosque quicumque veritatem de animalibus perscrutati sunt participationem rationis orationisque in animalibus comperisse. Apparere autem in hac diversitatem, ut Aristoteles quoque dixerit, in essentia minime differentem, sed per magis minusve diversitatem, quemadmodum plerique putent differentiam deorum in hac ad homines esse."

91. Ibid.: "Concedatur itaque secundum magis et minus esse in his different-iam rationis, neque tamen ratione animalia reliqua omnino priventur, neque ex eo, quod nos magis quam animalia intellegamus, propterea illa intellectione omnino privemus, sicut neque volare perdices negamus, quoniam astures velocius volent." (Porphyrius 324).

92. It was precisely his reading of the animality and not the humanity of ani-mals, says Porphyry, that turned the historical Pythagoras against flesh-eating; see quote in text.

93. *Comus* 459–63, in *Complete Poems and Major Prose*, ed. M. Y. Hughes (New York: Macmillan, 1957).

94. Lucretius, *De rerum natura* 3.127, 217 and elsewhere.

95. Marjara is undecided about what to say here: "One of the implications of the *creatio ex deo* theory was the equation between God and pre-creation matter" (*Contemplation of Created Things*, 98). "It would be preposterous to think that Milton, by asserting that Chaos is God-filled, equates God with Chaos" (99). The root of the confusion here is "equates"; it's not clear what it would mean for God to be "equal to" matter or Chaos. For God to create the world *out of* himself is for him (a) to be not matter, but a material being—that is (at a minimum), to be ex-tended in space and time; (b) to organize parts of this extension (viz., the embryon atoms) into wholes in their own right.

96. *Iamblichus de mysteriis,* 156. Translation mine.

97. Ibid., 262 (Proclus).

98. Ibid., 502–3 (Ficino's commentary on the Hermetic *Asclepius*). Transla-tion mine.

99. *Comus* 593–599.

CHAPTER 4. GOD'S HATRED

1. Aristotle, *Poetics* 49b9–20, in *Aristotelis De arte poetica liber*, ed. Rudolf Kassel (Oxford: Clarendon Press, 1965).

2. Fortunately for the Advocate's credit for literacy (not to mention grati-tude), he doesn't start by libelling his greatest mentors as "ethically defective" cheerleaders for "an inferior mode of heroism" (*pace* John M. Steadman, *Milton and the Paradoxes of Renaissance Heroism*, 23). By the time the Advocate moves on to chivalric epic, we already know that in his view the "chief maistrie" of the *Iliad* and the *Aeneid*, at least, has nothing to do with tediously "dissecting" (i.e., showing the dismemberment of) knights in battle (*PL* 9.29–31).

Homer doesn't invite us to admire *any* kind of "refusal to be thwarted," only a refusal to be unjustly thwarted (*pace* Dennis H. Burden, *The Logical Epic*, 143–44). *Ate* and *hubris* aren't what make heroes admirable by Homeric or Virgilian standards. In fact, pious Aeneas commends himself by his dedication to the sur-vival of his people, and his submission to higher authority and principle. Milton never has his surrogate imply—least of all in the proem to *PL* 9—that pagan epic is essentially unheroic.

The question isn't whether there are proud or vengeful epic heroes (*pace* Evans, *Paradise Lost and the Genesis Tradition*, 230–31) but whether epic litera-ture endorses the "values" (ibid.) of heroes who act on illusions of superiority or grievance—especially when (as with Satan) the object of their resentment is somebody *they're* inferior to, and somebody with a real grievance against *them*.

3. See Michael Lieb's seminal article " 'Hate in Heav'n': Milton and the *Odium Dei*" *English Literary History* (1986), 519–39. Lieb sets himself the task of reconciling a "God of love" with a "God of hate," (521) both of whom manifest themselves in *PL*: "against those who are entirely reprobate, God's hate is everlasting" (525), yet somehow the "thematic center" of *PL* is the "triumph of 'Heav'nly love' over 'Hellish hate' [*PL* 3.298–301]" (519). Reconciling these two aspects of God calls for a "genuinely sympathetic treatment" of God's hate (522), a treatment that focusses on an episode that crucially exemplifies God's hate: in the final act of *PL* 6 the very same divine chariot expels the disloyal angels from God's presence forever and repairs the damage they did to heaven. In short, God's hate and love are "complementary aspects of the same idea" (532). *PL*'s "dialectic" solution to the problem of God's hate is that, in God, hate is "always ultimately restorative" (532–33). God's hate is "ultimately consummated in the realization of God's love" (535).

There is no contradiction in the chariot's dual function, and hence no need for a "dialectic" maneuver to resolve it. As Lieb himself notes, the hatred and love meted out by the Son's chariot illustrate a single "idea": on the Advocate's showing, the loved and hated, respectively, *deserve* love and hate. Unfortunately, this uncontroversial solution ends by giving us back the problem.

The God celebrated in *PL* loves even the *undeserving*—with some exceptions. His love—with some exceptions—triumphs over his *justice*; that's the point of the lines Lieb quotes from *PL* 3. On the universal Christian view, God loves all his creatures as creatures, even those he simultaneously hates as betrayers (Aquinas, *Summa Theologica* 1.20.2 ad 4, 1.23.3 ad 1; Calvin, *Institutio Christianae Religionis* 1.5.6). The problem with the received account of infinite magnanimity is the "some exceptions" clause: why is God's overflowing love overflowing enough to redeem some of those who don't deserve redemption, but not all?

The alienated theologian in *Waiting for Godot* has been driven mad by the notion of a being who "loves us dearly with some exceptions for reasons unknown." Short of supplying the reasons, the minimum requirement for carrying out the second half of the Advocate's task is (a) to show the existence of those reasons, and (b) to show that the reasons vindicate God's love rather than his justice all over again.

4. *Summa theologica* 1.83.2, in *S. Thomae Aquinatis Summa Theologica* (Turin: Sacra Congregatio, 1922).

5. Ibid., 1.64.2, 2 ad 1, 2 ad 2. Gardner, *A Reading of "Paradise Lost,"* 101, cites *Summa Theologica* supplement 16.3 to the same effect.

6. Gregorius Magnus, *Expositio Moralium* 2.6, in Migne, *Patrologia Latina* 75.

7. Cf. Martz, *Poet of Exile*, 107.

8. John Steadman, *Milton and the Paradoxes of Renaissance Heroism*, 116: "The 'fixt mind' that scorns to 'repent or change' can be called heroic constancy; but it may also be diagnosed as 'hardening of the heart.' " It isn't clear that there's *any* tradition of "heroic constancy" (available to the advocate, at least) devoted to celebrating "constant" malice and "constant" treachery. "May be diagnosed" seems to suggest that the text leaves this issue up for grabs; in fact the diagnosis

is supplied categorically (and insistently) by the narrator, and confirmed by his narrative.

In *The Muse's Method*, 30–31, Joseph Summers compares Henry James's and Milton's handling of characterization. "Milton makes the natures of his [reprehensible] characters clear from the beginning and provides us with far more warnings than [Henry] James"; by withholding clarity at the outset and cutting down on warnings, James "managed to seduce all but the most attentive readers into identifying initially with a point of view which seems sensible and, if not absolutely good, at least human and sympathetic." One need not, in short, be very inattentive to miss the sparse warnings in James or be taken in by the initial ambiguity of evil—whereas to be seduced by Satan, on Summers's showing, requires a deaf ear to many warnings and a blind eye to a lot of initial clarity in the presentation of evil. Yet Summers goes on to claim that "[Milton's] presentation of "the 'heroism,' the 'reason,' and the 'freedom' of Hell" anticipates James's seduction technique.

On Summer's showing, Milton's seduction technique differs from James's in a crucial respect: Milton's calls for an incompetent reader; far from taking steps to seduce the "fit audience . . . though few" (*PL* 7.31), he has taken steps (clarity of presentation and frequent warnings) to keep competent readers unseduced. Meanwhile, thanks to the theory, he gets credit, without lifting a finger, for generating the misreadings of incompetent readers.

Those who are struck by this critical insight are welcome to it.

Summers is entitled to his lapses (if, as I think, the seduction theory is a lapse); in my judgment, *The Muse's Method* is one of the few indispensable books in the canon of Milton criticism. A relevant case in point: "Satan comes near to such a state [of nonentity] in all his roles: as the tyrant who claims an absolute power which he does not possess, as the rhetorical warrior and seducer who argues confidently from false analogies and from his own experience (on the assumption that all natures are like his), as the liar, and as the pervert who gains his only pleasure from destruction" (55).

9. *Eikonoklastes* 9 in *The Student's Milton*, p 806b.

10. Juvenal: "Nil habet infelix paupertas durius in se, / quam quod ridiculos homines facit" (Satire 3.152–53), in *Satirae* ed. C. F. Hermann (Leipzig: Teubner, 1865).

11. Cf. Aquinas: devils know themselves damned (*Summa Theologica* 2–2.18.3); their hell is the knowledge that hell is what they deserve (1.64.4 ad 3).

12. See Aristotle, *Politica* 1285a19–22.

13. Ibid., 1314a33–38.

14. "Scilicet omnes / consensu populi stantque caduntque duces: / quem si de medio tollas, discordia praeceps / aduolat, et secum regia fata trahit" (Andreas Alciati, [Lyons: Mathieu Bonhomme, 1551], sig. C7r).

15. For a different way of reading Satan as a "Moses figure," see Michael Lieb, *The Dialectics of Creation*, 130–31.

16. In *The Full Voic'd Quire Below* (Lund: CWK Gleerup, 1982), 52–69, Claes Schaar coins the semantic notion of a "vertical system" of "infracontexts" to qualify his arbitrary collection of classical and Biblical analogues as part of the meaning of the simile. The "infracontexts" help him to the insight that the point of the simile is twofold: the redemptive power of baptism and the saints' joy in the meting out of justice to the damned.

17. Stephen M. Fallon, *Milton and the Philosophers* (Ithaca: Cornell University Press, 1991), 203–4.

18. Descartes, *Oeuvres*, 7:425, 133.

19. Herodotus, *Persian War* 7.8; I have consulted *Herodoti historiae*, ed. Charles Hude (Oxford: Clarendon Press, 1913).

20. See Fallon, *Milton and the Philosophers*, 219.

21. *Ethica Nicomachea* 1152a20–24.

22. Failure to grasp this point undermines David Weisberg's Foucauldian argument in "Rule, Self, Subject: The Problem of Power in *Paradise Lost*," *Milton Studies* 30 (1993), 85–107. On the strength of twentieth-century usage, Weisberg takes it for granted that "the notion of 'permission' rules out determination" (88); in Hell "one's physical body is confined, but thought is free" (99). On the contrary, the notion of 'permission'—in *PL*, at least—*presupposes* both determination and (given determination) the unfreedom of demonic thought. It's quite true, as Weisberg says, that in Hell one "simultaneously chooses for oneself and is ruled from the outside" (106), but since hellish choice is unfree to start with, there is no interestingly "modern" paradox here of freewill channelled, like the initiatives of a rat in a maze. What's getting channelled is automatism.

23. Cf. Burden, *The Logical Epic*, 25: "God did not will Satan's escape but merely permitted Sin to achieve it." Burden takes God's mock-consternation at *PL* 3.80–86 literally. Cf. also Martz, *Poet of Exile*, 98: "God's apparent lack of control over Satan, we can now begin to see, represents part of God's view of every creature's freedom to break the bounds that are prescribed, not forced upon us."

24. Origen, *Perì archôn* 3.1.10–11 (Migne *Patrologia Graeca* 11.265–70); Erasmus, *De libero arbitrio*, 47–48 (IIIa3).

25. Erasmus *De libero arbitrio*, 50 (IIIa6).

26. Ibid., 47 (IIIa3).

27. Luther, *De servo arbitrio*, 709.

28. Calvin, *Institutio Christianae Religionis*, 1:158 (1.18.3).

29. Ibid., 1:159 (1.18.41).

30. Luther, *De servo arbitrio*, 18:711.

31. Augustine, *Ad Bonifacium contra duas epistolas Pelagianorum* 2.9, Migne, *Patrologia Latina* 43.

32. Luther, *De servo arbitrio*, 18:753.

33. Geraard Vossius, *Historiae de controversiis quas Pelagius eiusque reliquiae moverunt libri vii* (Leyden: Jan Patius, 1618). In "*Paradise Lost* and *De doctrina* on Predestination" (*Milton Studies* 34 [1997], 45–60), Paul R. Sellin endorses an Arminian objection to the two-tiered scheme: God can't be giving irresistible grace to some unless he's giving inadequate grace to the others (53); on the strength of this argument, Sellin confidently claims that God's tribute to free will in *PL* is mere lipservice (ibid.). The logic of the argument escapes me. In any case, Arminius is objecting to the "disregard of actual sin and merit in assigning election and reprobation" (57). But in *PL*, God will reward actual endeavor and punish actual neglect (*PL* 3.191–93, 198–99). And far from giving something inadequate, he's giving "what may suffice" (*PL* 3.189).

34. Vossius, *Historia de controversiis*, 546.

35. Targum Jonathan at Gen. 4:7–8.

36. This is the fatal weakness in Neil Forsyth's argument that the Pauline-Au-

gustinian world view is inadvertently Manichean. See *The Old Enemy*, 254, 417–18. According to Forsyth, Christianity oscillates between the belief that "the world in fact is ruled by Satan" and the belief that "Satan is himself ruled and thwarted" (417f.). No oscillation is necessary; "rule" is a weasel in this context. Satan rules humanity only by a free consent that God declines to rule out, but will bring to a just issue. In this respect at least, Goethe's Mephistophelis is a better guide to the Christian view of history; he introduces himself to Faust as "a part of that power that never ceases to will evil, and never ceases to do good" (*ein Teil von jener Kraft / die stets das Boese will und stets das Gute schafft*"). Translation mine, from text of *Faust* in *Goethes Werke* (Stuttgart: J. G. Cotta, 1882), 5:50.

37. See John Stachniewski, *The Persecutory Imagination* (Oxford: The Clarendon Press, 1991), 337, 356. Stachniewski helps himself wherever convenient to the assumption (which he elsewhere contradicts) that Calvin's determinism is an evil novelty, and that Satan's despair is inconceivable without it.

38. Stachniewski knows this on page 327 of *The Persecutory Imagination*, but contrives not to know it on page 357.

39. John of Damascus, *De orthodoxa fide* 2.4 in Migne, *Patrologia Graeca* 94; Aquinas, *Summa theologiae* 1.63.6 ad 3, 1.64.2 fin., 1.64.2 ad 5, 1–2.80.4 ad 3, 3.4.1 ad 3, 3.6.2 ad 2, 3.46.1 ad 4, *Supplementum* 3.16.3.

40. Augustine, *De libero arbitrio* 3.10.29; Aquinas, *Summa Theologiae* 1–2.80.4 ad 3.

41. *Doctrina Christiana* in *The Works of John Milton* (New York: Columbia Univ. Press, 1933) 14:102.

42. Ibid., 14:140.

43. Ibid., 15:40.

44. Augustine, *Tractatus* 58 on the Gospel according to St. John, in Migne *Patrologia Latina* 35.

45. Aquinas, *Summa theologiae* 2–2.132.

46. Ibid., 1.44.4 ad 1.

47. *Doctrina Christiana* 14:72.

48. See, e.g., the well-known exposition of this kind of view in Aquinas, *Summa theologiae* 1.19.3, 10 ad 2. God necessarily does whatever is best; if there were only one best, he would be restricted to it of necessity. But in fact, what he's restricted to of necessity isn't a *single* choice, but a *defined range* of choice.

In " 'To Act or Not': Milton's Conception of Divine Freedom," *Journal of the History of Ideas* (1988), 425–49, Stephen M. Fallon, argues that this broad-band necessitarianism is "nothing more" than a way of insisting that calling God's deeds "good" isn't merely calling them "done by God" (442). But this tortures the text; God's deeds can be non-tautologically good without being the only kind of deed available to God. In the absence of a textual cue to the contrary, "necessity" keeps its face value.

Fallon also argues that broad-band necessitarianism is a corrective to what he takes to be the Neoplatonist claim that God's goodness functions as an "efficient cause" of his acts of will (440). But as we've already noticed in chapter two, the goodness of God in Neoplatonism is not an event at all, much less an event that (à la billiard ball collisions) causes later events; on Neoplatonist assumptions, "efficient cause" doesn't apply to the ultimately real things.

The illustrative passages Fallon quotes from Cudworth, Spinoza, and Aquinas

(432, 436, 440) fail to sustain Fallon's efficient-cause reading. In particular, Cudworth says that goodness is the measure or rule exemplified by God's will. A property is a formal, not an efficient, cause of what exemplifies it.

49. Erasmus, *De libero arbitrio*, 20 (IIa2).

50. Anselm, *Proslogion* 10 in Migne, *Patrologia Latina* 42.

51. Aquinas, *Summa Theologiae* 1.21.3 ad 2.

52. For Puritan attempts at theodicy inspired by the failure of the Good Old Cause, see Christopher Hill, *The Experience of Defeat* (New York: Viking, 1984), chapter 10, section 3 ("God on Trial").

53. Cf. Martz, *Poet of Exile:* "The resolution of this paradox [mankind's preference for evil] is made more difficult, not easier, by Milton's insistence upon the doctrine of the freedom of the will as a principle that he cannot bear to renounce. It may well seem, as it sometimes seems to Adam, that only a faulty piece of workmanship or planning on the part of God could have led to such an overwhelming number of wrong choices. Milton's last book forces the cruel paradox upon us." (182). Freewill can hardly make the paradox harder—or easier, for that matter; freewill *is* the paradox: a causally unbiased process somehow shows a bias— invariance would be more like it; unlike Einstein's God, the Advocate's God seems to play dice with the universe, and the dice seem to be loaded.
The paradox is resolved by noticing that there's no law of logic (much less nature) that requires dice to obey the laws of probability.

54. Martin Chemnitz, *Examen concilii tridentini* (Frankfurt am Main, 1590), 1:185.

55. *The Student's Milton*, 738.

56. Ibid.

57. Cf. Targum Jonathan at Gen. 3:24 in *Miqr'aoth Gᵉdoloth: Sepher Bereshith* (New York: M.P. Press, 1972). Werman, *Milton and Midrash*, 84–85, cites the Targum passage as generally relevant to "ideas in *Paradise Lost*," but, curiously, without reference to the *PL* treatment of precisely the same episode in Genesis.

58. Pun intended.

59. "O certe necessarium Adae peccatum, quod Christi morte deletum est! O felix culpa, quae talem et tantum meruit habere Redemptorem!" (*Missale romanum* (Rome: Desclée and Co., 1962), 249–50.

60. I.e., to be a *furcifer*.

61. T. S. Eliot, "Preludes," in *The Complete Poems and Plays* (New York: Harcourt, Brace and World), 13.

Bibliography

Alciatus, Andrea. *Emblemata domini.* Lyons: Mathieu Bonhomme, 1551.

Allen, D. C. "Milton and the Creation of Birds," *Modern Language Notes* 63 (1948): 263–64.

Anselm. *Proslogion,* in Migne, *Patrologia.*

Aquinas. *Compendium summae totius theologiae.* Rome: Sancta Congregatio,

———. *Summa contra gentiles.* Notre Dame, Ind.: University of Notre Dame Press, 1975.

———. *Summa theologica.* Edited by Bernardo De Rubeis, Charles Billuart, et al. Turin: Pietro Marietti, 1922.

Aristotle. *De anima.* Edited by W. D. Ross. Oxford: Clarendon Press, 1959.

———. *De animalium motione.* Edited by V. G. Jäger. Leipzig: Teubner, 1913.

———. *Ethica Eudemia.* Edited by R. R. Walzer and J. M. Mingay. Oxford: Clarendon Press, 1991.

———. *Ethica Nicomachea.* Edited by I. Bywater. Oxford: Clarendon Press, 1959.

———. *Poetica.* Edited by T. G. Tucker. London: D. Nutt, 1899.

———. *Politica.* Edited by F. Susemihl and O. Immisch. Leipzig: Teubner, 1929.

Arminius, Jacobus. *Opera theologica.* Frankfurt: William Fitzer, 1631.

Athenagoras. *Athenagorae libellus Pro christianis: Oratio de resurrectione cadaverum.* Edited by E. Schwartz. Leipzig: J. C. Hinrichs, 1891.

Augustine. *De civitate Dei.* Edited by J. E. C. Welldon. Toronto: Macmillan, 1924.

———. *De correptione et gratia* in Migne *Patrologia Latina* 44.

———. *De libero arbitrio.* Edited by W. M. Green. Berlin: Tempsky, 1956.

———. *Ad Bonifacium contra duas epistolas Pelagianorum* in Migne *Patrologia Latina* 43

———. *Tractatus de Joanne 58* in Migne *Patrologia Latina* 35

Beckett, Samuel. *Waiting for Godot.* New York: Grove Press, [1954].

Bennett, Joan S. *Reviving Liberty: Radical Christian Humanism in Milton's Great Poems.* Cambridge, Mass.: Harvard University Press, 1989.

Boethius. *Consolationis philosophiae libri.* Hack: Leyden, 1671.

———. *De persona et natura:* see above.

Buber, Martin. *I and Thou.* Translated by Ronald Gregor Smith. New York: Scribner, 1957.

Burden, Dennis H. *The Logical Epic: A Study of the Argument of Paradise Lost.* London: Routledge and Kegan Paul, 1967.

255

Calvin, John. *Institutio christianae religionis.* Edited by A. Tholuck. Berlin: Gustav Eichler, 1834.

Chemnitz, Martin. *Examen concilii tridentini.* Frankfurt am main, 1590.

Danielson, Dennis Richard. *Milton's Good God: A Study in Literary Theodicy.* Cambridge: Cambridge University Press, 1982.

Dennett, Daniel. *Consciousness Explained.* Boston: Little, Brown and Co., 1991.

Descartes, René. *Oeuvres de Descartes.* Edited by Charles Adam and Paul Tannery. Paris: Leopold Cerf, 1897–1910.

Donne, John. *The Works of John Donne.* With a memoir of his life by Henry Alford. London: John W. Parker, 1839.

Eliot, T. S. *The Complete Poems and Plays, 1909–1950.* New York: Harcourt and Brace, 1952.

Erasmus. *De libero arbitrio diatribe sive collatio.* Edited by Hans von Walter. Leipzig: Deichert, 1935.

Evans, J.M. *Paradise Lost and the Genesis Tradition.* Oxford: Clarendon Press, 1968.

Fallon, Stephen M. *Milton and the Philosophers.* Ithaca: Cornell University Press, 1991.

———. " 'To Act or Not': Milton's Conception of Divine Freedom," *Journal of the History of Ideas* (1988): 425–49.

Forsyth, Neil. *The Old Enemy: Satan and the Combat Myth.* Princeton: Princeton University Press, 1987.

Gardner, Helen. *A Reading of Paradise Lost.* Oxford: Clarendon Press, 1965.

Herodotus. *The Persian Wars.*

Hill, Christopher. *The Experience of Defeat.* New York: Elizabeth Sifton Books/ Viking, 1984.

Hobbes, Thomas. *The English Works of Thomas Hobbes.* Edited by William Molesworth. Reprint of the 1840 edition. Aalen: Scientia, 1962.

———. *Thomae Hobbes Malmesburiensis Opera philosophica quae latine scripsit omnia.* Edited by William Molesworth. London: Longman, Brown, Green and Longman, 1845.

Iamblichus. *Iamblichus de mysteriis, Proclus de anima atque daemone, Idem de sacrificio et magia, Porphyrius de divinis atque daemonibus, Michael Psellus de daemonibus, Mercurii Trismegisti Pimander, eiusdem Asclepius, interprete Marsilio Ficino.* Leyden: Ioannes Tornaesius, 1570.

John of Damascus. *Joannis Damasceni De orthodoxa fide libri quattuor in Migne Patrologia Graeca 94.*

Juvenal. *Juvenalis satirae.* Edited by C. F. Hermann. Leipzig: Teubner, 1926.

Kerrigan, William. *The Sacred Complex: On the Psychogenesis of Paradise Lost.* Cambridge, Mass.: Harvard University Press, 1983.

Levy, Raphael, ed. *Trésor de la Langue des Juifs Français au Moyen Age.* Austin: University of Texas Press, 1964.

Lewalski, Barbara Kiefer. *Paradise Lost and the Rhetoric of Literary Forms.* Princeton: Princeton University Press, 1985.

Lieb, Michael. *The Dialectics of Creation*. Amherst: University of Massachusetts Press, 1970.

————. " 'Hate in Heav'n': Milton and the *Odium Dei*," *English Literary History* (1986): 519–39.

————. *Poetics of the Holy: A Reading of Paradise Lost*. Chapel Hill: University of North Carolina, 1981.

Locke, John. *An Essay Concerning Human Understanding*. Edited by Alexander Campbell Fraser. New York: Dover Publications, [1959].

Lucretius. *De rerum natura*. Edited by W. E. Leonard and S. B. Smith. Madison: University of Wisconsin Press, 1942.

Luther, Martin. *Luthers Werke*. Edited by A. Freitag. Weimar: Boehlau, 1908.

MacCallum, Hugh. *Milton and the Sons of God*. Toronto: University of Toronto Press, 1986.

Maimonides, Moses. *Mishneh Torah*. Edited by Philip Birnbaum. New York: Hebrew Publishing Co., 1944.

Marjara, Harinder Singh. *Contemplation of Created Things: Science in Paradise Lost*. Toronto: University of Toronto Press, 1992.

Marlowe, Christopher. *Doctor Faustus*. Edited by John D. Jump. Cambridge, Mass.: Harvard University Press, 1962.

Martz, Louis L. *Poet of Exile: A Study of Milton's Poetry*. New Haven: Yale University Press, 1980.

Marvell, Andrew. *The Poems and Letters of Andrew Marvell*. Edited by H.M. Margoliouth. "A Dialogue Between the Soul and the Body." Oxford: Clarendon Press, 1952.

Milton, John. *Areopagitica*. New York: Payson and Clark, 1927.

————. *Complete Poems and Major Prose*. New York: Odyssey Press, 1957.

————. *John Milton's Writings in the Anglo-Dutch Negotiations 1651–1654*. Edited by Leo Miller. Pittsburgh: Duquesne University Press, 1992.

————. *The Student's Milton*. Edited by Frank Allen Patterson. New York: Appleton-Century-Crofts, 1957.

————. *The Works of John Milton*. Edited by Frank Allen Patterson. New York: Columbia University Press, 1937.

Missale romanum. Rome: Desclée and Co., 1962.

Molina, Luis de. *Epitome de praedestinatione*. In Friedrich Stegmueller, *Beitraege*, q.v.

Origen, *De principiis*, in Migne, *Patrologia Graeca* 11:115.

Orpheus. *Orphica*. Edited by Gottfried Hermann. Leipzip: Caspar Fritsch, 1805.

Plantinga, Alvin. *God, Freedom, and Evil*. New York: Harper and Row, 1974.

Pliny the Elder. *Naturalis historiae libri 37*. Edited by Karl Mayhoff. Leipzig: Teubner, 1892.

Plotinus. *Enneades*. Edited by Emile Bréhier. Paris: Les Belles Lettres, 1963.

Pomponazzi, Pietro. *Mantuani libri quinque de fato, de libero arbitrio et de praedestinatione*. Edited by Richard Lemay. Lucania: Thesaurus Mundi, [1957].

————. *Tractatus de immortalitate animae.* Edited by Gianfancesco Morra. Bologna, 1954.

Prudentius. *Prudenti opera omnia in usum Delphini recensita.* London: A.J. Malpy, 1824.

Quintilian. *Institutionis oratiae libri duodecim.* Edited by Ludwig Rademacher. Leipzig: Ludwig Rademacher and Vincent Buchheit, 1959.

Rosenblatt, Jason. *Torah and Law in Paradise Lost.* Princeton: Princeton University Press, 1994.

Rumrich, John. "Milton's God and the Matter of Chaos," *Publications of the Modern Language Association* 110 (1995): 1035–46.

Sellin, Paul R. "*Paradise Lost* and *De doctrina* on Predestination," *Milton Studies* 34 (1997): 45–60.

Schaar, Claes. *The Full Voic'd Quire Below: Vertical Context Systems in Paradise Lost.* Lund: CWK Gleerup, 1982.

Shakespeare, William. *The Riverside Shakespeare,* 2d ed. Edited by G. Blakemore Evans et al. Boston: Houghton Mifflin, 1997.

Spinoza, Benedictus de. *Benedicti de Spinoza opera quotquot reperta sunt.* Edited by J. van Vloten and J. P. N. Land. The Hague: Martin Nijhoff, 1913.

Stachniewski, John. *The Persecutory Imagination.* Oxford: Clarendon Press, 1991.

Steadman, John M. *Milton and the Paradoxes of Renaissance Heroism.* Baton Rouge: Louisiana State University Press, 1987.

Stegmüller, Friedrich, ed. *Geschichte der Molinismus.* Beiträge zur Geschichte der Philosophie und Theologie des Mittelalters, vol. 32. Muenster, 1935.

Stillingfleet, Edward, Bishop of Worcester. *Origines sacrae.* London: Printed by J.H. for Henry Mortlock, 1680.

Summers, Joseph Holmes. *The Muse's Method.* Cambridge, Mass.: Harvard University Press, 1962.

Swinburne, Richard. "Does Theism Need a Theodicy?" *Canadian Journal of Philosophy* 18 (1988): 287–311.

Targum Jonathan, in *Miqraoth Gᵉdoloth: Sepher Bᵉreshith.* New York: M. P. Press, 1972.

Thomas a Kempis. *Thomae a Kempis C.B. Ordinis S. Augustini de imitatione Christi libri quattuor.* Parma edition (ex imperiali typographia) of 1807.

Van Inwagen, Peter. *An Essay on Free Will.* Oxford: Clarendon Press, 1983.

Vossius, Geraard. *Historiae de controversiis quas Pelagius eiusque reliquiae moverunt libri vii.* Leyden: Jan Patius, 1618.

Weisberg, David. "Rule, Self, Subject: The Problem of Power in *Paradise Lost,*" *Milton Studies* 30 (1993): 85–107.

Werman, Golda. *Milton and Midrash.* Washington, D.C.: The Catholic University of America Press, 1995.

Wier, David A. *The Origins of Federal Theology in Sixteenth-Century Reformation Thought.* Oxford: Clarendon Press, 1990.

Yolton, John W. *Thinking Matter: Materialism in Eighteenth-Century Britain.* Minneapolis: University of Minnesota Press, 1983.

Index